Walking on Thin Ice

Also by David Hempleman-Adams

TOUGHING IT OUT
The adventures of a Polar Explorer and Mountaineer

Walking on Thin Ice

IN PURSUIT OF THE NORTH POLE

David Hempleman-Adams

with Robert Uhlig

ORION BOOKS
The Daily Telegraph

First published in Great Britain in 1998 by
Orion
An imprint of Orion Books Ltd
Orion House, 5 Upper St Martin's Lane, London WC2H 9EA
and *The Daily Telegraph*
1 Canada Square, Canary Wharf, London E14 5DT

A CIP catalogue record for this book is available
from the British Library

ISBN 0 75281 797 3

Typeset in Great Britain by Selwood Systems, Midsomer Norton
Printed and bound by Butler & Tanner Ltd, Frome and London

Grateful acknowledgement is made for permission to quote from
The Four Quartets by
T. S. Eliot, © Faber & Faber Ltd. And to BBC Video Diaries
for the use of their title, *Walking on Thin Ice*

For my girls

Contents

Acknowledgements

OVER 200 PEOPLE, ranging from friends and sponsors to acquaintances and virtual strangers, have helped me greatly by giving me invaluable advice, assistance and encouragement over the years since I embarked on the first expedition of what would later become the Adventurers' Grand Slam. There is neither space nor time to acknowledge them all individually here, but I thank each and every one of you for your friendship and assistance.

However, there is one person without whom there would be no story: my Norwegian partner Rune Gjeldnes. This is as much his story as it is mine, and I owe him an immeasurable debt.

I would also like to thank the 'backroom boy and girl': my long-suffering sidekick Rachel Clarke, who keeps me on the straight and narrow at the office in England; and John Perrins, our faithful and hard-working base manager at Resolute Bay and the unsung third member of the North Pole expedition team. My thanks too to my editors Yvette Goulden and Selina Walker, and Sarah Yorke in publicity, for their support and enthusiasm for both my books.

My wife Claire, and Alicia, Amelia and Camilla, my daughters, have tolerated beyond the call of duty my frequent absences from home, and I thank them deeply.

Finally, I would like to thank my co-author Robert Uhlig, for his patience, perseverance and guidance in the writing of this book.

Robert, in turn, would like to thank Hilary Curtis for her unflagging encouragement, support and affection; and Paul Grover, for the good humour which made six weeks in Resolute Bay a lot more tolerable.

The Road to the Grand Slam

August 1980	Mount McKinley.
August 1981	Kilimanjaro.
March 1983	The Geographic North Pole, failed solo and supported attempt.
February 1984	The Magnetic North Pole, first solo and unsupported expedition.
April 25, 1992	The Geomagnetic North Pole (79°12′N; 72°12′W), first successful expedition (with Steve Morris, Jock Wishart, Richard Mitchell, Hugh Ward, Neill Williams).
October 9 1993	Mount Everest.
August 14 1994	Mount Elbrus.
February 1995	Aconcagua.
December 1994	Mount Vinson.
May 1995	Carstensz Pyramid (seven summits completed).
November 7 1995 to January 5 1996	The Geographic South Pole, first Briton solo and unsupported.
February – March 1996	The Magnetic South Pole.
March 5 – April 28 1997	The Geographic North Pole, failed unsupported attempt with Rune Gjeldnes.
March 5 – April 28 1998	The Geographic North Pole, first successful British-Norwegian expedition, supported with Rune Gjeldnes.

What we call the beginning is often the end
And to make an end is to make a beginning.
The end is where we start from . . .
We shall not cease from exploration
And the end of all our exploring
Will be to arrive where we started
And know the place for the first time.

T. S. Eliot, 'Little Gidding' from *The Four Quartets*

Prologue

'**W**E LOST THE POLE.' With these four words, uttered in the depths of disappointment while floating on pack ice 291 miles from the top of the world, my 1997 expedition to conquer the North Pole ended and the 1998 assault began.

After seven weeks of battling across the shifting ice that floats precariously on the freezing Arctic Ocean, I had to admit that once again the most beautiful and most demanding of terrain had vanquished my dream of becoming the first Briton to reach the North Pole unsupported. My hopes of entering the record books as the first person to complete the Adventurers' Grand Slam, the fifteen-year odyssey that has dominated my adult life, lay in tatters on the Arctic ice.

On day forty-five, our ingenuity, good luck and determination had run out. A few yards in front of the fibreglass chunk from the wrecked sledge, one of Rune's socks lay in the snow, and further ahead lay more of Rune's clothing, equipment and provisions. Rune, meanwhile, was oblivious to this, happily skiing ahead, unaware that our expedition was over.

I ripped the sledge harness off my shoulders and skied the thirty feet between us, tapped him on the shoulder and pointed to what lay behind. Rune looked me in the eye and shrugged. 'First, David, a cigarette,' he said. 'Then we decide what to do.'

We turned the sledge over to discover that the hole ran from one side to the other. It was no great surprise – we had been patching it up for days, hoping it would hold.

There was nothing further we could do. We couldn't carry all our provisions on one sledge. We didn't have the material to make rucksacks, and even though he is as strong as an ox, Rune could not carry 200lb on his back.

He turned to me as the tears streaming down my face froze within seconds on my bare cheeks and encrusted my shaggy moustache and beard. 'David, it's not so bad,' he said. 'We will be back next year and this time I promise we will do it. No problem.'

I was heartened by his words, but I had to be sure that once again Rune would accompany me through this living hell. We had started the journey almost as strangers, but in the past forty-five days we had become the closest of friends. If there was anybody I could do it with, and in whose hands I would trust my life, it was this shy, self-effacing Norwegian marine who had kept me going so far.

'Today – right now,' I said to Rune, 'North Pole 97 ends and North Pole 98 starts. Agreed?'

'Agreed, old man,' he answered, his usual roll-up cigarette smouldering between his lips. 'Now let's go home.'

1

All Roads Lead North

The Route to the Grand Slam

I F ALL HAD gone to plan, in mid-May 1997 I would finally have laid to rest the burden of the legacy that had come to haunt me ever since my first foolish attempt to reach the North Pole on foot failed in 1983. In the few moments when I am totally honest with myself, I realise that I am extremely lucky to be alive today after that first expedition.

I had little knowledge of the kind of conditions that lay ahead of me then, and I thought I could turn a lack of funds, equipment and experience to my advantage. Other expeditions, I reasoned, had struggled to push and cajole dogs and snowmobiles through rubble and pressure ridges – a hellish chaos of jumbled blocks of ice which lie scattered across the Arctic as ice floes the size of several football pitches crash into one another, buckle and create giant frozen hedgerows. So instead of relying on canine or combustion power to drag my provisions and equipment across the first 200 miles of the debilitating terrain of the cap, I would don crampons and drag a sledge behind me. In this way, I reckoned, I would become the first person to walk solo to the North Pole.

Once this spirit of simplicity had gripped me, I was determined to make the journey as pure as possible. I would discard all high-tech modern fripperies, I decided, and guide myself by the stars and the sun, using only a sextant to plot my position each day. In any other environment my naivety might have seemed quite charming, but in the Arctic such ignorance can be a death sentence. Fortunately, the Canadian authorities refused outright to allow me to embark without a lightweight Argos electronic satellite navigation system.

Quite why I thought I could make it to the North Pole in one piece back then I find hard to envisage today. The reason for my confidence – I'm sure some called it cockiness at the time – lay in my mountaineering accomplishments in the three years leading up to that first polar expedition. In 1979, after several years of climbing some of the highest and most challenging peaks in the Alps, I trekked as far as the base camp of Everest. Although only at the foot of the fabled mountain, it was 18,000 feet up and it whetted my appetite for bigger and more ambitious climbs.

In August 1980 I travelled with Steve Vincent, a student friend, to Alaska to climb Mount McKinley, at 20,320 feet the highest summit in North America. Climbers like nothing better than to surround mountains with myths, and McKinley is no exception. Some of the stories would have you believe it is the only mountain on Earth where you can be chased by grizzly bears on the slopes and hunted by polar bears around the base. Other stories tell of McKinley's massive and frequent avalanches, often precipitated by minor earthquakes. But there is one thing every climber knows is true of McKinley: it is criss-crossed by a spider's web of some of the largest and most fearsome crevasses on any mountain.

As McKinley's many glaciers slide slowly like white treacle towards the mountain's base, the glaciers' surfaces split into gaping crevasses at every turn and on each undulation they ooze across; at times, the frozen waves and troughs of the glaciers seem to create more expanses of crevasses than of solid ice. To make matters worse, in the winter it snows almost continuously on McKinley, hiding many of the crevasses from view. In some cases the covering is only a light dusting which creates a formidable and deadly trap; in other cases the snow can be many tens of feet deep, and will have frozen sufficiently to support the weight of a man. But as summer advances, the structures can crack under the surface snow, and nobody knows with which footstep the bridges will crumble and crash, taking any passengers with them to a no-return destination hundreds of feet below.

Received wisdom has it that the McKinley climbing season begins in April, when the coldest weather ends, and extends to July, by which time the heat of the sun has opened or weakened most of the crevasses. We went in August. We were told many times that it was madness to attempt to climb McKinley in the middle of summer, but with its formidable reputation and its status as the highest mountain in North America it was too much of a challenge for us to resist.

Steve and I set out on a fine day and made good progress. On the second night we camped at a spot that I believed was well sheltered from anything the mountain could throw at us during the night, but in the small hours we were woken up as our tent began to shake. I looked at Steve, and by the look on his face I could tell we were both thinking the same thing: earthquake. The shaking soon stopped, but it was replaced by an even more ominous sound: all around our tent we could hear the rumbling and rushing of avalanches. I stuck my head out of the tent to see what was going on, but the weather and the cloud of snow-dust thrown up by the avalanches had conspired to whisk up a white-out – a fearsome condition in which it is impossible to distinguish between the snow-covered ground and the cloud-filled sky. I could see no further than a few yards in front of the tent.

Until then, because of my mountaineering and skiing experiences in the Alps, I had thought I could always spot a likely avalanche path, but I came to realise my limitations on McKinley. We had crossed dozens of avalanche fields, and any one of our many steps could have sent several hundreds of tons of snow hurtling down the slope, carrying us to a probable death. We had camped in the middle of a highly precarious snow field, and in the morning we discovered that fewer than fifty yards from us an avalanche had come to rest. There was no reason, other than our good luck, to explain why the avalanche had stopped short of sweeping our tiny tent away. Again, I was reminded of the most valuable lesson a mountaineer or explorer can learn: never underestimate the terrain and don't take anything for granted.

With this scare behind us, we hared up the mountain, reaching the summit in an astonishing four days, but our flirtation with death was not over. On the way down from the summit, the weather worsened considerably; within hours we were caught in another white-out. One wrong footfall would mean stepping into nothingness. We continued onwards, weary and desperate to reach base camp. With our faces adorned with tentacles of frozen perspiration and driven snow, I became convinced Steve was leading the wrong way and turned left of the track we were on. Steve shouted at me, telling me that I was mistaken.

'Bollocks!' I shouted back in the driving snow and wind, 'this is the route.' We had rarely argued before, but this time I was sure I was right. He stopped dead and insisted he knew the way. He told me he was basing his conviction on no more than gut feeling, but he said it with such belief that I went with him. Fortunately he was right, and a few minutes later we were safely at our base camp.

When Steve Vincent and I had climbed Mount McKinley, the first of the seven mountains that would later form the backbone of the Grand Slam, there was no such thing as the 'seven summits'; it wasn't until 30 April 1985 that Dick Bass, an American businessman, reached the top of Everest and claimed to be the first person to have climbed the highest peak in each of the seven continents. I had first set my sights on the seven summits in 1994 at the instigation of Rebecca Stephens, the first British woman to climb Everest, who pointed out that at that time I had already completed four of the seven: McKinley, Kilimanjaro, Everest and Elbrus in the Caucasus Mountains.

Back home after climbing McKinley in 1980, Steve and I were soon restless. We knew we had to settle down and earn some money and had plans of starting a business with a mutual friend, Jerry Scriven, importing ski and mountaineering clothing and equipment. But before we started a life on the straight and narrow, we promised ourselves one last treat: Kilimanjaro, the 19,340-foot-high pride of Africa. It turned out to be probably the safest and dullest climb of all the seven summits, but it was not without its dangers. The volcanic ash underfoot made it hard work, but it was nevertheless more of a hike than a climb, and we reached the summit within a few days.

Shortly thereafter, in the late summer of 1981, I picked up a copy of *National Geographic*, and read with some envy and longing of the successful expedition to the Geographic North Pole by Naomi

Uemura, a Japanese explorer. At the time Sir Ranulph Fiennes was about to set off on his Transglobal Expedition, which planned to take in both geographic poles, and Reinhold Messner had just climbed Everest solo and without the aid of oxygen. Although I had vowed to settle down, these incredible exploits soon set me dreaming, and within days I was determined to be the first Briton to reach the Geographic North Pole solo.

I had made dozens of successful climbs and I thought the North Pole was within my capabilities. For nearly eighteen months I devoted every spare moment to preparing and planning for the expedition. Steve and I closed down the import business we had set up in New York, I rented a flat in Bristol with Claire, then my girlfriend and now my wife, and while we lived on pennies I raised tens of thousands of pounds for my polar assault. Along the way I met some of the legends of adventuring, including Sir Ranulph Fiennes, who gave me a mass of invaluable advice, as did Wally Herbert, a Briton who in 1969 had traversed the North Pole on dog sleds.

Towards the start of February 1983, I set out for Resolute Bay, Canada's second most northerly community and the High Arctic venue for most explorers' last preparations for expeditions to the geographic and magnetic poles, as well as some to Baffin Island and Greenland. Expeditions to Baffin Island, at 184,000 square miles the largest island of the Canadian Arctic archipelago, and to the Magnetic North Pole normally serve as training runs for the Geographic North Pole, but I was eager to tackle the big one – the top of the world in every sense – and I set my sights on that point – 90° North – where all the lines of longitude meet.

The last time it was pinpointed, in 1994, the Magnetic North Pole was located on the Noice Peninsula, a promontory on the south-west side of Ellef Ringnes Island. The Magnetic North Pole is the point towards which all magnetic compasses point. For centuries, before they knew that there is no land at the Geographic North Pole, mariners believed a magnetic mountain at the Geographic North Pole was the source of attraction for compasses.

In 1831 Sir James Clark located the true hub at Cape Adelaide on the west coast of Boothia Peninsula in the Canadian Arctic. Nobody knows for sure why there is a magnetic pole at this point, but it is believed that it is generated by electrical currents that originate in the hot, liquid outer core of the Earth. Since it was first located the Magnetic North Pole has moved around 1110 nautical miles, or 1285 statute miles, towards the north as the complex flow of electric currents in the Earth's liquid core changes.

Reaching the Magnetic North Pole is considerably easier than getting to its geographical cousin because it is within striking distance of civilisation, around 250 miles from Resolute Bay, and involves crossing both land and the frozen pack ice of the waters surrounding the Arctic Archipelago. The waters are in fjords, and consequently the currents are much weaker than in the Arctic Ocean, so the ice is generally flat with little rubble and few pressure ridges. By contrast, a trek to the Geographic North Pole, the northernmost point of the world's axis, is a mission of defiance against the forces of nature. The North Pole is at the centre of the Arctic Ocean, 482 statute miles from Ward Hunt Island in Canada. To reach the Geographic North Pole by foot one has to walk on water, a feat possible only from early March to mid-May each year when the pack ice is thick and sufficiently intact to make the long race against the thaw possible.

For my first assault on the Geographic North Pole Steve Vincent agreed to set up a base camp with my old school friend Giorgio 'Mac' Matranga at Eureka, a weather station beside a frozen airstrip battered by winds and dotted with a couple of tin huts. This remote and beautiful spot, three hours' flying time from the nearest civilisation, was to be my base manager's home while I walked to the North Pole. The only other living things nearby were wandering herds of musk oxen, caribou and polar bears. The monotony of the weathermen's routine was broken only when a maniac such as myself stopped off on the way to Cape Columbia, my starting point at the tip of Ellesmere Island, the most accessible for North Pole expeditions.

In the first week of March 1983 I waved farewell to the Twin Otter aircraft that had carried me to Cape Columbia and bedded down for my first night on the ice, on the brink of learning the toughest lesson of my adventuring career. Feeling desperately lonely – I was the only person attempting the North Pole in 1983 – I planned to complete the 482 statute miles in forty days, needing to average eleven miles a day. The folly of that target soon became apparent when, at the end of day one, I had covered just one mile.

It had taken me *three* hours to get ready in the morning. In the extreme cold, I found everything took longer because I had to think carefully before making any movements to avoid catching frostbite. In addition to my caution, my body was in shock, which slowed me down further. In extreme cold the human body protects itself by shutting all operations down to 80 per cent of normal operating speed to conserve energy. Once I got out of my tent, I found the going exceptionally tough. There is nothing else on the face of the planet that can prepare you for the incessant cold, fields of rubble and the immense pressure ridges of the North Pole. Every advance of ten yards was to me a momentous achievement. My sledge had to be hauled across blocks and reefs of ice that intersected one another and traversed the pack ice as far as I could see. It was like dragging several hundred pounds across a shifting obstacle course with barricades that crumbled as I attempted to breach them.

Within the first few days I came to a bitter realisation. I had already lost any hope of reaching the Pole in record time. In my first three days I hadn't even managed five miles; about four weeks later, when I fell off a fifteen-foot ridge and cracked two ribs, my mission was over. I had lasted thirty-two days and covered only 230 miles, but I was relieved that the end was in sight. I thought I would soon be back in the warmth of the High Arctic boarding house at Resolute Bay and then on my way home to be reunited with Claire in Bristol. Little did I know that my ordeal was not over yet.

I radioed the base station at Eureka and told them what had happened. They arranged for a plane to come and collect me, but the nearest Twin Otter ski-plane was at Resolute, where a storm had set in. Two days later the storm moved on to Eureka, where the Twin Otter would have to refuel. When the storm cleared at Eureka, it hit the ice-cap. In all I spent ten days in my tent clutching my ribs, cursing that I had run out of painkillers and waiting desperately for a rescue. In the end Mac and Steve persuaded a plane from Operation Caesar, a Canadian scientific research project located on a floating ice island above the Lomonosov Ridge, an underwater mountain range near the Pole, to pick me up. I returned home chastened and humbled. I'd done well considering my inexperience, but I had failed, and that I found difficult to accept. The beginning of my long and exhausting battle with the North Pole had begun.

I started to plan my second Geographic North Pole trip as soon as I topped Carstensz Pyramid in Irian Jaya in May 1995. It was a fairly routine climb but a particularly satisfying achievement as it was the last peak I needed to conquer to complete the seven summits.

My polar adventuring career had lain dormant for the best part of eight years since reaching the Magnetic North Pole in 1984, a personal success that restored much of my confidence and self-respect after my problems the year before. Business and family had kept me from my first love, but from 1992 I returned with a vengeance, completing a hard and at times desperate trek to the Geomagnetic North Pole as part of a team. The year after climbing Carstensz Pyramid was my busiest year for expeditions yet. On 5 January 1996, fifty-nine days after setting off from Hercules Inlet on the west side of Antarctica, I made it to the South Pole solo and unsupported, an expedition that tested my mental and physical stamina to the limit. A month later, in February, I set off from Tasmania with a crew of nine to sail across the iciest part of the South Pacific Ocean. On 19 February, with our yacht the *Spirit of Sydney* dripping ice from its rigging, our satellite navigation system flipped, indicting we had just passed over the Magnetic South Pole. Then, in April, I led a group of ten fairly in-experienced adventurers to the Magnetic North Pole, a once-in-a-lifetime opportunity called the Ultimate Challenge that gained me the distinction of becoming the first person to visit three poles in six months.

However, these expeditions, although highly demanding and significant in their own rights, were merely appetisers before the main course. The South Pole had been exceptionally tough, but I knew it was nothing in comparison with what awaited me at the top of the world. I could no longer avoid the simple fact that there was only one other task that lay ahead. Maybe I had been putting off the venture I feared the most until last, but I knew that I had a unique chance to complete the Grand Slam – the seven summits plus the Geographic and Magnetic North and South Poles. No other person had come close to this series of eleven tasks because adventurers tend to be either mountaineers or polar explorers, seldom both. After spending the best part of six months in the Antarctic and Arctic, I believed I was ready for the conditions and hardship.

In some ways my expedition to the Magnetic North Pole in 1984 had been much harder than a trek to the Geographic North Pole was likely to be. The Magnetic North Pole expedition was unknown territory; no solo and unsupported outing had succeeded before me. By comparison the Geographic North Pole was not a mystery. There are no charts to show the conditions ahead, the terrain changes by the hour, and I knew it would be bloody hard, but I knew what lay ahead of me. I also knew many other explorers had made it, supported and unsupported, alone and in groups, on foot, on snowmobiles and with dogs, since Robert Peary came close enough to claim he had reached the top of the world in 1909.

Whatever the Arctic could throw at me I thought I could take, not least because this most inhospitable place had become a drug for me and I was determined to gain the upper hand on my addiction. It was fourteen years since my last failure at the North Pole, and despite the harder terrain, drifting ice and much colder temperatures of the North Pole, I believed my South Pole and Magnetic North Pole experiences would give me a good chance, provided my luck held out. Nevertheless, the omens were not as good as they could have been. Several British attempts had failed shortly before I set out: Sir Ranulph Fiennes had aborted trips four times, Rupert 'Pen' Haddow had been unsuccessful twice. If I was to succeed, I would have to surpass these extremely experienced men.

My second consideration was that, after being driven quite literally up the pole by the desperate rigours of solitude on my trek to the Geographic South Pole, I would be better off with a companion. The only question was who. The British adventuring community, although ostensibly very fraternal, simmers with competition below the surface. I could think of no suitable partner to accompany me and abide my company for seventy-five days and who would not, in turn, drive me to distraction. It was while contemplating these three factors – the relative lack of success of British polar explorers leading up to 1997, my need for a companion and the rivalries among British explorers – that I hit on a solution: I would seek a Norwegian as my accomplice.

Britain and Norway have been arch rivals in polar exploration since before Captain Roald Amundsen beat Captain Robert Falcon Scott to the South Pole in 1911, and there had never been a joint British-Norwegian polar bid. Norway was considerably more successful than Britain with many firsts to its name, including Roald Amundsen and

Liv Arnesson, the first woman to reach the South Pole solo and unsupported, yet it was a rare occurrence for a Briton to seek advice from a fellow Norwegian explorer. I have always believed we Britons have a lot to learn from the Norwegians in terms of surviving extreme conditions. Their clothing and equipment are based on a heritage that goes back to Amundsen, one that has proved its worth. They seem to have a better approach to diet and lose less weight, and consequently maintain their strength for longer on the ice. Norwegians are generally more experienced – and I trust their methods because I have used them before and they've always worked – and have a common-sense approach to exploring that is less gung-ho and more reassuring.

My first choice was Borge Ousland, a legend among polar explorers and a man I feel privileged to call a friend. He had passed on a lot of good advice to me in the past, and as one of the world's most accomplished explorers had immense experience. I called him in Oslo and asked him to accompany me, but he had recently failed on a Norwegian crossing of Antarctica and was hell-bent on returning there to cross the continent unsupported shortly before my North Pole trip. If all had gone to plan, Borge would have reached the South Pole with a week to spare before leaving with me for the North Pole. The schedule was too tight and did not leave any room for delays or injuries. If Borge picked up any frostbite in the Antarctic or anything more serious, my expedition would be in jeopardy.

I told Borge I wanted a Norwegian and he agreed that it would be a good thing if Britain and Norway could at last bury the hatchet. If Borge would not come with me, could he at least suggest a fellow countryman, I asked. Without hesitating he advised me to call Rune Gjeldnes, a member of Norway's Marinejegerkommandoen – the Norwegian equivalent of the Special Boat Service – and the explorer Torry Larsen, a close friend of Rune. At first I was a little reluctant to go with a military man. Historically, professional adventurers have come from one of two backgrounds – the aristocracy or the military. As an amateur part-time explorer, I have had to fight against the resulting prejudices in the mountaineering and adventuring establishment.

Although some people assume my double-barrelled surname means I have a privileged background that has afforded me the time and money to indulge my passion for exploring, the opposite is the case. I was born a Hempleman in Swindon in 1956, my parents divorced when I was eight, and when my mother remarried my surname changed to Adams, the name of my stepfather. I soon got used to my new name, but when I was twenty-four, to reflect the admiration and love I still felt for my father and the pride I felt at being a Hempleman, I changed my name by deed-poll to Hempleman-Adams.

I had further reason for concern about a military man. For all its virtues, in my experience a military training can instil an arrogance and a false sense of pride that can be counter-productive in explorers. Soldiers and sailors tend to think civilians are not tough enough for the rigours of survival, yet as many military expeditions fail as civilian ones. I was worried that a military man, with the pride of his regiment weighing heavily on his shoulders, might make the wrong decision in a moment of crisis. I was also concerned that a soldier or sailor might have all the misplaced courage that I knew could be so hazardous in an environment as unforgiving as the Arctic. I knew from bitter experience that a little too much enthusiasm, like insufficient knowledge, can be a dangerous thing. The last thing I needed was a hot-headed aggressor when circumstances called for cool consideration.

Borge quelled my concerns when he told me that Rune, like me, had become interested in expeditions at fifteen and was passionately committed to a life outdoors. When I was a teenager growing up in the West Country, my love for the outdoors was sparked by Mansell 'Jesse' James, my PE teacher at Writhlington Comprehensive near Bath. He took an interest in me, maybe because I was the only child with divorced parents, and suggested that I have a go at the Duke of Edinburgh Award scheme. It was his encouragement and guidance that led me to where I am today.

'Give Rune a ring at his parent's farm,' Borge said. 'I think you'll like him and get the response you want.'

Despite Borge's recommendation, I called Larsen first, but he, although flattered by my interest, turned me down because he was returning to the Norwegian Navy. I then called Rune up out of the blue. Or at least I thought it was out of the blue – I didn't know that Borge, the old devil, had forewarned him.

'Do you want to go the Arctic?' I asked. 'I'm a British explorer and I'm looking for someone to accompany me to the North Pole.' From what Borge had told me, I thought the invitation would be a formality and he would leap at the chance.

'No, not really,' Rune answered. 'Sorry, I'm not interested. Too busy.'

After such a swift reply, I expected to hear the instant click of the receiver. Maybe he has a low opinion of British explorers, I thought. Or maybe he is joking, I told myself, and took this as a good sign that he had a sense of humour.

Rune, however, was deadly serious.

'There's little you could say that would make me go to the North Pole. I'd like to do it one day, but now is not the right time. Sorry.'

I refused to take no for an answer, particularly as his straightforward honesty had caught me with my guard down and impressed me. Most explorers would grab greedily at the chance of an all-expenses-paid trip to the North Pole, yet here was this cheeky young twenty-six-year-old turning it down. At his age I would not have looked such a gift horse in the mouth, and so, intrigued by his insouciance, I insisted on flying to Norway to meet him.

We arranged to go out for a drink in a bar in Bergen near his home where, I hoped, I would be appalled by his arrogance and naivety and count myself lucky that he had not accepted my invitation. But that evening at the appropriately English-named Dickens bistro one beer turned into two, two turned into many, and long before the evening was out I realised he was my ideal companion.

Rune, who first skied at the age of three, had just completed the longest unsupported cross-country ski trek in history. In 1994 he had crossed Greenland from Umanaq to Isertoq, 550 miles in thirty-one days. However, this was a mere training trip for the following year's G2 expedition. With Torry Larsen, Rune had parachuted into Greenland and skied down to the southern tip where the pair kayaked from the east to the west side. They then traversed Greenland, the largest island on Earth, by the longest route possible, from south to north, covering 1830 miles in eighty days, and yet Rune was not talking about it. It was a good sign. We appeared to have similar personalities, uninterested in boasting about past achievements and more engrossed in what lay ahead.

I knew Rune was my best bet for getting to the Pole. I could make a solo attempt again, but it would be hellish and my chances would be better with a companion. I thought back to my South Pole and Mag-netic North Pole trips. On both I had come perilously close to giving up because of sheer loneliness, fear or despair. On my way to the Magnetic North Pole I had lost my nerve after falling through the ice into water, and was at the time determined to return to the comfort and warmth of Resolute Bay. It was only after a stern talking to by John Burgess, my base camp operator, that I continued the trek to the Magnetic Pole. Had I been making the journey with a companion, I would probably not have made the radio call to John in the first place. Until just before the 1997 North Pole expedition I still had nightmares about falling through the ice into the freezing water. If I had been able to share my fears at the time with a partner, I may have coped better with the trauma. On the march to the South Pole I had become so lonely that I was concerned I would lose my mind. It was only by giving names to my skis and sledge and talking to them that I managed to maintain morale, but even this did not stop me from executing a particularly vicious attack on 'Boy' – as I had christened my sledge – when my frustrations got the better of me.

With all these memories of isolation and despair flooding back, I knew I had to persuade Rune to join me. Although we were by now getting along like old friends, he remained impassive whenever I broached the subject. I plugged away and cajoled him, but he didn't want to shift. He was on a lecture and book tour after his Greenland trip and far too busy, he said, for another expedition. Several beers later his reluctance appeared to be waning, but he still seemed inherently unwilling. He told me he was worried that he would be unable to devote enough time, attention and energy to preparing for the expedition, and that I would be better off looking elsewhere.

This honesty impressed me all the more. Many other men in his position would in their zeal have failed to mention any such obstacles. I liked this young man, fourteen years my junior, immensely on first meeting and believed that by that stage I had hooked him. He was definitely interested but wary, and kept making provisos. He warned me that because of his book and lecture tour and other commitments he could promise no more than to turn up on the day we were to leave for Canada. I assured him that it would not be a problem. All he had to do, I said, was commit himself to full focus on the ice.

It was getting late, and I needed a definitive answer. I pressed him to make up his mind. 'If I come,' he said, 'then I have to do all the cooking. I like to do the cooking and I don't trust your English food.'

I thought I was in a dream. He had almost agreed, and he wanted to take care of the chore I liked least.

We decided to think about it for ten days. I knew it would work with him; I had a gut feeling, but I didn't want him to feel pressurised. I flew back to England and waited. It was hard to hold back for the ten days, but after they were up I phoned him.

Rune picked up the phone, said hello, and then 'Why not?'

The scene was set for the first joint British-Norwegian attempt on the North Pole.

2

Learning Lessons
the Hard Way

*Last Days of the 1997
North Pole Expedition*

Day 40: Monday, 21 April 1997

Argos report

00165	84.749N	71.537W	1	112/0005Z–112/0033
(3)	–.17211E+2	85	85	00

Position: 84°44'58" North; 71°32'14" West
Temperature: −17.2°C (inside tent)
Windchill: −39°C
Hours of sunshine: 24
Nautical miles covered today: 7
Nautical miles so far: 97
Nautical miles to go (*in a straight line*): 318
Status: Storm

Today we decided we had to get going whatever the weather. Yesterday was wasted, a horrible day stuck in the tent with thirty-knot winds whistling around our tiny encampment, sending us drifting east at an alarming rate. No choice but to get out and face the elements, but I wonder to what purpose? For the last two days I have been harbouring grave doubts of ever reaching the North Pole unsupported. We are not significantly behind on our schedule, but we are down on our food. We spent eight valuable days sitting at Ward Hunt Island at the beginning of the expedition. It was valuable time, and we paid the price by eating more of our rations than we should have done and burning more fuel than planned.

I find myself sitting here now ruing those wasted days and elementary oversights. Rune was extremely embarrassed that he had left his blue bag on the Twin Otter ski-plane that dropped us on the ice at Ward Hunt Island. He insisted that we forget it, that we should set out for the Pole straight away, but I knew it was vital that he had the bag with him. As well as personal items such as his diary, a bible – admittedly somewhat incongruous for a trained killer in the Norwegian marine corps – some pictures and cassettes, it contained the single most important provision for a heavy smoker such as Rune: ten weeks' supply of tobacco. Rune appeared to show little inclination to wait for his bag to arrive with a Dutch expedition due to land at Ward Hunt Island a couple of days later, but when I saw him smoking the rolled-up pages of my diary I knew we had to wait for his treasured baccy.

The Dutch should have arrived the next day, but the weather closed in on what should have been day two of our expedition. Blizzards, high winds and zero visibility engulfed our tiny tent. We were stranded a mile off Ward Hunt Island for eight long and drawn-out days, keeping ourselves amused by spring-cleaning the tent, telling stories and listening to the BBC World Service. The only consolation was that we would have made scant progress had we set off in that weather.

On Thursday, 13 March, a day when the cold was so extreme that I had felt numb all day and any movement was an ordeal, a tiny Twin Otter landed a couple of miles away from our tent on the beach at Ward Hunt Island. On the tiny plane came the Dutch expedition, one of whom was carrying Rune's cherished blue bag, followed by an unexpected visitor – Alan Bywaters. Dave Spurdens, our base man, had radioed from Resolute in a panic the night before when he realised I had forgotten to sign the consignment of travellers' cheques he was holding at Resolute Bay for our pick-up flight. In the worst case the money would be needed for an emergency medical evacuation or rescue flight, but Dave was unable to pay for anything without my signature. I had no choice but to pay the price for my oversight: a two-and-a-half-mile walk back to the landing strip to sit in the hut and laboriously sign each cheque one by one, so that they could be collected by a later flight and returned to Resolute. However, it was a blunder commensurate with Rune forgetting his blue bag, so in some way we were back on an equal footing, and if Rune had not forgotten his bag, I reasoned, I would not have been able to sign the cheques. We should not have needed reminding at that early stage that the smallest oversight can have near fatal consequences on the Arctic ice, but already we had made two slip-ups. Maybe we should have seen these events as ominous warnings.

The day after that we started out on the tortuous trek and made reasonable progress. But within days Rune's sledge had begun to show the first signs of damage from being pulled across the rubble and over pressure ridges. We had ordered carbon-fibre sledges but because it was impossible to examine them closely at Resolute Bay we failed to notice that the sledges were made of much weaker fibreglass. Our only option since then has been to reduce the weight on Rune's sledge and relay all of our equipment and provisions through most of the last ninety-seven miles.

For every mile we have clawed our way towards the Pole, we have had to walk at least three. First we carried half our load to a suitable clearing in the tangled maze of blocks that made up the first one hundred or so miles of our journey. Then we unpacked the sledges and dragged them back empty to our starting point, loaded them up with the remaining equipment and carried it through the jumbled frozen landscape to the clearing. It wasted time and energy, and as a consequence we now need more food, more fuel and, most importantly, a new sledge if we want to get to the Pole. Every night, after walking for up to seven hours in the biting winds, we have pitched our tent and then fought against overwhelming fatigue to patch up the cracks in Rune's sledge. We have drilled holes with a Swiss Army knife and used wire, tape, string and shoelaces to hold the pieces of Rune's sledge together.

Forty days after leaving Ward Hunt Island, I'm not sure how much longer Rune's sledge can hold, nor when the right moment is to ask for a resupply. I have even more doubts about our ability to cross leads of open water with the broken sledge. I wish I still had Richard Weber's data from his expeditions with Misha Malakhov with me.

In 1990, Borge Ousland and Erling Kagge made the first unsupported journey to the Pole by ski, a journey we are attempting to replicate. Then, in 1995, Richard Weber and Mikhail Malakhov went one better when they became the first men to walk from Ward Hunt Island to the North Pole and back unsupported. It was a phenomenal achievement, driven by Weber's belief that, in his words, 'going on an expedition to the North Pole, then taking a plane out is like climbing Mount Everest and getting helicoptered off the top'. Although we are not attempting to emulate Weber and Malakhov's return trip – for me reaching the Pole is all that counts – they did keep some of the most reliable and detailed records of weather conditions and distances covered each day, and it would be useful to compare our experiences with theirs.

After deciding our strategy, Rune and I had deliberately chosen to set off without any records of other expeditions, other than the memories of the experiences of our predecessors – William Parry, James Clark, Fridtjof Nansen, Robert Peary, Roald Amundsen, Wally Herbert and Ernest Shackleton – etched into our minds. However, just nine days and eight miles out from Ward Hunt Island we came by Weber's records in the strangest and most unexpected of ways.

On that day, 21 March, we had spotted the first damage to Rune's sledge, a crack along one of the Teflon runners underneath the fibreglass shell. It was not serious but the crack was wide enough to ensure the sledge would no longer float on water. We stopped a few hours later, earlier than usual because we were both depressed by the realisation that the crack represented the first serious threat to our chances of reaching the Pole.

The Arctic days were short at that time of year and it was soon dark. Several hours after darkness had fallen, we heard footsteps approaching our tent. We both feared at once that it was a polar bear, one of the world's largest carnivores. Knowing that the staple diet of polar bears is seals and explorers, Rune was out of the tent in a flash with our customised Sabatti rifle in his hand. He had expected to come face to face with a furry trespasser; instead he was confronted by a shivering, terror-stricken man. Alan Bywaters, a twenty-one-year-old student from London, tumbled into our tent and collapsed, clearly suffering from acute frostbite.

We had first met Alan Bywaters, who called his expedition Solo North, at the High Arctic boarding house at Resolute Bay where, like us, he had been preparing for an unsupported polar assault. He had boasted that despite his inexperience and lack of funds, he would 'reach the pole or come back in a box'. Despite his bold words we were not surprised to see him; it was obvious to any onlooker that Alan was inexperienced by polar expedition standards. Many had feared he would lose his life, and several of the locals attempted to persuade him not to set off from Resolute, but he had refused their advice.

We had suspected for some time after setting off from Ward Hunt Island that Alan had been following our ski tracks. There is no shame in following other expeditions' tracks; all explorers do it as it makes more sense to trail others who have gone ahead and possibly found an easier route through the quagmire of frozen rubble. But when he stumbled into our tent that night, Alan told us he had been making good progress through the rubble until he had fallen into a lead of open water and seen his sledge, with his radio – vital to any expedition – slide off the ice into the Arctic Ocean. Knowing that he faced certain death if he could not locate shelter, he had searched for our tracks in the snow and followed them for six hours through the rubble. Weak and suffering from severe frostbite, he had stumbled across the ice in temperatures of −39°C – around −60°C with windchill – until he found our tent.

Rune and I struggled to keep him warm. We knew that if his body temperature dropped any further he would soon be dead. That night, Rune and I huddled together in the tent and sandwiched Alan between our two bodies to fight the hypothermia that was threatening to overwhelm his body. Rune cooked some soup, propped him up in a sleeping-bag and fed it to him like a nurse with a stricken patient, while I clutched his limbs between my hands and in my armpits to encourage blood to flow through his frozen flesh. We knew we had to be careful; it is dangerous to massage frostbite injuries and we knew we should not attempt to thaw the flesh until we could be sure it would not freeze again.

As the weather deteriorated outside, we erected a radio antenna and called for a medevac emergency plane to rescue him. We were told to radio again in the morning, when the sun was up and we could assess the weather outside. It was a long night. Alan did not take long to drop off to sleep – his body was shutting down as hypothermia overpowered him and ice crystals formed in the cells of his body, drawing water from his tissues and triggering dehydration. He woke several times in the night complaining that he could not feel his toes. I examined them, and they were hard or wooden to the touch. It was a clear indication that he had severe frostbite and might lose his toes.

At six o'clock the next morning Alan woke up; much to our amazement he was as bright as a spark. Again we radioed First Air, the air company at Resolute and passed on our local weather report. While the radio operator told us to stand by for further instructions, Rune made Alan some more soup and tended to his terrible feet, by this time black and covered with blisters from frostbite. After a short while, the radio operator informed us that a rescue aeroplane had left Resolute and would be with us within a few hours. As soon as Alan heard that he was on the way home, his body collapsed in front of our eyes.

Rune spent the rest of the day preparing a meticulous landing strip, stamping on uneven blocks of ice and marking the edges with bags of snow and a flare. A couple of hours later we heard the drone of the rescue plane's propellers, but it could not land near us because of ice crystals in the air, so it set down around thirty miles north of our location and waited for three hours for the air to clear. When John O'Connell, a very modest pilot, finally landed on his third attempt, he commended Rune on his 600-foot-long strip and said it was as good as touching down at Edmonton airport. We strapped Alan into a sledge and carried him across a mile of uneven, broken-up ice to the landing strip, loaded him onto the plane, wished him well and waved him goodbye. As the door closed on the medevac plane it was very difficult to resist the temptation to climb on board ourselves and end the frozen torture.

The take-off was spectacular. With Alan's extra weight and what remained of his equipment on board, the plane needed the entire length of the ice floe to gather sufficient speed. We watched, our mouths wide open in astonishment as the plane struggled to build up enough speed to clear a pressure ridge of ice boulders at the end of the strip by just six inches.

We walked back to our tent and celebrated with brandy, pork scratchings, salami and soup. We had expended a lot of our food and fuel on Alan, and lost valuable time, but he had done us one favour: he had been trained by Richard Weber and left us Weber's 1992 schedule. Much to my relief, I found we were as far north as Weber had been at the same time during his expedition with Malakhov. This information quelled my concerns that we would never make it to the Pole and reassured me that we should soon be progressing faster.

A few days later, in my never-ending quest to cut weight to the minimum, I dumped Weber's schedule, and now I am regretting it. We are stuck here in a snow storm. Rune's sledge is severely damaged and I fear that we are running out of time, food and fuel. To make matters worse, yesterday we floated two and a half minutes south during the day. By this morning that distance had increased to three minutes, or three nautical miles. There is nothing we can do but pray the weather will improve so that we can make up the lost distance as soon as possible.

We broke camp at around eight this morning into a total white-out. This strange, moody light disconcerts me, particularly when there is a lot of new rubble to stumble across. I've got a bad back, mainly from pulling my sledge. Although it is lighter now it weighed around 300 pounds when we started out and now I am paying the price for pulling all that weight across the ice. It is very easy to make a wrong step in these conditions, and every time I slip, stumble or lose my balance, searing pains shoot up my back.

At last it has begun to feel warm once we get moving. After weeks of long hours of darkness, the sun has not set for several days now and spring seems to be on the way. This twenty-four-hour sunshine is a mixed blessing – it is a relief after the extreme cold of the first few weeks, but it heralds the start of the thaw and any leads of open water in the ice-cap will take longer to set.

Despite our troubles with the sledge, our injuries and the terrible weather, we set a new record today – seven miles, another milestone on our journey north and enough to warrant a celebratory nip of brandy in the tent tonight. Thirty miles so far this week; if it had not been for the storm it would have been forty.

Now we are inside the tent and Rune is cooking our dinner. I have opened the forty-day letter from my wife, containing messages from my three young daughters and memories of home. 'In a couple of days Alicia and Camilla will be at school and it is getting warm outside, so get on with it and hurry home,' Claire has written. Home seems a very long way away and right now there is no place I would rather be.

Day 41: Tuesday, 22 April

Argos report

00165	84.881N	71.253W	2	113/0610Z–113/0655
(3)	−.19116E+2	85	85	00

Position: 84°52'50" North; 71°15'10" West
Temperature: −19.1°C (in tent)
Windchill: −90°C
Hours of sunshine: 24
Nautical miles covered today: 8
Nautical miles so far: 105
Nautical miles to go (*in a straight line*): 310
Status: Storm

The ice is a mess after the high tides of the full moon a couple of days ago and we are drifting substantially west. We heard the women's relay team, Polar Relay, over the radio tonight. They are doing extremely well and it looks like they will go all the way. Hyoichi Kohno, who is attempting a solo trip to the North Pole from Ward Hunt Island, should be finished this week. Lucky sod.

It is blowing a gale today and we ought to stay in the tent, but after yesterday's record we decide there is nothing for it but to get out on to the ice and try to set a new record. The task has not been made any easier by the terrible night we had last night. It seemed exceptionally cold to me and consequently my feet have been frozen all day. Sometimes you forget what the warmth of the sun can feel like. The cold up here is unlike anything else, it soaks any vestiges of heat from deep within my muscles and joints, and I feel as if I will never be warm again.

I stick my head outside the door of the tent and I instantly have second thoughts about stepping outside. Snow is blowing over my frostbitten nose at twenty to twenty-five knots. The temperature outside the tent is −51°C, but in the full force of the elements, the windchill takes it down beyond −90°C. All I want to do is crawl back inside my sleeping-bag, but I remember what Geoff Somers, the plain-speaking base-camp manager on my 1996 Geographic South Pole expedition, had said when I wanted to give up: 'Get out and try. It's better than sitting in the tent and drifting five miles east.'

Buoyed by the thought of Geoff's words from yesteryear, we set a second record in two days today – eight miles covered and with it the sublime ritual of a celebratory snifter of brandy for the second night running. Once we get to 85°N, a little over seven miles ahead, we will step up our work-rate to eight hours a day. That should give us an extra mile a day. It's good to see some progress at last and I'm feeling more confident.

Day 42: Wednesday, 23 April

Argos report

00165	84.889N	70.646W	1	114/0805Z–114/0833
(3)	−.19200E+2	85	85	00

Position: 84°53'21" North; 70°38'48" West
Temperature: −19.2°C (in tent)
Windchill: −85°C
Hours of sunshine: 24
Nautical miles covered today: two-thirds of a mile
Nautical miles so far: 106
Nautical miles to go (*in a straight line*): 309
Status: Storm

Another terribly frustrating day. Yesterday I was on top of the world, thinking we could walk in any weather, but today was without question heavy work. Sharp winds, gusting 30 to 35 mph. It's hard to stand up straight.

We drifted half a degree west overnight – extremely worrying. As the weather warms up, the winds are getting stronger. Sometimes it seems as if we are walking on a giant rudderless galleon, with the pressure ridges as sails. Every time the wind blows, it pushes the ice further from where we need and want to go.

We were talking about the perfect holiday today and I hope to take my girls on one when I get back. I plan to whisk Claire off to Venice and Verona for the opera festival, and Alicia, Amelia and Camilla to Norway to visit Rune at his family's farm. If there is time I would also like to squeeze in a long weekend at the beach in Devon or Cornwall with my daughters. Right now, the thought of lying on a beach, basking under a warm sun, is immensely appealing.

I am thinking also of poor Ron, Claire's father who died recently, a lot on this trip – especially while walking. What a terrible stupid waste it was. Then I wonder what we are doing here. I think of Jim Lovell, when he missed the Moon in Apollo 13; we are pretty close to missing the Pole. We can always come back of course, or get a resupply, but what a way to live.

The Kid – Rune – is truly good company, except that his Walkman broke today, so no more Van Morrison on Sundays.

By the end of the day, after walking for seven hours in atrocious conditions and pitching the tent when we feel we cannot take another step, I discover that we have drifted back further than we have walked. We are now at 84°53'16" North, admittedly only five seconds further south than the point at which we started, but nevertheless that leaves us a twelfth of a mile further from the Pole than this morning. If it were not for the wind we would be ten or twelve miles closer to the Pole tonight. This is a rare form of torture.

Day 43: Thursday, 24 April

Argos report

00165	85.025N	68.822W	2	115/0125Z–115/0200
(3)	–.19830E+2	85	85	00

Position: 85°01'30" North; 68°49'20" West
Temperature: −19.8°C (in tent)
Windchill: −79°C
Hours of sunshine: 24
Nautical miles covered today: 8
Nautical miles so far: 114
Nautical miles to go (*in a straight line*): 303
Status: Storm

We drifted even further back overnight. When we wake up, we are at 84°52'38" North and 69°25'37" West, almost a mile south and some way east of where we were at seven o'clock last night.

Still I wake up feeling hopeful. The 85th Parallel is in sight, and I am determined this morning to get there. Once we leave camp I realise that the task will not be easy – a bloody hard day in total white-out again. To say the weather is debilitating is a massive understatement.

I think of Camilla all day. It is her first day at school, and I should be there with her. I hope she got my flowers and had a nice day, my little girl.

We struggle through gale force winds, and we are rewarded when I get the GPS out to read our position. Rune is ecstatic when I tell him we are a mile and a half beyond 85°N, especially as this milestone warrants a nip of brandy as a reward for both of us. Bliss. The sublime pleasure of these little luxuries is worth more than their extra weight in our sledges. A taste of home is such a pleasure out on the ice.

Tomorrow, a new hurdle. According to plan we should go up to eight hours a day on the ice. We're getting used to the extra hours afforded by the midnight sun and feel ready to take advantage of the long hours of daylight. I have almost forgotten the misery of those endless hours of darkness in the first few weeks of the expedition. Maybe that is the secret of a good adventurer: we forget the misery quickly enough to want to do it again. Our fitness, strength and morale are picking up, and I feel it's about time we faced up to fighting the wind for a least ten hours a day.

No leads of open water today, but we are still subject to a big drift east.

Day 44: Friday, 25 April

Argos report

00165	85.121N	67.534W	1	116/0015Z–116/0033
(3)	–.21902E+2	85	85	00

Position: 85°07'17" North; 67°32'04" West
Temperature: –21.9°C (in tent)
Windchill: –79°C
Hours of sunshine: 24
Nautical miles covered today: 6
Nautical miles so far: 120
Nautical miles to go (*in a straight line*): 295
Status: Storm

Our worst weather to date, but nevertheless we make the plunge and emerge from the tent into a ferocious storm. A total white-out – I cannot see Rune six feet in front of me. Absolutely terrible conditions which make me wonder what the hell I am doing here.

A slow, cold day during which we are very lucky not to fall into the water. Three times Rune stops on leads of open water covered with fresh snow, and on each of them we could very easily drop through the fragile frozen membrane into the icy water.

I am also nearly stranded on an island of ice while crossing an open lead. Rune leads the way, using a large floe as a stepping stone. When I step on to the ice floe, there is a creaking sound as the ice holding the floe in place splinters, and Rune seems to float away from me. Then I realise that he is the stationary one and I am floating away from him – petrifying, particularly as I am a weak swimmer. Rune runs along his side of the lead, unable to control his laughing, and shouts at me to jump. When he stops running and laughing, and shouts urgently with a concerned look on his face, I realise there is nothing for it but to make a leap for Rune's shore. I land at his feet – a narrow escape. When I calm down and look at the lead I can see how lucky I have been: about thirty yards further east it opens up to around twenty feet across, far too wide for anyone to jump.

We are now camped in a particularly dangerous spot. There is open water on two sides of us and a pressure ridge on the third, which indicates we are sited on a small drifting pan. Too much movement tonight and we could be stranded, a pair of polar castaways.

The perilous position of our tent reminds me of a similar occasion on my South Pole expedition in 1996. I was so tired after a day of laboriously picking my way through and across dozens of crevasses that I pitched my tent without being too concerned about my exact whereabouts. Shortly after nine o'clock, when I had cooked and eaten, then de-iced my mittens and outer clothes by warming them on the stove, I performed the same ritual I completed every night before going to sleep. I stretched down into my sleeping-bag for my plastic pee bottle and paid a last call before bed-time. Then, as usual, I tipped the contents into the outer tent. This last action was the most important of all in the ceremony. My urine would normally freeze in the bottle if left overnight in the sleeping-bag.

As I tipped out the contents of my bottle I did not at first register that there was no sound. Usually, I would hear a fizz as the snow melted and then set within seconds around my pool of urine. If there was no snow, only ice, I would at least hear a slight crackle as my effluent hit the taut, frosted surface. But this time there was silence, and that concerned me. Tucked up, warm and secure in my down sleeping-bag, I really did not relish getting up to discover the reason for the silence, but the quietness worried me. Despite my fatigue as a result of another exhausting day, I clambered out of the bag and took a look.

I could see nothing. Where there should have been a trace of urine or a spot of crusty snow, there was a deep blue gaping orifice. My befuddled brain struggled to work out the implications, then they hit me like a bombshell. I had camped on a narrow ice-bridge across one of the many crevasses I had been gingerly side-stepping all day. Fortunately for me, by this point there was twenty-four hour daylight. If it had been dark and I had taken two steps in front of my tent, I would have plummeted to the bottom of the crevasse.

While trying to keep my nerve, I considered my options. My full weight plus the tent, fuel and food were balanced on a precariously thin layer of snow on an ice-bridge that could give way at any moment. However, I reasoned that if it had held so far it was likely to hold for the rest of the night, and I've always believed in the adage that if it ain't broke, don't fix it. My position above the icy abyss seemed as safe as it could be, and in my exhaustion I did not want to contemplate the prospect of packing everything up, getting dressed and then looking for another suitable place to camp, which could be an hour's walk or more away.

Maybe there was something else at work. I'm not a particularly religious person, but like most explorers I am consumed with superstitions and, at times, feel that in some way the spirits of my illustrious predecessors accompany me in my darker moments. At that moment, my admittedly somewhat unhinged and drowsy mind reasoned, the Antarctic and all who had battled with her would decide my fate. If I am meant to go now, I thought, then there is nothing I can do about it. If not, I might as well stop worrying about it and go to sleep.

At times, when one is on the ice it pays to ignore rational thought and rely on gut instinct. There is the danger that one might fall into the trap that Henri-Frédéric Amiel warned against, that 'A belief is not true because it is useful', but all the latest technology employed by modern-day explorers is no substitute for the wisdom and judgement gained from experience in the field. And that night, experience told me it was safe to sleep on the ice-bridge.

Tonight, while Rune and I float on this small pan of ice three hundred miles from the North Pole, I hope we are wise to spend the night in this precarious position.

Before I slither down into my sleeping-bag, I reflect on what has been a very strange day, and hope for good weather tomorrow.

Day 45: Saturday, 26 April

Argos report

00165	85.153N	67.103W	1	117/0105Z–117/0133
(3)	−.1660E+2	102	102	00

Position: 85°09'10" North; 67°06'12" West
Temperature: −16.6°C (in tent)
Windchill: −59°C
Hours of sunshine: 24

Nautical miles covered today: 6
Nautical miles so far: 126
Nautical miles to go (*in a straight line*): 291
Status: Damaged equipment

At 3.30 p.m. today, we lose the Pole. The bottom of Rune's sledge finally gives in. Several big patches of fibreglass fall off in the rubble and two runners collapse. We make our way to a pan and decide what to do.

At first I am livid that we have been let down by the sledge, but now that my initial anger has subsided I feel extremely frustrated and very disappointed. We decide we have no choice but to call up a rescue aeroplane. It would take days for the base camp to prepare for a resupply with a new sledge and equipment, and we are floating east at an alarmingly fast rate.

Before I call up the rescue plane, Rune turns to me and says: 'Remember David, it will take us a very long time to get back to where we are today, but it will take only two seconds to radio for rescue. We must make the right decision.' He is right. We are abandoning more than just forty-five days on the ice. It takes the best part of a year to prepare and raise sponsorship for an expedition, but today it is clear we have no option but to call it quits.

We radio Morag Howell, the base manager for First Air, one of the two companies that fly Twin Otters from Resolute Bay on to the ice-cap. She sounds delighted, probably because she doesn't have to fly all the way to the Pole. Both First Air and its rival, Borek Air, have aircraft at the Pole – they fell through thin ice in the 1970s when they came to a stop after landing. Morag says we are likely to be picked up some time on Monday. We have plenty of food left, and we don't mind waiting if it means we can share the flight with another expedition to save our costs. Morag tells me that we have covered the same mileage in the same time as Weber and Malakhov, and as Borge Ousland, who in 1994 became the first man to reach the Pole solo and unsupported.

These statistics are somewhat meaningless and provide scant con-solation when you are let down by your equipment, particularly as I am convinced we would have made it if our sledge had not collapsed. For the first one hundred miles we had to relay all our equipment because of Rune's broken sledge, so in mileage terms we would be within ninety miles of the Pole, but again this statistical detail means very little when you have to admit defeat.

Day 46: Sunday, 27 April

Argos report

00165   85.150N   66.913W   1   118/2220Z–118/2255

(3)   −.2012E+2   102   102   00

Position: 85°09'00" North; 66°54'47" West
Temperature: −20°C (in tent)
Windchill: −67°
Hours of sunshine: 24
Nautical miles covered today: 0
Nautical miles so far: 126
Nautical miles to go (*in a straight line*): 291
Status: Storm

It was very difficult to sleep last night, despite our exhaustion. I feel bitterly disappointed, especially as our failing was not our direct fault, but simply the result of a broken sledge. I am convinced we would have made it. At our current rate of walking it would have taken us twenty-eight days to reach the Pole and we have thirty-seven days' food left.

The fact that we will soon be heading home has not sunk in yet. We did discuss a resupply, but it would take weeks for a new sledge to arrive from Norway, by which time we would also need a new supply of dehydrated foods, which will also have to be ordered and prepared.

Maybe next year. Two months and a year to plan, but a lot of experience gained, no doubt about it. Rune is such a brilliant partner. I hope he will come back next year. He truly is superb in all areas, and I don't think I would have made it this far without him.

We are a very odd couple – he the droll, laid-back hippy on the surface but a highly experienced, extremely fit trained killer under-neath; me, the businessman and bumbling father of three who is obsessed with this mysteriously beautiful and unforgiving place – but an excellent team.

Rune seems to be over the worst of the disappointment. He is a bit withdrawn, but that all changes when he remembers that he has packed a massive Churchill cigar to smoke at the Pole. He turns to me, with a faint smile on his face, and says: 'I don't know what I'm waiting for. Fuck it, why don't I smoke it now?'

He scurries out of the tent and I hear him rummaging through the contents of the sledges. A minute later he is back in the tent with eight inches of Havana's finest clamped between his teeth, enveloped in maduro smoke and with a wry smile on his face. We shake hands, congratulate each other on having at least got this far, and decide to make a party of it. We polish off the last of the pork scratchings, suck several cubes of chocolate each, and wash it all down with the last of the brandy.

The alcohol makes me even more depressed, but it also helps to dissipate the tensions of the last few days, and I now feel very tired. The exhaustion of a month and a half on the ice and fourteen months' preparation has begun to hit me. Rune, as always, has managed to be sanguine about the whole sorry episode. He turns to me, with his cigar almost burnt to the stub, and says: 'David, there's always a good side to every story. Yesterday I ran out of tobacco – maybe the sledge was meant to break.'

Over the radio, we hear that the Dutch Nomad Nord Pol team and the women's Polar Relay team have not moved for most of the week, so at least we can say we had the best week in terms of mileage.

Day 47: Monday, 28 April

Position: Floating backwards – we've stopped taking readings
Temperature: −22.6°C (in tent)
Windchill: −66°C
Hours of sunshine: 24
Status: Damaged Equipment

The pick-up planned for yesterday did not materialise, so now we are stuck on the ice, relaying hourly weather reports to the whole of northern Canada. The sky is clear and the weather is fine, so it looks like we will be picked up at five p.m.

Inside the tent it is down to −5°C as we have the stove on, the warmest yet. Everything is changing quickly and summer is nearly here. Rune has marked out an exemplary landing strip again. He really takes pride in his strips.

We are getting bored waiting for the pick-up. Once we have left the ice I know I will miss it, but right now I just want to get home to see my wife and family, and get back to some kind of normality.

Rune and I agreed on Saturday to return next year, and since then we have drawn up a list of improvements to equipment and provisions that ought to make next year's expedition more successful:

1. The sledge must be lighter, smaller and stronger, with a better and lighter canopy. Next time we must double-check it to ensure that it is made of carbon-fibre, as ordered, and not fibreglass.

2. We both agree the tent should be smaller and lighter, and considerably easier and quicker to put up. We spent too much time struggling with this year's tent in high winds, increasing the risk of frostbite.

3. We need shorter skis – around 180 to 190 centimetres long. Although only thirty centimetres shorter than this year's skis, we think less length will make them considerably more manageable in the rubble. We both fell several times because our skis snagged in rutted and lumpy stretches.

4. Less maintenance equipment.

5. We need to find some kind of socks or tights with a vapour barrier to stop sweat percolating to the outer layers of clothing and footwear, where it freezes and becomes cold and heavy. If not, we need to find a way to stop the plastic bags we are using as vapour barriers from slipping as we walk.

6. We need larger sleeping-bags with an outer layer, a pocket to store night-time necessities, a vapour barrier layer, and no zips to let our warmth percolate out. A Thinsulate inner bag inside a goose-down outer bag would be ideal.

7. Better outer gloves, made of cotton or fur. This year's gloves froze rigid in the cold making it impossible to warm our hands by flexing our fingers.

8. We need larger micro-fibre jackets with bigger hoods, and they must be breathable to let the sweat out when walking.
9. We need to keep better records. A temperature chart with details of other successful expeditions' daily mileages and drift would be ideal.
10. Spices and herbs to pep up the food. The same six or seven dishes for two months becomes very boring.
11. More letters from my daughters to read along the way.
12. More music tapes.
13. Stronger aluminium ski poles – we broke three stumbling through the rubble and pressure ridges on the first few days. In the cold the ski poles become like glass and shatter very easily. We also need to stick more tape on the grips for better insulation. Even with three pairs of gloves on, a lot of heat is lost through the ski poles. My hands became very cold and I came close to frostbite.
14. Gaiters from ankle area of boots to below the knee to prevent snow and ice from entering boots.
15. A thermos for Irish stew, with cups and bowls.
16. Better boot insoles, with more support and thermal properties to reduce the amount of heat lost through the sole of the boot into the ski.
17. A larger piece of sheepskin to protect my frostbitten nose.
18. New ski goggles for both of us.
19. Good coffee, tea and cognac.

We spend most of the afternoon talking on the radio to anybody who will listen – the Polar Shelf project, Borek Air and, of course, the pilots on the way to pick us up. We've arranged flights to arrive back in England on Friday, so only two days to kill in Resolute. If we had succeeded in reaching the Pole, these would have been days of celebration and partying; now we will be bored rigid and embarrassed.

The plane arrives on time, shortly after five, spotted first as a dot in the sky but within minutes above us and circling, checking that the ice is strong enough to take its weight. The sight of the plane prompts a horrible feeling, really quite gruesome. For 46 days we have been walking alone on the ice, surviving by ourselves, and all of a sudden we have outsiders violating an environment that, although harsh and unforgiving, has become our home, safe from the gaze of the outside world. To make matters worse, they are arriving to ferry us back to civilisation as failures.

It doesn't matter what excuse we put forward, we have failed. We may have saved Alan Bywater's life; we may have survived fifty-five days; we may have kept to schedule despite broken equipment; and we may have told each other that we could have done it, but the bottom line is that we have failed. When we get back to England, people will make excuses and say, 'Oh, but this ... but that.' But in reality there are no buts, we have bloody failed.

As the aeroplane approaches, we promise each other a lot of things. I will go to Norway to see Rune's farm and meet his parents. As ever, I am very keen to keep to my promises as rhetoric can be so cheap when you are on the ice; as soon as you get back to civilisation all these undertakings are easily forgotten.

The plane lands and the pilots come over and try to cheer us up. 'Well, we'll see you next year,' says Russ Bomberry, the American Indian chief who is captain of the plane. He is right, and there is little else he can say, but it does little to assuage the overwhelming sense of dejection and disappointment we both feel.

For the last time this year we take down the tent, pack it up and lift it with the sledges into the Twin Otter.

'Jesus,' Russ says when he sees the underside of the sledge, stripped of both its runners and showing more fresh air than fibreglass. 'Why did you bother to keep going? Why didn't you stop?'

'Because you keep going until the tank is empty,' Rune answers, 'that's why.'

Rune and I look at each other in silence – there is little left to say – and cast one last look around the frozen landscape before climbing up the ladder into the plane. The moment when the co-pilot closes the plane's door behind me is probably the worst feeling I have ever had. I have conquered the seven summits, the Geographic and Magnetic South Poles, and the Magnetic and Geomagnetic North Poles, yet ultimately I am still no closer to my goal, the Adventurers' Grand Slam, than I was when I first failed at the Geographic North Pole in 1983. The North Pole, the hardest piece in the jigsaw, still eludes me.

Tears well up in my eyes as the plane takes off and I look down on the unforgiving icy ravages below. Fourteen years ago, when I was young and cocky, the Arctic had given me a sound mental and physical beating for having the temerity to try to conquer it on my own and without sufficient experience. I have returned older, wiser and more experienced, but the contempt with which the Arctic treated me in 1983 seems like a fair punishment in comparison with the defeat we have just suffered at the hands of bad luck.

Rune and I do not say much to each other as the plane begins the eight-hour flight home. As we fly over the pack ice and see the rubble, the pressure ridges and the leads of open water we have crossed, it slowly dawns on me how significant our achievement has been. Even with the aeroplane's tendency to compress time and space, obliterating the beauty and variation of any landscape it crosses and giving the impression of flat monotony and homogeneity, our efforts are impressive. 'Christ, we covered a large distance,' I think to myself. 'If it takes several hours to fly over the distance we covered on foot, then we certainly walked a long way.'

Rune turns to me from the other side of the cramped fuselage. It seems exactly the same thoughts have been passing through his mind. He shrugs his shoulders and says, 'What a long way to go with a broken sledge.'

Tuesday, 29 April

Shortly after midnight, with the sun low in the northern sky, we spot the landing strip at Eureka and touch down. Rune and I jump out of the plane, by now pleased to be back in relative civilisation with the promise of a hot meal and a soft bed ahead of us.

Eureka is one of the most desolate spots on Earth, but like most places in the High Arctic its loneliness in such magnificent surroundings conveys a rarely found beauty. Eight men live in isolation at Eureka in a string of Nissen huts at the bottom of a vast powder-white valley. This Canadian government weather station beside a frozen fjord, surrounded by satellite dishes and radio aerials festooned with blinking lights, is half a mile from the airstrip and three hours' flying time from any other living person. Their only company, besides the aircraft which land to refuel once or twice a week, are the musk oxen, caribou and Arctic wolves that come scavenging for food around their kitchens.

It is the kind of location that most people see only in James Bond movies. It is not difficult to imagine a camouflaged secret agent dropping in from a mission behind enemy lines, pulling off his gear to reveal an immaculate dinner jacket underneath. Unsurprisingly, it is prohibitively expensive to overnight at Eureka – the prices rival a five-star grand hotel. A spartan room with a single bed costs $350 a night, breakfast is $60 and the half-mile bus ride from the airstrip to the weather station is $198. There is a single communal bathroom, but the $350 charge does not even include a towel. But all these charges are academic to us – after seven weeks on the ice, the last thing we are carrying is money.

Accommodation is the least of our concerns anyway. More than anything we want something to eat. For over seven weeks we have survived on dehydrated foods laced with vegetable and soya oil. For the last hour of the flight I had been dreaming of a thick, juicy steak with a lobster tail on top, but now even a hamburger looks unlikely.

We walk down to the weather station along a road with signs that warn of lemmings crossing the carriageway, and explain that we have just been airlifted from the polar ice-cap with not a penny to our names. After explaining our predicament I decide to chance my neck and ask the cook if we can have a free meal. He shakes his head, so I attempt to appeal to his generosity with promises of presents from civilisation.

'I'll send you a postcard from England,' I say.

He is not impressed.

'I'll send you the money when I get home,' I offer.

The cook shrugs indifference.

'I'll send you a bottle of whisky,' I plead.

That does the trick. In a part of the world where alcohol is strictly controlled and the nearest liquor store is two flights and $1700 away, the promise of booze, it seems, can buy almost anything. We sit down to eat one of the most plain but best-tasting meals I can remember, a straightforward American cooked breakfast of eggs, bacon, sausage and pancakes washed down with several cups of freshly brewed coffee.

However, while we munch through the massive fry-ups it occurs to me that the weathermen are taking very little interest in us. After all, it cannot be that often that they receive visitors, let alone two polar explorers with tales of bravery and fortitude to tell. A few minutes later we realise the reason for their disinterest. The door of the dining-room swings open and four ebullient young women, clearly highly excited, come bursting in. They are one of the teams from the Polar Relay, an expedition to walk to the North Pole in relays of four British women at a time. Unsurprisingly, we stand little chance against this kind of competition. Having not seen a woman for maybe six months, the Eureka men have eyes only for one thing. As soon as the members of the Polar Relay team sit down to eat, the weather techies are around them like bees around a honey-pot – a salutary lesson to Rune and me on the priorities in life. There we were thinking we were something special for having survived on the ice for a month and a half, but to a handful of men in this Arctic wilderness it is nothing in comparison with the attractions of female company.

While out on the ice I had thought the Polar Relay team were taking the easy option, not making clear quite how they were getting to the Pole. Each relay team would fly out to Resolute, train for a couple of weeks, then fly out on to the polar ice-cap, walk for eight days towards the Pole and then hand on the baton to the next team.

But now that we have met the four girls in Eureka, I have to concede they are wonderful. They have really brought us back down to earth. They have been on the ice for eight days – none of them has even been to the High Arctic before – and they have loved it. They are bursting with excitement and full of the joy of their achievements. They have spent just eight days in the most inhospitable of environments, and they are not even part of the team that has the distinction of reaching the North Pole, yet they are quite obviously awe-inspired by the whole experience. They have cracked on, whatever the weather, and kept to their target of six miles a day. The only thing that has slowed them down has been waiting for the next resupply and switchover of teams. They have done a fantastic job.

The dining-room vibrates with the sound of their exuberance, while I sit in the corner like Ebenezer Scrooge at Christmas, begrudging them their achievements. 'You miserable old bastard,' I think to myself. 'Here you are getting sniffy about they way they are doing their expedition, yet they are clearly full of all the wonders of their exploits.' They are on the top of the roof and Rune and I are on the bottom of the floor, and to compound it all the weather techies have been getting themselves in a frenzy about these British women coming through. I realise that I have lost sight of why I started exploring all those years ago when I was a thirteen-year-old climbing in the Brecon Beacons. I have spent most of the previous two and a half years in the polar regions and I have lost some of the inspiration and enthusiasm that has led me to these remote places in the first place. The women turn out to be wonderful reminders of why I started exploring and have brought back to me with a jolt what expeditions are all about and how magical they are.

After we finish eating, the weather technicians cannot get rid of us fast enough. The first thing one of them says to us is, 'We'll give you a lift back up to the airstrip. You can sleep for free in the sleeping-bags in one of the huts up there.'

'It's okay,' I reply. 'We can hang around. It's all right, we want to unwind before we go to sleep.'

He is having none of it. 'Yeah, but we can give you a lift up free of charge.'

They usually charge $198, so I wonder what is going on. It ought to be obvious to me that the weather technicians want us out of the way, but after so long on the ice we seem to have lost the ability to pick up the subtle nuances of human interaction. When the penny drops, Rune and I toddle off with our tails between our legs and make our own way up to the airline hut up at the airstrip, which is at least heated so we can lay out our sleeping-bags.

By the time we get to the hut – a twenty-minute walk at the most – we are exhausted. Suddenly it has hit us. We have been battling the cold and the wind for every hour of fifty-five days and now we are worn out. Having not washed in all that time we are seriously smelly, our clothes are sticky with grime, our tempers are frayed and our resolve is shattered. But most of all we are dead on our feet. Without washing or taking our clothes off, we collapse on to the bunks and sleep around the clock.

Wednesday, 30 April

After a much-needed sleep we catch another short flight in the morning, this time back to Resolute Bay, the hub for all polar expeditions in the Canadian High Arctic. Although explorers often joke that Resolute is another name for hell, because it is so desolate and the starting-point for several months of self-inflicted misery and suffering, we are pleased to see it, not least because it is the penultimate destination before home.

We roll into Qausuittuq Inns North, the boarding-house where most polar explorers prepare for the onslaught of their expeditions, or repair to when the trial is over. Joy Rochen, the cook who dotes on explorers as they pass through, is waiting with lunch ready on the table.

'Don't bother washing. Sit down and tuck in. You must be starving,' she says, much to my surprise.

She is right. We are ravenous, but I am surprised she has not noticed how bad we smell. It does not take long.

'My God, you hum like nothing I have smelled before,' she says as she brings the food over to us. 'That's bad enough to curdle milk.'

We are summarily dispatched to the showers to wash the best part of two months' sweat, grime, anxiety and toil from our bodies. Cleanly scrubbed, we return to the table.

Over the next few hours the humiliating rite of explaining our failure begins and never seems to end. The boarding-house is busy with other expeditioners, including Geoff Somers, who accompanied me on the Ultimate Challenge, an expedition we led with ten novices to the Magnetic North Pole in 1996. He cannot believe the damage to the sledge, but his amazement that we did not give up and continued to push towards the Pole makes little difference – there is nothing worse than having to explain why you did not succeed again and again and again.

Other explorers seem to have made a virtue of failure; in Britain, it seems, failure is perceived as being more heroic than success. If you fail, people seem to reason, it must be difficult; if you succeed, then it must have been easy. Well I am ashamed of failing. Forget the easy, reassuring rhetoric, we failed and that's the end of it. It is horrible. There is no excuse. We failed. If you are an adventurer you go out and do something, and that's it. If you try to climb Everest and you're attempting to get to the summit and you don't get up, you have failed. You can say, 'Well it was cold and it was windy, and it was the worst weather in a hundred years', and that's a good excuse, but ultimately you have still failed.

That evening, already sick of explaining ourselves, we catch a plane south, across the Arctic tundra to Toronto. I take Rune up the CN Tower and we have a meal at an oyster bar. The day after the 1997 General Election we arrive back in Britain to face our sponsors, friends and families, and to go through the whole sorry process of explaining our downfall all over again.

As we collect our baggage at Heathrow's Terminal Four, we watch Tony Blair's triumphant entrance to Downing Street on television with a mixture of astonishment and bewilderment. After two and a half months in the High Arctic, cut off from any news from the outside world, Britain has changed substantially – and so, it seems, have we.

3

Be Prepared

*Getting Ready for
North Pole 1998*

I T WAS WONDERFUL to return home. While I had been away my wife
and children had moved into a new house, and they welcomed me
back into our new home. My daughters, Amelia, Camilla and Alicia,
clambered all over me. Although this was extremely delightful, it
brought home to me just how much they missed me and made me
feel very guilty. Rune and I felt pretty lousy, but fortunately nobody
else seemed to care. They were just pleased to see us, and in their eyes
it was a major achievement to have got as far as we did. I'm lucky in
that I have a group of friends who do not care what I do, or how
successful I am, and within a couple of weeks Rune returned to
Norway and I returned to normal life.

However, before I could finally wind down the 1997 expedition I
had to visit the sponsors. I did the rounds straight away, trying to get
the money in, and it was quite plain they were not all going to play
ball. The main sponsor, Typhoo, was very good. Rajiv Wahi, the
managing director, was marvellous. He said that they had always seen
it as a long-shot and he committed there and then to backing us in

1998. Tom Shebbeare of the Prince's Trust was equally supportive, as was Peter McPhillips at Buxted. To my relief all the other sponsors at least offered to back me the next year, but it meant I would need to find some new funding for the 1998 expedition.

In all, I collected about two thirds of the funding I had been promised – more than I expected. Those that did not pay up said that the sponsorship had been specifically for reaching the North Pole, and that I would get the money when I reached the goal. Fair enough. It is rare to be paid in full if you have not completed a job in any profession, and although I am not a professional explorer in the strictest sense, I still have to respect the fact that in my sponsors' eyes I had not achieved what I had been paid to do. However, it made raising the funds for the 1998 expedition all the more difficult.

Although we were very dejected, ultimately we felt quite good because we were convinced we would have made it to the Pole – weather permitting – if our equipment had not failed. Polar exploration is at best a fifty-fifty gamble. There are so many variables to contend with, ranging from how cold it is and how much the wind blows to the stamina of the explorers and the sturdiness of their equipment, that any departing polar expedition knows its fate is not entirely in its own hands. In the Arctic, where there is no land between the departure point and the destination, the odds are stacked even more against the explorer than in the Antarctic, where the climate is colder but at least most of the ice covers solid ground. Every explorer hoping to conquer the Geographical North Pole knows that his destiny depends as much on his luck with the shifting thin ice that forms his route to the top of the world as on his preparation, experience and determination.

Trying to raise North Pole expedition sponsorship from businessmen used to dealing with certainties, or at least calculable risks, is difficult, so, like other explorers before me, I decided to capitalise on the fact that I had failed twice before. Failure can often seem a more interesting story than untrammelled success. Surprisingly, this policy worked. The media seem to love nothing more than a fighter who, despite repeated setbacks, continues to battle his personal demons, and undoubtedly the fact that Rune and I had rescued Alan Bywaters had helped to raise our profile.

With this in mind I contacted the BBC, who since 1983 had covered some of my previous expeditions, and the *Daily Telegraph* because I was impressed by the support they had given to Richard Noble and Andy Green's attempt to set a supersonic land-speed record in ThrustSSC on the desert flats of Nevada. I also told them of my plans to fly Alicia, my eight-year-old daughter, and my wife, Claire, to the North Pole to meet me if we made it. As far as I could find out, Alicia would be the youngest person ever to set foot on the Geographic North Pole. A reporter and photographer from the *Daily Telegraph* and a camera crew from the BBC agreed to accompany us to the High Arctic for the departure from Ward Hunt Island in early March, for a resupply five weeks later, and to fly to the Pole for our arrival in early May.

With television and press coverage promised, it was easier to arouse interest from sponsors. They realised we had not failed because we were not experienced enough, nor because we had fallen out or made some crass mistakes or poor decisions. We had no frostbite to show for our troubles, and it was clear we had been fit enough and had got into the right routine to make it to the Pole.

I decided to take a break from organising North Pole 1998 in June and July to give myself some time to make good every one of my promises that I would treat my wife and children and pay back many friends who had helped me in the Arctic. During the 1997 expedition I had kept a meticulous record of all the pledges I made, not least because talk is cheap, especially when you are thousands of miles from home, but also because the treats offered the promise of gratification at the end of all the hard slog. In May and early June, I took several groups of friends to various restaurants around the country. Scott and Shackleton had a tradition of meeting for a meal at Simpson's in the Strand in London after an expedition, and in the interests of maintaining the tradition I took Rune there for a slap-up meal. Bit by bit I worked through the rest of the list, ticking off the undertakings I had vowed to keep.

Best of all, I spent a lot of time with the children, and did indeed take them on holiday to Norway to see Rune on his farm in the mountains of Trollheimen. It was good to see where my friend had grown up, particularly because we had often talked on the ice about where he lived, his friends, his parents and his brothers. He showed us where he had learned to climb mountains and canoe on the lakes, gaining experience in how to deal with the cold in Norway's severe winters.

In July I fulfilled another promise by taking Claire to the opera festival at Verona, and to visit Venice. In the last few years I had spent a large portion of my time away from my wife and now she needed spoiling to thank her for persevering with my adventuring, and to show her that she is far from forgotten when I am away. If anything, expeditions to remote parts of the world have served to make me realise how easy it is to take family and friends for granted when one is at home, and I always return filled with resolve to make more of an effort with everyone.

When Claire and I returned from Italy, Rune and I learnt that we were to receive bravery awards from the Royal Humane Society for our rescue of Alan Bywaters. We had not heard a word from Alan since our return from the Arctic, but this announcement made up for it. I had also been told while on the ice that the Royal Scottish Geographic Society had decided to bestow its prestigious Livingstone Medal on me. In October I travelled up to Glasgow for the ceremony, held on the same day as the society's annual dinner, with the bust of one of the world's greatest explorers residing nearby in the committee room.

I received the medal in recognition of my efforts in exploration and work in other fields, such as the contributions I had made to the advancement of science when I traced the position of the Magnetic North Pole in 1984 and measured the largest magnetic declination on record, and through my association with the Prince's Trust. To say I was honoured and very proud would be an understatement. The medal is not awarded every year, only when the society sees fit, and when I looked at the list of my forebears, which included Robert Peary, Robert Scott, Ernest Shackleton, Roald Amundsen, Lord Kitchener, Sir Edmund Hillary, Wally Herbert, Neil Armstrong and Sir Francis Chichester, I was humbled.

It was truly a great honour, and all the more so because the Royal Geographic Society in London had always given me the cold shoulder. In my twenties I had been told by an RGS fellow that I would never be asked to lecture at the RGS because I had been educated at a comprehensive school. In 1983, before my first North Pole bid, I approached the society to seek official recognition and approval for my expedition, but I was received by a condescending committee whose members asked me if I knew how to change a valve on a radio – forty years after the birth of the transistor – and enquired whether I would be wearing string vests. In that short interview they made it quite clear that I did not have the right background for their patronage. Now, after over thirty expeditions, I still have not received support or approval from the RGS.

A few weeks after the Livingstone Medal ceremony I joined Peter McPhillips, chief executive of Buxted, one of my main sponsors, for a charity bicycle ride to raise funds for research into the debilitating affliction Friedrich's ataxia. We flew out to Dublin and had a raucous night on the town, training for the ride by drinking six pints of Guinness and eating a dozen oysters. That night I made a pact with Peter and two of his friends, Mike Beard and Richard Wood, that if I finished the bike ride they would come to Resolute Bay and meet me at the North Pole.

The next morning I woke up with a dreadful hangover. My head was spinning and my knees were weak, and the thought of cycling fifty miles on a clapped-out bicycle made me feel even more ill. Any thoughts of keeping Peter, Mike and 'Woody' to the pact soon evaporated when I tried to walk downstairs and felt extremely sick. I managed to pull myself together and dragged myself to the start line on a heavy old mountain bike that I knew I could never propel across some of the most mountainous stretches of County Wicklow. Then Peter turned up and I realised where my salvation lay.

Peter had the most amazing high-tech bicycle, a beautiful light-weight machine, and was proudly decked out in all the latest cycling gear. I asked him if I could try on his helmet and gloves and give his bike a spin, promising to return at the end of the first straight, about a quarter of a mile away. Once we had started, I am sorry to say I instantly forgot any intention of returning the bicycle. It was too good and comfortable, and I justified my decision by reasoning that Peter would one day thank me for using the bicycle that allowed me to force Woody, Mike and him to come to Resolute Bay in the High Arctic with me.

The ride was harder for me than climbing Everest, especially as a downpour of rain began ten miles into the fifty-mile distance. Eventually I finished, some two and a half hours behind the fastest participants, but pleased that I had survived for a second Guinness and oyster competition after the race.

In early August preparations began in earnest for the next expedition. As with any major business project the trick is to plan meticulously, and Rune and I sketched out a critical path analysis. After foundering in 1997 because of a simple equipment failure, this time we decided we would be supported. We planned on two re-supplies, one after fifteen days, the next twenty days later, with a third resupply pencilled in for an emergency.

The resupplies were planned to allow us to start with a relatively light sledge over the hardest part of the course, the first sixty-five miles to 84°10'N. The second section, which should be flatter and easier, was longer and therefore we would have heavier sledges carrying more food. By the time we reached the final third we reasoned we would be fit and strong, so the third segment of the expedition was planned to take twenty-five days, carrying thirty days' food. We also had to take the cost of resupply flights into account. Beyond 86°30'N the cost of a flight doubles, so we had to reach this point, 205 miles from Ward Hunt Island, within thirty-five days – no more, and ideally no less. It was a tough challenge, but we reckoned it was within our capabilities.

While I chased sponsors, Rune, who had not had the time the previous year, used the lists we had made on the last few hours on the ice to gather equipment and busied himself checking tents, sleeping-bags and skis. Having already spent over seven weeks on the ice together and gelled as a team, there was little that needed discussing. We now knew whether we liked each other's food, and we had dis-covered which pieces of equipment were not up to the job, simple things like the ski poles. Rune had brought them especially from Norway, praising their strength and lightness; I broke three of them in the first couple of weeks, trying to pick my way through rubble. In low temperatures, if the pole becomes caught between two blocks of ice and you twist it, it snaps like a stick of rock. To be fair, Rune did not break any of his poles; I am clumsier than he is, but it was clear his special Norwegian sticks were not up to my rough treatment.

Another obvious change was the sledge. We went to a different manufacturer that Rune knew, and double-checked that it was made of carbon-fibre Kevlar. We also changed the tent. Our 1997 tent was like a warehouse; although there was plenty of space, it flapped in the wind and took too long to put up. Rune chose a smaller, lighter design that he thought would be more durable.

Another of our decisions was in favour of shorter skis; our 210-centimetre skis had snagged and jammed between the frozen blocks and ice gravel. We plumped for 180-centimetre to 190-centimetre skis with skins for traction, which would be more manageable and mobile.

Rune and I both preferred to wear proper cross-country polar ski boots made in Norway, rather than the mukluks worn by most expeditions. Traditional mukluks are based on the sealskin or caribou-hide boots worn by the Inuit Eskimos. Most modern mukluks are made of soft rubber and thick cotton with two layers of felt lining and a mesh between the insole and outer rubber sole to stop heat draining from the sole of the foot into the ice. They are extremely good boots, the best of which are guaranteed to −90°C, but they are bulky and unwieldy. Most expeditions use mukluks clipped to their cross-country skis using large plastic bindings, much like the old-fashioned strap-on roller-skates. The bindings are notorious for breaking and don't allow as much movement as proper Nordic ski bindings.

A lot of our clothing was based on Norwegian experience. The best sequence of layers is a contested science, but after six polar expeditions, much advice – in particular from Borge Ousland who has walked solo to both geographic poles – and some custom alterations to off-the-shelf clothing, I've arrived at a system that works for me.

Inside the boots we wear a thin pair of wool socks next to our feet, followed by a plastic freezer bag as a vapour barrier, then a thicker sock and strengthened boot linings. In essence it is the same combination Roald Amundsen wore to beat Sir Robert Scott to the South Pole but without the plastic. The vapour barriers prevent our sweat from spreading to the outer layers of socks and the boot, where it will freeze. Frozen sweat not only makes your feet cold, it also makes the boot heavier. Over the course of a few weeks the boots can gain several pounds in weight from frozen sweat (and you can lose several toes to frostbite as a consequence), so it is imperative to prevent sweat from escaping. The only drawback is that our feet stew in their own sweat all day and come out looking like white prunes. Consequently we have to be careful not to contract trench foot, and we check and nurse our feet every evening. For the same reasons of tried and tested traditional technology, we wear canvas boots rather than leather. Leather cracks in the cold and does not allow moisture to escape as efficiently as canvas.

We use the same vapour-trap principle with our sleeping-bags: first a vapour barrier – essentially a large bin bag like a condom – then a thin synthetic sleeping-bag, followed by an outer goose-down sleeping-bag. Every year expeditions fail because the adventurers do not use a vapour barrier; their sweat seeps into the outer layers and within a week the sleeping-bag is rigid with frozen sweat, adding ten or more pounds to its weight. Its incumbent does not sleep at night, becomes exhausted and never warms up, increasing the risk of frostbite or hypothermia. On our 1997 expedition we learnt the hard way. We did use vapour barriers but they were not good enough and within a couple of weeks our sleeping-bags had gained weight by at least ten kilograms and were rock solid. We could hold them up and they would not bend. Then, when we turned in for the night, they took two hours to thaw out.

The first layer of our clothing is untreated Norwegian lamb's wool. The wool's natural oils have not been washed out, so the knitted long-johns, long-sleeved vest, underpants and headover – a concertinaed neck-warmer pulled over the head – all smell strongly of sheep. The underpants are particularly itchy and take a couple of days to get used to, and consequently are not changed for the entire expedition. As always there is an explanation for our discomfort: wool acts like a wick, drawing sweat and moisture away from the skin, keeping us warm. In addition, the natural oils in the wool improve insulation. On top of these woollen thermals we wear a thin Polartec fleece layer and then a windproof jacket and trousers which we have made to our specifications with wolverine fur, one of the few furs that does not freeze at −50°C, sewn around the hood of the jacket to act as a heat curtain, keeping the warmth close to our faces and protecting us from sidewinds.

The most important component of the outer layer is the zipper, which we meticulously lubricate with graphite. It might seem a minor detail, but we must be able to close zips almost instantly without needing to take off our gloves. The consequence of not being able to do this is frostbite, either on our fingers and hands or on the exposed flesh under the zip, such as a leg or armpit. It's only when you've struggled with a zip in 30mph winds at −50°C that you realise the stark necessity of having reliable zips with large tags that can be tugged with gloves on. If the zip on our trousers snaps, exposing our legs to the cold long enough for the flesh to freeze – under fifteen seconds at −50°C – then the trip will soon be over.

Compared with the 1997 expedition, this time we had a lot more time to prepare. Again Rune took care of most of the food and I organised the sponsorship and made sure all the badges were sewn on to our jackets, hats and sledge canopy. In 1997 we had stayed up deep into the night attaching sponsors' badges to our equipment once we were in Resolute, depriving ourselves of sleep and preparation time in the vital few days before we set out for the ice.

My overriding personal priority this time was to make sure I was physically fitter than before the 1997 expedition. I have never been particularly keen on training before an expedition, preferring instead gradually to acclimatise myself once I am on the ice or on the foothills of a mountain. In this way I can start out slowly when it is still very cold and the hours of daylight are short; by the time it is warmer and the sun is up for longer I am fit and raring to go. This policy has always worked well when I have been on my own, such as on my solo and unsupported treks to the Geographic South Pole and the Magnetic North Pole. It has also worked well on mountain climbs too because it is essential to start off slowly to avoid altitude sickness. However, in 1997 this course of action had frustrated Rune. He was so fit and such an accomplished skier that my lack of speed clearly held him back.

Rune was almost born on skis. He is the youngest of four brothers and was only three years old when his elder siblings first strapped a pair of Nordic skis to his feet, and while I trudged slowly across the ice, he scooted ahead of me with ease. I once asked him what he thought of my skiing, on a day when I thought it had all clicked and I was doing exceptionally well.

'Not bad, David,' he said. 'Your skiing is as good as my Norwegian nephew's.'

'Oh thanks Rune,' I said, pleased to receive his praise. 'And how long has your nephew been skiing?'

'About six months. He's four years old, David,' came the withering reply.

But Rune's joke had a serious side. Three days after we had set out from Ward Hunt Island, Rune told me that he was worried we would never reach the Pole if I did not get a move on. Because of my slow progress he was becoming dangerously cold waiting for me to catch up every twenty to thirty minutes. As a member of a partnership, it was incumbent upon me to do something about my fitness.

The only way to prepare for dragging a 100 to 150lb sledge for six hundred miles is to tie a couple of large rubber tyres to a rope, attach it to a harness, strap yourself in and drag the tyres for mile after mile over rough ground. I had made myself such a harness and tried to train whenever I found time, but I knew that by the time I had gained enough stamina using this technique I would have little inclination then to drag a sledge across the Arctic ice.

As well as spending several evenings sitting in a Buxted deep freeze store near Swindon to acclimatise to Arctic temperatures, I bought myself a Nordic ski trainer, an indoor cross-country skiing machine, in an attempt to improve my technique. Hour after hour I would plod away on the infernal machine, trying to better my rhythm and stretch the length of each stride, but I soon tired of the monotony. In the end I found the most effective training was to load up a rucksack with eighty pounds of weights and go for a regular ten-mile hike at a brisk pace. At least I was outdoors, and not ploughing up and down the garden with a tyre dragging behind me.

The only parts of the training I can honestly say I gained enjoyment from were pulling my daughters around on tyres and putting on two stones of extra weight. It was particularly satisfying to be able to tell Claire that I was going out training when I was going down to the pub – every pint sunk meant a few more ounces towards my optimum fighting weight.

While I was struggling to get fit, Rune continued with his normal regimen of bodily abuse. As usual he was eating the most unhealthy foods, and when not smoking sixty cigarettes a day was consuming tin-loads of chewing tobacco. It often seemed to me that Rune's sole purpose in life was to see how far he could push his body, but so far it had shown not the least sign of complaint. He is the fittest, most alert and strong man I know, and he thinks nothing of his daily ten-kilometre runs and cross-country ski treks. His reactions are so fast that he admits he sometimes surprises himself when he realises how fast he has responded to a threat.

With the preparations in hand, the sponsorship and press coverage organised and the fitness programme under way, by the end of December 1997 I could start to think about the expedition itself. This is the most dangerous time for any explorer. I am often asked why I go on expeditions. It is not an easy question to answer and I have spent many hours walking across ice or climbing a rock-face trying to figure out a valid response. Without a doubt there are many moments when I wish I did not have this strange drive to go where nobody, or few other people, have been before. I am just one of those people that have to have a goal to work towards. I have built my own home and built up a business, and adventuring is similar. Deep down, mountains and poles are places I have to visit, and hopefully conquer, simply because they are there. If I have not been there, or if I haven't done it, there is a very strong feeling inside, like a burning, that I just have to do it. Whenever I go on an expedition I carry 'Dauntless Quest', one of Robert Service's poems, with me in my diary. It was given to me by a friend and comes closest to explaining why I fill driven to explore:

> Why seek to scale Mount Everest,
> Queen of the air?
> Why strive to crown that cruel crest
> And deathward dare?
> Said Mallory of dauntless quest:
> 'Because it's there.'
>
> Why yearn with passion and with pain
> To storm the sky?
> Why suffer, sullen goals to gain,
> And fear defy?
> 'Tis not for glory or for gain
> We darkly die.
>
> Why join the reckless roving crew
> Of trail and tent?
> Why grimly take the roads of rue,
> To doom hell-bent?
> Columbus, Cook and Cabot knew,
> And yet they went.
>
> Why bid the woolly world goodbye

To fellow far,
Adventures under evil sky
And sullen star?
Let men like Mallory roar,
'Because they are.'

All the trips and expeditions I have undertaken have started with an idea which then becomes a persistent pipe dream. I am a terrible daydreamer to the extent that I will often be hatching plans for other deeply unpleasant and exhausting journeys while in the midst of an arduous expedition. This dreaming process is very dangerous for me – once I start it I know that at some time in the future I will embark on the journey. It is an incredibly strong driving force, and may be the strongest power inside me.

The idea of an expedition and the daydreaming that surrounds it is very seductive. At first I cannot think about the drawbacks or impediments; all I can think about is that it is something I would like to do, then it becomes something I must do. Strangely, after a while this drive becomes a kind of anger. Often I don't like the train of thought and action that I have started, but there is no way back once I've started daydreaming about it. I have to continue.

The next stage is a continuation of the daydream, but the daydreams become a self-deception. Essentially I am lying to myself about how easy and enjoyable it will be. At this stage I do not focus on the pain, suffering, discomfort and misery, but I soon realise when I'm out on the ice or on the side of a mountain how much better the dreams are than the reality. I become a much more pessimistic person when I am on an expedition than I am at home, and I often think the depressions and despondency I feel out on the ice or on a mountain are triggered by just this fact, the realisation that the expedition is far less easy than I imagined it might be.

Ironically, within two weeks of returning home after an expedition I will have forgotten all the painful and unpleasant aspects of being out on an expedition. From talking to other explorers, I think the ability to forget the discomfort and focus only on the goal is a common trait. For most people the journey to the destination is the most important thing, but for explorers the journey is merely a means to an end. For me, reaching the destination is ultimately the only part of the journey that matters. I spoke to Rune and he told me that he goes through a similar process before an expedition, but added that this time, for the first time, he was very relaxed and had not daydreamed at all. He was very focused and said that he knew he just had to do it.

By the end of January 1998 everything was in place. We made a last-minute switch of clothing sponsors to Karrimor, which necessitated some rushed re-ordering of our outer and fleece clothing. In mid-February we held a press conference in front of a life-size ice sculpture of a polar bear and announced our plans to make a bid for the Pole. Before the two previous expeditions in 1983 and 1997 I had posed for photographers in front of Robert Falcon Scott's statue at Waterloo Place in London, but this time I decided against it. Maybe it was a bad omen to pose with Scott; he had lost the race to the South Pole after all, and I had failed twice. This time I was determined it would be third time lucky.

In the last week before I set off for the High Arctic in Canada's Northwest Territories, I again went through the agonising process of saying goodbye to my family and friends. This is always the worst part of an expedition, much more harrowing than facing a polar bear or the threat of losing a finger or toe to frostbite. I took my daughters to the cinema to see the Spice Girls movie, and then for a meal at McDonald's. On the last evening I took my wife out for a meal, fully aware of the stress and worry I was yet again asking her to endure and feeling guilty about neglecting my duties as a father. Since my first daughter was born, I have been away for extended periods each year, and this year was scheduled to be one of my busiest yet.

On 26 February I visited my grandmother, Doris Hempleman, to bid her farewell. She has always worried a lot when I go away. I visited her in an attempt to quell her fears and to impress upon her the need to accept reverse-charge phone calls from strange parts of the world.

When I became the first Briton to walk alone and unsupported to the South Pole, I tried to contact my family by telephone from the American polar base where twenty-seven particularly unfriendly scientists are holed up. I had injured my leg trying to avoid falling down a crevasse, my face was like a rhinoceros hide after a severe battering at the hands of the Antarctic winds and I had lost 20lb in weight. I was desperate to hear a voice from home and wanted to let my family know I was relatively fit and healthy, but because of the exorbitant cost of making satellite phone calls from their base, the scientists granted me permission to make one call, and then only if the charges were reversed.

My first attempt to ring home to Lacock ended when I heard my own voice on the answerphone. I racked my brain for other numbers – after fifty-nine days alone on the ice with no support or resupplies it was hard enough to remember the names of my relatives, let alone their phone numbers – and seemingly out of nowhere my grandmother's number came to me, so I passed it on to the operator. I heard the call go through, and a lady whom I believed to be my grandmother picked up the phone. She asked the operator where I was calling from and was told the South Pole. I then heard her say, 'The boy is stupid, I'm not paying that much for a call.' With that the phone went down with a click, and I was left grinning sheepishly at the scientists standing around me. It was only when I got back to Punta Arenas in southern Chile that I managed to let my family know that I had reached the Pole and was alive and well.

By Friday, 27 February all the planning and preparation was over so I did the first thing I always do before embarking on an expedition and tied my lucky Z stone around my neck with a piece of dental floss, the only suitable piece of cord I could lay my hands on at the time. The stone goes on the day I leave home and doesn't come off until I get back.

All explorers have strange superstitions. With your fate so dependent on the weather and Lady Luck, it is difficult to ignore anything that you believe could help you beat the odds. I have worn the Z stone on every expedition since I climbed Mount Everest in 1993, when at Nache Bazaar, the capital of the Khumbu region in Nepal, I ran into a former Sherpa climber who was running a tea shop and stall in the local market. He was selling the Z stones, said to be lucky mascots for climbers, at $200 each, but I blanched at the price, mainly because it amounted to half the Nepalese national average annual wage. I wanted to buy one of the stones, so I made a deal with the Sherpa: I would pay him fifty upfront and if I made it to the summit of Everest and the stone lived up to its claim of guaranteeing a safe return I would pay him the remaining sum; if I didn't make it to the top, the price would remain at fifty. Neither of us spoke about the possible third outcome. He accepted the offer, I made it to the top, and I quite happily paid him the outstanding $150.

After breakfast on the Friday morning I said goodbye to my girls. It is always extremely difficult for me because I am aware that I have to spend an equal amount of time bidding farewell to each of them. This time they were even more upset because Rune had become a member of the family and the favoured bed-time story reader to boot, and they were also having to wish him *bon voyage*.

My youngest daughter Amelia was due to go into hospital to have a small lump in her throat examined, and for the first time in all my adventuring days I felt I really should not be leaving home that morning. My wife, who is normally very brave at partings, broke down in tears, and I felt a complete hard-hearted bastard leaving her to cope with Amelia on her own. I asked Claire if she wanted me to cancel; of course, she said I should not even consider it. I drove out of the gates of my home feeling very guilty and not particularly excited about the journey ahead.

As Rune and I drove up the M4 motorway towards London and Heathrow airport, I hoped this would be the last time I left home for such a critical expedition. This would surely be the last chance I would have to reach the North Pole. At forty-one years of age I felt I could no longer punish my body as I had in the past, nor could I justify the time away from my three young children. I was well aware that my daughters would worry more and more as they grew older and came to a better understanding of the dangers I have to combat every day walking on the thin ice of the Arctic.

But deep down I knew there were other rationales at work. If I did not succeed this time, my credibility as an explorer would be shot. The North Pole would have beaten me three times. This time, I had to emerge the victor.

4

A Shock to the System

The Departure

Friday, 27 February 1998

As my brother Mark drives Rune and me off the M4 at the Heathrow exit, we overtake the Thrust supersonic car on the back of a low-loader. It seems like a symbol of good luck – one British success story hopefully passing on the mantle to what I hope will be another. A few minutes later we are in Terminal Four to meet with the third member of our expedition squad, John Perrins, a retired policeman who has agreed to be our base-camp manager. For sixty days he will be our only lifeline and contact with the outside world. Also waiting in the terminal are two television news crews from the BBC and ITN and a reporter and photographer from the *Daily Telegraph*, who will accompany us north.

With all our expedition baggage it takes ages to check in at the Canadian Airlines desk, but the biggest problem is our gun. We need the shotgun as a last resort against polar bear attack, but even with a gun permit it is difficult to persuade the security authorities at Heathrow that we need to travel with it. Once we manage to assuage them, we hand it over to an official, only to run into yet more problems.

I pass through customs and immigration with relatively little trouble. The immigration official takes a look at my passport and asks, 'Not any relation to that idiot explorer are you?' I think of a smart answer, but judge that from the look on his face it is probably best to deny all and answer, 'What, are you nuts?' I then report, as instructed, to the customs and security desk to present my firearms certificate. This is where my problems begin. All the luggage had been checked through on one person's airline ticket, including the gun. According to the customs official's document the gun had been checked in by Paul Grover, the *Daily Telegraph*'s photographer, but I am the person with the firearms certificate. It is all too much for customs bureaucracy. Even with both Paul and me standing in front of him, the official will not let the gun be put on the aircraft. It is only with the help of Kelvin Ogunjimi, a Canadian Airlines concierge, that we can extricate our weapon, without which we would not have set out for the North Pole.

Cursing the petty restrictions of red tape, I run for the plane and get to my seat with only a minute to spare before we are due to take off. The long flight to Calgary is made much more pleasant by the upgrade to business class, but from past experience I am well used to the fickleness of airlines. In 1983, I was upgraded from economy to first class on the way out to Canada for my first attempt on the North Pole, but they made me wait until every passenger had boarded before they gave me a stand-by seat in a half-empty economy class on the return flight.

Aware that this could be my last chance to drink champagne and dine on lobster, I eat and drink far too much, and as we fly over the majestic mountains of Greenland, many of them unclimbed and unnamed and a powerful magnet to any ambitious mountaineer, I begin to feel quite hung over. Looking down on Greenland, covered in places by a blanket of 1000-foot-deep snow as if a giant down duvet had burst above it, I speculate on what lies ahead. Already I am thinking of the expedition and hatching plans for future trips with Rune.

Once we are over Canada, I ask permission to visit the flight-deck where the captain prints out a weather report from Resolute Bay. It reads:

YRB CYRB 272315
201011
TAF CYRB 272231Z 272323 12030G40KT 1/8SM IC ?BLSN
SCT004 TEMPO 2 323
1/2SM BLSN BKN004

From this jumble of letters and numbers he extracts a weather report that in the comfort of the business-class cabin is frighteningly brutal: 'the wind is blowing at forty knots and the temperature is −32.3°C, making a windchill of −72°C. There is scattered visibility due to strongly blowing snow. The captain says the weather could be poor enough to block aircraft landings.'

Eight hours later we arrive at Calgary, collect our luggage and board a small propeller plane for the short hop to Edmonton. By eight p.m., after eleven hours of travelling, we finally arrive at the Nisku Inn. Edmonton is shrouded in freezing fog, and the temperature outside is −12°C. The cold cuts through to my bones as we unload the van at the hotel, but it is nothing in comparison with what lies ahead.

Inside the hotel no one would know the weather outside was cold enough to bring on hypothermia in fifteen minutes. This odd building, with few outside windows, has a string of rooms built around a fake tropical garden under a ceiling painted purple. Staying at the Nisku Inn is one of the superstitions I have to adhere to before a polar trip. When I stayed in 1983, I was so impoverished that I stole the cutlery and sachets of jam and butter.

The final step in the pre-polar ritual is to sink a few pints in the appropriately named Last Chance Saloon, a country and western bar at the inn, where it is best to avoid catching the eye of the local oil workers if you want to keep out of trouble. As I sip my beer, I reflect that it seems as if every act I have undertaken in the last few days will be the last of its type for a very long time, and the pitcher of beer that Rune and I share in the Last Chance Saloon is no exception. Tomorrow we will be flying to the High Arctic where alcohol is very strictly controlled, a prohibition that makes our final beers for two months taste particularly good, and which helps to drown Rune's incessant snoring on the first of the many nights we will sleep side by side.

Saturday, 28 February

After a year's preparation we are finally back in Canada and on the way to the High Arctic for what I hope will be the last time I have to walk across the thin ice of the frozen Arctic Ocean to the North Pole.

This journey has become my personal nemesis. In twenty-six years of mountaineering and polar adventures few of my expeditions have failed. Compared with the South Pole and the Magnetic North Pole, where I succeeded solo and unsupported on my maiden attempts, on paper this trip would seem much easier: I have a companion and we will be supported. But that detracts from the true challenge of the North Pole: there is no map or chart to show the route, the terrain changes every day, and no one can predict what lies ahead.

A large breakfast this morning. I now weigh fifteen and a half stone, two and a half over my usual weight to keep me going to the Pole. By the time I reached the South Pole in 1996 my weight was down to eleven stone, but I soon managed to put it back on. While I am gorging myself on carbohydrates, Rune and John go shopping for two personal stereos and sixteen packs of rolling tobacco.

When we leave the Nisku Inn, the scenery outside really lives up to the winter wonderland description. The fog has frozen to the bare branches of the trees overnight, and everything is frosted in white. It looks beautiful as we make our way to the airport for the long flight to Resolute Bay on a Boeing 737 equipped with a gravel-guard on the nose-wheel to prevent stones on the runways from spraying into the jet engines. Inside the plane the cabin is split in half across the fuselage to take cargo in the front half and passengers at the back. The pilot warns us that we may not make it to Resolute as the airport is covered in thick fog, but he takes off all the same, though not before I go through my customary ritual of losing my boarding pass. Rune may have a point when he teases me, 'If you can't even get on a flight, how do you expect to get to the North Pole?'

We pose for photographs on the tarmac and then board the plane which is full of miners returning for a two-month stint at the Polaris Mine, about sixty miles north of Resolute. The remaining seats are taken up by an Inuit mother carrying her child wrapped in a blanket tied to her back, and Japanese tourists bound for Yellowknife, the self-acclaimed Northern Lights capital of the world. Until thirty or forty years ago the Aurora Borealis could be seen from Hokkaido, the northernmost of the four islands of Japan, but now that the Magnetic North Pole has moved north the Japanese have to travel to Yellowknife to see the celestial light show. They apparently believe it is good luck to conceive under the Northern Lights, and there are several honeymoon couples on board the aircraft.

I sit next to a female miner who tells me about her strange life at the Polaris Mine. Every morning she drives to work, one mile into the Earth's core, where she works an eleven-hour day for six days a week. She often works the seventh day if she is on night shifts as there is little to do during the daytime in the permafrost outside the mine; the miners have built a nine-hole golf course but it can only be played in the summer, and even then, with no grass it is entirely unlike any other golf course. The fairways are rocky and the greens are made from brushed gravel, but at least there are no sand bunkers, she says. The golfers carry a piece of astroturf with them around the course, she tells me, and they place the ball on the carpet before each shot. If the ball hits a rock after a drive, it can bounce off at ninety degrees, making for a very unpredictable round of golf.

By the time we get to Yellowknife, a former gold- and diamond-prospecting town, the temperature has dropped to −16°C and we see trees for the last time for over two months. None of the trees is above thirty feet in height because of the short growing season. I feel apprehensive as we fly further north and the terrain becomes more desolate. I start to realise there is no going back.

At Cambridge Bay, our next stop, the ground is covered in permafrost, the temperature has dropped to −21°C with 25mph winds, and my nostril hairs freeze inside my nose. The short walk from the aeroplane to the terminal is enough to make the tip of my nose glow bright red and throb, a legacy of the frostbite I picked up during my South Pole trek. The tiny airport is no more than a red corrugated iron shack beside an airstrip, and we are now within the Arctic Circle. Within this imaginary line that encircles the North Pole at 66°32' North, there is at least one day a year during which the sun never sets and one day, during the winter, when it never rises. At this time of year daylight has only recently returned to these isolated northern villages, but on the ice-cap where we are headed it is still permanently dark and consequently even colder.

An hour's flight later, when the stewardesses have handed out certificates confirming we have entered the Arctic Circle, we are crossing the Arctic Archipelago. This group of islands was made famous by John Franklin in 1845 when he commanded a voyage to search for the Northwest Passage. For years sailors had hoped to find a way from the Atlantic through the Arctic to the Pacific to provide a quicker route to the Far East. Franklin and his crew almost discovered one but died in the process when their ship became encased in ice and they were poisoned by lead in their tinned food. This archipelago at the top of Canada is dotted with names strangely familiar to a West Country boy, such as Devon, Somerset and Cornwallis Islands, named by William Parry, a British explorer form the south-west of England who tried to reach the North Pole in 1827 and who made detailed explorations of the area from 1818 to 1825.

We are headed for Resolute Bay where the locals say, 'It's not quite the edge of the world, but you can see it from here.' In the winter this frost-encased hamlet on the south coast of Cornwallis Island, with a mostly Inuit population of 200, is dark for two months and the temperatures plummet to forty below, without taking into account the chill from the whistling winds that blow 300 days a year. In the summer the temperatures lift just above freezing, the sun does not set for four months and the snow is blown away to reveal barren rock through which a few wild flowers poke. It is no wonder we adventurers call Resolute Bay 'Hell on Earth'.

As we disembark the aircraft it is late afternoon and has been dark for some time, and the brumal cold slaps me in the face and takes my breath away. I think I will never get used to the first moment of a renewed encounter with such extreme cold, particularly as I am dressed in clothing suited to a heated aircraft. As I walk across the tarmac, covered in several inches of ice and snow, the −30°C cold makes my eyes water and I notice the moisture freezing in my eyelashes in the short time it takes to reach the tiny airport building.

Inside the terminal it seems as if most of the hamlet has turned up to see the plane come in; during the winter, aircraft are the only link with the outside world and bring all supplies to the tiny hamlet. Consequently, an apple costs the equivalent of a pound sterling at the Co-op, the hamlet's only store. During some summers the sea ice does not melt sufficiently to allow ships to berth at Resolute, and cars and other large goods ordered in the south of Canada have to wait another year before they are delivered to their buyers in Resolute.

But a plane arrival at this time of year, only ten days after the period of permanent round-the-clock darkness has ended, warrants more than a cursory visit to the airport. In late February, when there are around four hours of sunlight and two of dusk, an aircraft arrival is a social event. Resolute turns out to meet up, chat and speculate on the relative merits of the mad men who turn up to head for the magnetic and geographic poles as the dark season ends and the silly season begins.

Inside the airport building, a former military shack, we meet Sergeant Sean Chapple and Corporal Alan Chambers, two Royal Marines who by now should have left on an unsupported expedition to the Geographic North Pole. They have been held up in Resolute by bad weather at Ward Hunt Island, the departure point for North Pole treks. We shake hands and wish one another good luck. They seem well prepared after last year, when they came to Resolute but abandoned plans for a North Pole expedition when they realised how extreme the weather can be and how tough it would be. This time they have done their homework, spoken to other polar explorers who have been successful, and have developed a good strategy. They will leave before us, but we know as well as they do that we will overtake them within a few days because they will be unsupported and hauling much heavier sledges.

Resolute Bay is one of the most inhospitable inhabited places on Earth, but there is a strange beauty in its grim windswept austerity. In January and February the temperature can plummet to fifty below, in spring the bay is enveloped in thick fogs, and in summer the mercury rarely rises above freezing point. An air-raid siren is used to remind people to go to bed in the twenty-four-hour sunlight.

The airport is nestled beside a string of high hills and is connected to the hamlet and the rubbish dump by the only two open roads on the island. The ride from the airport to Resolute Bay is many people's first and only view of the High Arctic, and at the end of February it can be a frighteningly daunting trip through a frozen monochrome landscape. It often seems as if there is no colour in the Arctic, only light and shade on a white ground and sky. Since we left Yellowknife, the colour seems to have drained from the terrain. Where two hours ago there were green trees and brown mud dotted on the ice and snow, now there is just white ice, grey and black rock, and the occasional glimpse of an emerald-green isle of thick, cracked, multi-year ice on the bay. On the left as we approach Resolute is Signal Hill; to the right is the frozen ocean bay with only refractions, Arctic island mirages, on the horizon.

In the 1950s, when the Cold War was at its height and Resolute supported an American and Canadian Air Force base, there were plans to enlarge the hamlet to accommodate up to one thousand people. But those plans were abandoned in the late 1970s when an administrator decided Iqaluit, formerly known as Frobisher Bay, would be a better headquarters. Now that the Soviet threat has disappeared, the hamlet supports the airport – a link to the polar ice-cap and nearby Polaris Mine – and a few hundred Inuit hunters. The only local employment is working for the hamlet or the state, at the school or airline companies, at the Polar Shelf research project or at the weather station. Most of the Inuits hunt. It is not uncommon to see a handful of polar bear skins strung out like stiff cardboard cut-outs outside the houses nestled in the bay, or to look through a window to see an Inuit family cutting up a seal in their living-room while watching cable television.

Keeping a community alive in this frost-bound environment is expensive. It costs ten million Canadian dollars a year to supply water to around fifty households, a school, a shop, a church and a handful of government offices or businesses. The water has to be kept heated and circulating in warmed pipes to prevent it freezing in the permafrost. If a pipe bursts, the hamlet may have to be evacuated.

We are headed for the Qausuittuq Inns North boarding-house, where most polar expeditions make their final preparations and check their equipment before the flight to Ward Hunt Island and the long trek to the top of the world. Staying at the boarding-house is very unlike any other hotel. All meals are taken strictly at set times, seated at a long table in the kitchen. The food is plentiful and excellent; no choice, but the kind of traditional home cooking – such as sausages, mash and salad followed by cherry pie and ice cream, washed down with orange squash – that is so necessary to build up strength to ward off the cold outside. It is good to see Terry, the manager and an old friend, and Joy, the cook, again. As usual Joy jokes that explorers always say when they get back from the ice that they've been dreaming of her bacon and eggs. 'Never me, just my cooking,' she adds. The only thing that is missing in this dry town is a bar, but as outsiders we are allowed to bring our own whisky, brandy and beer.

At dinner I bump into my old friend Thierry Petry, who is about to lead a French-Canadian and Italian expedition to the North Pole. He is extremely experienced and usually very well prepared – he had his appendix removed before his South Pole expedition – and we compare notes on our plans and proposed schedules. Thierry has recently walked to the base of Everest so we also talk about our respective experiences on the mountain. After dinner Rune, John and I push and cajole our wooden crate containing all our equipment into the garage and begin the long process of unpacking, checking and preparing equipment. Everything, except for our secret stash of whisky and brandy, has frozen in the crate.

The Marines both seem very anxious. They have been waiting for three days to set off. Their sledges are on the plane and they are studying satellite pictures from the Internet (the weather site we were looking at is at ftp://gis.lter.alaska.edu/LoRes_Archive/daily_composite.gif). The picture shows a massive build-up of cloud layers over Alaska, indicating a massive snowfall is on the way and headed for Ward Hunt Island. More worryingly, we can also see a very large pressure ridge about forty-five miles north of Ward Hunt Island.

I am wary of relying too much on satellite pictures. The one overriding characteristic of the polar ice-cap is that it is impossible to predict from one day to another what the conditions will be like. By the time we get to Ward Hunt Island the one thing we can be sure of is that the ice will have moved around, there could be new leads of open water, and the present ones will have frozen over or closed up.

Sunday, 1 March

In characteristic fashion, Resolute Bay greets us on our first full day in the High Arctic with a display of typically appalling weather. It is relatively warm for the time of year, only −25°C, but the wind is blowing the snow around so hard that we cannot see further than six feet in front of us. The bad weather has again delayed the Marines'

departure, and in the driving wind Nigel Bateson, the BBC cameraman, is struggling to set up a satellite dish on the roof of the garage. I
hope the inclement conditions do not endanger our flight to Ward
Hunt Island on Thursday.

To make things worse, I have slept fitfully and wake up feeling
rotten. I think I'm getting a cold, the last thing I need on a polar
expedition. The Canadians say that an exceptionally virulent flu that
has killed over twenty people is doing the rounds this year. My head
feels like an over-inflated football, my nose and ears are blocked, and
my joints and muscles ache. If I've got the Canadian flu, we will have
to postpone our departure.

Feeling so rotten, I have little inclination to do anything but lie in
bed, but before we leave on Thursday we have to prepare our equipment and check it has survived the journey from England. As Nigel
keeps reminding me from his days in the South African Army, the
seven Ps are all-important: 'Prior planning and preparation prevents
piss-poor performance.' The sledge harnesses, made of rubber bungee
ropes to cushion the jolt on our backs as we drag our carbon-fibre
sleds, must be cut to length; our pre-packaged dehydrated food must
be divided into daily rations; and we need to test our clothes, tent,
radio and Argos satellite position locator beacon.

By early morning the garage floor is strewn with black bin-liners as
Rune divides up our food into five-day packs of muesli for breakfast,
powdered drinks and soup for lunch and a dehydrated meal for the
evening. Each meal has been laced with butter, olive and soya oils,
and the vacuum-sealed packs look disgusting – dried food swimming
in grease. We also have packs of Mars bar and milk chocolate with
nuts, cut up into chunks. Simply taking the wrappers off the food
saves considerable weight on twenty or thirty days' food supplies, but
for a reason I cannot understand some expeditions set out with tins of
food in boxes.

I have designed a new apparatus for the radio aerial, but Rune
thinks it is too heavy to justify the improvement over last year's system.
We shall see. Last year, it sometimes took us half an hour to stretch
the radio antenna between two skis and link it to the radio. My new
apparatus has large clips that should attach quickly to the tops of the
skis. The aerial wire is coiled around the clips for storage and quickly
unfurled when putting up the aerial. I've spent several months making

and testing it at home, and I am convinced it is much better.

This year we are also carrying Bluefox ice-spikes, an emergency measure in case we fall through the ice into the ocean. The blue handles of the titanium spikes clip together to form a rectangular plastic block which can be carried in a chest pocket. If either of us falls through the ice, we can snatch the block apart and embed the titanium spikes into the ice at the edge of the hole to stop ourselves slipping under. I last fell through the ice on my solo walk to the Magnetic North Pole and have only recently stopped having night-mares about the terrifying moment I felt myself disappearing through what I had thought was terra firma.

I put on my full Arctic kit for the first time, and will not remove my underwear or wash from now until we get back from the polar ice-cap. We also prepare, check and test out our new shorter skis. Tomorrow we will take them out for a spin on the ice, but before then we have to get our base station working. John Perrins, our base-camp manager, is struggling to get the computer working and the Argos position beacon, which is meant to pinpoint our position to within one hundred yards, is telling us that the garage is moving west at a rate of several knots an hour.

Monday, 2 March

I wake up feeling even worse than yesterday. I should have gone to bed earlier, but there was too much work for an early night, and I now feel totally gripped by the cold.

My biggest fear is illness on the ice. My first North Pole attempt in 1983 ended when I fell over and cracked a couple of ribs. In 1996 I almost abandoned my trek to the Geographic South Pole on day six when I fell backwards while dragging my sledge over some particularly large sastrugi (ridges of snow formed by the wind) and jarred my coccyx. The pain was acute and piercing and I had doubted my ability to continue, but I spurred myself on because I had battled through injury before when I climbed Mount Everest. Half-way up that mag-nificent mountain I started to cough so hard that I cracked two ribs. I survived the final ascent to the summit of Everest only through sheer will power, so with the Everest experience in mind, this time I will play safe and visit the local clinic for a check-up.

After the disappointments of last year, and then all the preparation, fund-raising and anticipation of this year, I am now seriously concerned that the expedition could be sunk by something as minor as a chest infection. The last thing I want is to find out on the ice that I have some serious ailment and need to be airlifted out. I would not normally bother going to a doctor with a cold, but I am paranoid now that I'm in the High Arctic. At the health centre in Resolute the nurse tells me I have high blood pressure – not surprising, considering the stress I am under and the excess body weight I am carrying. She prescribes Fisherman's Friends and a course of antibiotics, but I am reluctant to take them unless the cough becomes worse, so I pack them in our medical kit for the journey across the ice.

Our preparations continue in the afternoon when we take our sledges out on to the ice of Resolute Bay for a first test-drive. Afterwards we check that my gun is working. Rune is much more at home with a gun than I am as a result of his military training, and I have delegated all polar bear defence responsibilities to him. This is, as always, a last-resort tactic; the last thing either of us wants to do is shoot a polar bear. They have more right to be on the polar ice than we have.

As darkness falls we hare up to the airport to see off Sean and Alan, the two Royal Marines. The storm has lifted somewhat and the pilots think they might be able to land at Ward Hunt Island tomorrow morning. Sean and Alan are flying to Eureka tonight, where they will overnight before flying, weather permitting, a further four hours north to Ward Hunt Island at dawn tomorrow. Sean and Alan have set themselves a high target of averaging two and a half miles a day for the first month, and Rune and I wait out by the plane to shake their hands and wish them luck. Sean and Alan have devised a plan to pull enough food and equipment to last eighty days on two smaller sledges each. They think this combination will be easier to manoeuvre through the ice rubble and pressure ridges which dominate the first one hundred miles from Ward Hunt Island. They plan to drag one sledge each for an hour, putting markers along their path, then attach a kite to the deposited sledges and walk back to collect the second pair of sledges. They both have extensive Arctic experience from their Marine training regimes in Norway and plan to work ten or eleven hours a day to maintain their target mileage, reaching the Pole in seventy-six days. However, they cannot afford to be confined to their tents by bad weather for very long as they are carrying only four days of emergency spare rations.

In the evening we again study satellite images of the ice-cap, but I remain sceptical of the merits of modern technology and I joke with Paul Grover, the *Daily Telegraph* photographer, that I am more interested in using his computer to look at pictures he has taken of Ginger Spice. We will be walking on shifting ice and it's dangerous to have preconceived ideas before setting off. We just have to go with the flow – literally. All we know for sure is that we are setting off on a neap tide, but a week later the ice will be subjected to the huge forces of a spring tide. What the ice will be like after that is anybody's guess.

Tuesday, 3 March

I still feel rotten and the Argos satellite position beacon locator is continuing to play up. Every hour we get a reading from the satellite system's Washington DC office that is more off-course than the last. Once out on the ice, this small metal box of electronics should be our most dependable link with the outside world, and it is meant to provide definitive confirmation that we have reached the Pole.

Every night we will switch the Argos beacon on for two hours. A constellation of French satellites passing overhead will pick up our transmitter's signal and should plot our position to within at most a quarter of a mile. It will send the record of our position to Toulouse and then via Washington to our base camp at Resolute Bay. If and when we reach the top of the world, the Argos should confirm to the outside world that we are standing at 90° North. In the past there has been considerable controversy over some adventurers' claims, in particular those of Robert Edwin Peary, but the Argos beacon is meant to put an end to any dispute. However, at the moment it is up to forty-eight miles off target. If we cannot fix it, verifying that we have reached the Pole will be the least of our problems; if our radio also fails we will also not be able to receive resupply flights or call in an emergency medical evacuation in the event of injury.

I clamber up on to the roof of the garage to fiddle with the beacon, which we have left up there for the last two days. While on the roof I use the satellite phone to call my wife and daughters. It is bitterly cold in the wind and I keep the conversation as brief as possible, but the locals say −30°C is extremely warm for this time of year.

The boarding-house is awash with suggestions and rumours that the El Niño weather system that has brought freak storms to North America and the warmest winter months on record to Britain is affecting the local weather and causing the polar ice-cap to melt sooner than it should. Although I do my best to conceal it, I am very concerned that we have chosen the wrong year to head for the Pole, that the ice will melt earlier and quicker than it should, and that we will have to abandon our bid because we encounter open water too wide to negotiate.

Later in the morning we test the fuel pumps and the MSR stove, one of the most essential examinations before the expedition. Sir Ranulph Fiennes's attempt to cross Antarctica failed in part because he had not tried out his stove before setting out; he discovered on the first night that he had taken a burner with a screw thread attachment that could not accommodate his fuel bottle. Our stove burns dirtily at first, producing carbon monoxide which can asphyxiate the occupants of a tent, but after several hours' work we have got all three of our stoves burning cleanly.

Then, in the afternoon, we head out on to the ice again to put up the tent. At long last the weather has lifted, it is a beautiful day and there is a dog-star rainbow overhead. At the top and bottom of the world, rainbows are spectacular. Instead of a semi-circle, the rainbow is a three-quarter circle and the ends bend inwards as they approach the horizon. At times like this the task ahead seems less daunting and the journey worthwhile. If only we could be sure that the weather would always be like this.

The week of blizzards and high winds has created a log-jam of expeditions waiting to leave from Resolute. The Marines have made it to Ward Hunt Island today and Thierry's French-Canadian and Italian team is now waiting for the green light to follow them north; they are already bickering before they have left and still have not decided which equipment to take. The pilot says it was −40°C at Ward

Hunt Island, with no wind. Last year it was below −60°C when Rune and I were dropped off.

All the talk at dinner is of El Niño and the unpredictable effect it might have on the ice. After years of planning all the explorers know they have only a short window of opportunity between March, when the sun first shines in the Arctic Circle, and May, when the perilous thaw comes to a head.

After eating we head up one of Cornwallis Island's two open roads to the airport to weigh our sledges. On my solo unsupported trek to the South Pole my sledge weighed around 285lb, a considerable liability that would have catapulted me down a crevasse had I fallen down one of the many gaping ice chasms. Last year, because we were attempting to reach the North Pole unsupported, each of our sledges weighed 300 to 325lb. The Marines are dragging over 300lb, and Thierry Petry's team are dragging two sledges each, the lightest combination they have weighs 420lb. It is with some considerable satisfaction that I find my sledge weighs just 106lb and Rune's tips the scales a little short of 150lb. Rune has elected to drag a heavier sledge than me. He says it will keep him warm and help even out the discrepancies in our skiing speeds. Ironically, seeing the other teams' sledges makes me feel optimistic. I cannot lift even one end of one of Thierry's sledges, but I can lift the whole of my sledge. It seems we have done our homework and we've got it right. These are the fruits of our preparation and I feel very good about it.

We return to the boarding-house to hear that the pilots who dropped off Thierry's team and the Royal Marines at Ward Hunt Island have spotted Peary's Lead around eight miles off Ward Hunt Island. Apparently the open water is between one and three miles wide and stretches for maybe twenty miles east and west of the island. It is followed by several other leads of open water. Peary dreaded such sudden breaks in the polar ice-cap as a 'nightmare ... the unknown quantity of polar exploration'. In 1906, during his first and unsuccessful expedition to the North Pole, Peary encountered what he called the 'Big Lead'. He nicknamed it the 'Hudson', after the river that runs along the west side of Manhattan Island, the seat of the Peary Arctic Club. At 84°38'N and approximately 74°W (his navigation has since been proved to be somewhat inaccurate and did not take any drift east or west into account) he encountered, on 26 March, according to his journals detailed in the book *Nearest the Pole*, 'a broad open lead extending east and west across our course, father than we could see'.

Rumours and counter-rumours of open water are extremely dispiriting before setting off on an expedition. I never know which of them to believe, or how much consideration to give to information which might be irrelevant within a couple of days. But right now I am very worried. We can cross water on our sledges, but not three-mile-wide stretches.

Wednesday, 4 March

I wake up feeling a lot better. After Joy's mothering and huge doses of paracetamol and vitamin C, the cold appears to have lifted, but I now have a chesty cough. I wonder if I ought to start on the antibiotics, but I am reluctant to do so. Most people advise me against taking the pills, not least because antibiotics could upset my gut flora shortly before I embark on a diet of dehydrated food on top of heavy exercise in extreme cold. I am not going to take any medication if I can help it. I am going to try to let it pass, but I am still worried that if it gets bad when I am on the ice then we'll have a re-run of Everest in 1993.

If all goes to plan and we leave for Ward Hunt Island tomorrow, today is our last chance to solve the mystery of our malfunctioning Argos transmitter, and to get our radio to work. It remains our biggest problem. The Washington Argos office has been sending us position reports via our transmitter on the roof of the garage, but they are still consistently off the mark by anything up to forty-eight miles. There is no point in leaving if the Argos is not working. John has been on the phone to Washington for the last three days trying to sort out the problems.

Shortly before lunch, Borge Ousland phones and I speak to him in the kitchen. He wishes me good luck. 'This is the big one for you,' he says. 'Go for it.' After lunch we receive a four-page e-mail with the positions for several of the most recent Argos readings from Peter Griffith in Washington:

Subject: Accuracy
Date: Wed, 04 Mar 1998 11:28: 54–0500

From: 'Peter Griffith' griffith@nacls.com
Organization: North American CLS Inc.
To: 'Sparks, Jennifer' <jsparks@nacls.com>

The Argos class, a measure of accuracy, follows the longitude field in each position report. Class 3 is accurate to 150 meters, class 2 to 350 meters, class 1 to 1,000 meters and class 0 over 1,000 meters. Most of your locations have been class 1 or 2 with an occasional class 3. The latest 4 positions have been class 0, including the last one, which is indicating alarm status. Please check the TAT3 to see if it is obstructed, and if the alarm switch is on, and let us know what you find. Thanks!

00165 74.683N   94.963W   1   062/0035Z–062/0033
(3)   −.2540E+2   17   17   00

First Number = Platform No.
Second + Third numbers = Positions
Fourth number = Accuracy code
Fifth number = Day of year and time (four digits after first slash is Zulu time, i.e. GMT)
Seventh number = Temperature in Celsius
Eighth number = Position of switch

Having read the e-mail it suddenly becomes apparent why our readings are so inaccurate. We have been reading the latitude and longitude as degrees and minutes, a scale where each degree is split into sixty minutes and each minute into sixty seconds. However, nacls is sending the positions to us in decimal degrees, where each degree is split into a thousand decimal points. We do a few quick calculations and instantly discover that the Argos is spot on; John is the one who has been getting it wrong. It is a relief to know the Argos is working, but it confirms my worst suspicions that you need a bloody physics degree to get to the Pole these days.

The Argos also has a position switch that we can use to pass on short messages using previously agreed codes. Our set of codes is:

17 = Everything OK
34 = Poor weather – pick-up not possible
51 = Moving pack ice/back drift
68 = Injury – need pick-up (urgent)
85 = Storm
102 = Damaged equipment
119 = Open water
136 = Injury Rune – continuing
153 = Injury David – continuing
170 = Injury – need pick-up (non-urgent)
187 = Landing strip nearby, 1200ft
204 = Good weather for pick-up
221 = Need resupply
238 = Polar bear sighting
255 = Polar bear kill
0 = Man in water – continuing

Most of the remainder of the day is used to finalise the expedition logistics. We need to decide precisely when we will have our resupplies and where. The first resupply should be no earlier than fifteen days after leaving Ward Hunt Island, but before passing 84°10' North – any further north will cost more and break our budget. According to our schedule we should be around 83°39' North at some time between 20 and 25 March, a good time for the first resupply; the second should follow twenty days later, around 86° North, some time between 12 and 18 April. If we're very much behind we may need a third drop. There's no point in going back because we run out of money.

I tell John that we will attempt to stop on a piece of ice on which the aircraft can land a day before the resupply, but if the plane cannot make the flight because of bad weather we cannot afford to hang around for long because we could float southwards at a rate of five miles a day. We will be totally reliant on John to bargain with the air companies on our behalf and find some way of minimising the cost, whatever the weather and position. The worst thing that could happen is that the plane flies all the way up to the ice for the resupply and the weather closes in as it passes Ward Hunt Island. In that scenario we still have to pay for the flight, so Rune and I will have to make the final choice on whether the aircraft should come up on a particular date.

We have also set up a radio schedule. Initially we will speak to John at base camp at seven p.m. every other day. John, using the call-sign Typhoo Base, will make five attempts to call us – British Typhoo – at 1900, 1915, 1930, 1945 and 2000 hours. If we make no contact in the evening, John will try again at 0700 the following morning. If we can make no radio contact on the high frequencies 5281.5MHz and 6553.0MHz, then we shall switch to the Argos and communicate exclusively on that.

At dinner, our last proper meal for sixty days, Joy has made a farewell cake, but I have lost my appetite. My nerves are getting the better of me and I feel quite shaky as we pose around the cake for last photographs in the boarding-house.

After dinner we load our sledges onto a hired pick-up truck for the journey to Resolute Bay's airstrip, but the truck's gearbox has frozen and we cannot move. Eventually, after fifteen minutes' cajoling and gunning of the engine, the gearbox thaws and we get going. On the way to the airport we stop at the weather station to watch Wayne Davidson, the local meteorologist nicknamed Wayne the Weathervane, launch a helium balloon to measure ozone levels in the atmosphere. After several days of relative warmth of around thirty below, it suddenly becomes extremely cold and a wind picks up. It is as if we are being warned of what lies ahead of us, in plenty of time to let us change our minds before setting off in the aeroplane tomorrow.

At First Air, the company which will be ferrying us to Ward Hunt Island, I talk to the pilot to find out when the best time to land will be, and to ask if we can land some way west of the island to avoid the lead of open water. The pilot says the meridian at Ward Hunt Island is at eleven a.m.; this is the time of brightest sunlight, and he warns me that the full moon on 12 March will create massive tides that will mash up all the ice. I've been through it before – everything moves and it is bloody scary. The bad news is that, according to the weather report tonight, visibility is very poor at Ward Hunt Island. The top of Elles-mere is shrouded in low cloud and the pilots do not want to risk a landing west of the island. They say they will land only on the ice-covered beach at Ward Hunt, and may have to turn back tomorrow if the weather becomes worse. I decide to take a risk and go for it tomorrow. Despite the danger of an aborted flight and the attendant expense of overnight accommodation at Eureka, I am itching to get going. It is better to go for it when you known there is a chance instead of waiting for perfect weather. Last year the Dutch team waited eight days for the right conditions at Ward Hunt.

After checking in for the flight, we return to the boarding-house and Wayne the Weathervane turns up with a new set of satellite pictures of the polar ice-cap. A long, vertical lead to the west of Ward Hunt Island appears to have become longer and wider. It would be a dream if this lead were to freeze sufficiently for us to walk on as it would create a gloriously wide motorway of flat ice pointing northwards. There is no sign of Peary's Lead from the air. Wayne thinks it might have moved east, have frozen over, or maybe the Marines misdiagnosed it. I feel somewhat relieved, particularly in the light of the pilot's refusal to land west of Ward Hunt Island.

Sean and Alan, the Royal Marines, have covered four miles in their first two days on the ice, a very good mileage. They are still on the ice-shelf before the rubble and pressure ridges start, but it's a good distance to cover at this time of year.

At long last the preparations are almost over, and we are ready to knuckle down to 600 miles of frigid torture. The preparation is just as important a part of a successful expedition as being able to survive temperatures that drop off the bottom of the thermometer, but I find the weeks and days leading up to the departure more nerve-racking than the time on the ice.

I do not know whether to take a shower. It would be nice to set off tomorrow not feeling sticky, sweaty and filthy, but the received Inuit wisdom is that it is best not to wash so that your body builds up a protective layer of natural body oils. However, I feel extremely uncomfortable and decide to have one. I will find out in the next few days if this was a mistake.

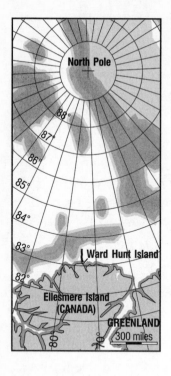

5

The Agony of the Arctic

The First Week

Day 1: Thursday, 5 March

Rune and I are up at 4.30 a.m. to finish a job we started exactly a year ago. No washing this morning before a breakfast of ham and eggs. It is dark outside and we eat in silence. Spirits are subdued by the tension of the moment and it feels like a condemned man's last meal.

It is strange to think of people back home rushing to work when we are about to head off into half a million square miles of nothingness. It's certainly a long way to go to get away from the traffic jams on the Chiswick flyover.

After our last visit to a civilised toilet for the next sixty days we cram into Pete Robinson's crew van and drive to the airport in pitch-black darkness. There are eight people in the van but nobody speaks for fifteen minutes. Even Nigel Bateson, normally the source of a stream of jokes and wisecracks, is silent; Rune, normally cheerful, is staring out of the window. He looks pensive and worried. I know how he feels.

There is a sense that our time has finally come and the chance to turn back has been passed. Now the sheer magnitude of the task ahead strikes home. I have a horrible feeling at the bottom of my guts that the pressure is definitely on. I have to do it this year because if I come up here three times and screw up then it's goodnight.

At Resolute's tiny airport we pass a pick-up truck carrying our sledges to the de Havilland Twin Otter aeroplane. 'There they go, your lifelines,' says Charles Rhodes, a BBC reporter, as the truck passes us. We squeeze into an office for the pilot's briefing. He warns me that a landing on the barren, unmanned, iced-over airstrip at Ward Hunt Island looks unlikely under the current weather conditions. The island is cloaked in thick low cloud which makes a touchdown at Ward Hunt more dangerous than usual.

Once on board the plane, Rune takes the front seat and slouches against the bulkhead with a cheeky grin on his face and his Walkman on his ears and starts to sing.

'I can't get no satisfaction,' he sings. 'Who's that by?'

'The Stones,' I answer. 'Have you got it playing on your Walkman?'

'No,' he says, 'something else. But you know the song. It's good isn't it?'

As the plane taxis to the runway, its propellers roaring, Rune bounces up and down in his seat, turns to me again and says in his half-Norwegian half-cockney accent, 'I've got the feeling I've been here before.' The plane builds up speed quickly, and very soon is in the air, Rune still singing his bastardised version of the Stones classic. 'This time you'll get it, kid,' I think as the plane climbs into the dark sky, lit only by a shimmering half-moon. 'This time there is no second chance.'

The flight to Eureka is wonderful, across a terrain like a white desert with the snow hanging like fog between the mountains. The open water between the mountains and islands is frozen ice, and above it all the sun is rising over the short Arctic winter day. At this high latitude the sunrise accompanies us for hours as we fly northwards and the golden globe struggles to lift itself above the horizon. I've made this journey several times before over thousands of mountains that have never been climbed and which will one day be named after the people who first reach their summits. It is always awe-inspiring.

As we fly into Eureka at the south end of Ellesmere Island to refuel

I spot some musk oxen and, just beside the airport, a junkyard of cars covered in ice. We land on snow and ice for the first time since last year. Outside on the airstrip it is −31°C and my eyes water as I get out of the plane; within half a minute my eyelashes are glued together by ice crystals. It is freezing cold, but warmer than last year, and the cold does not detract from the beauty of the sunrise over the mountains beside the airstrip. There is little to see that is man-made, just a couple of huts and corrugated iron shelters, but snow covers everything like giant white sand dunes and ice crystals glint in the air like diamonds.

Rune and I walk along the airstrip together, but we do not talk much. I tell Rune that I am still very nervous about the sixty days ahead. He does not answer, but I know he is thinking the same thoughts, of surviving the first ten days and getting into a routine. They are always the hardest. If we have forgotten our radio or some other piece of equipment then we have just got to get on with it and make do. The last time we saw Eureka we had just failed, and as I stand beside Rune, surrounded by the desolate beauty of the High Arctic with so much ahead of us, I think to myself that I hope the next time I come through here my thoughts are that it has been a successful trip.

Forty-five minutes later we have refuelled and the plane is in the air. The pilots inform us as we leave Eureka that visibility at Ward Hunt Island is down to less than one mile, but as we approach the island the cloud we had feared clears. John Perrins points out that the Moon is directly ahead of us and the sun is below the right wing at a right angle to the Moon, indicating a classic neap tide. 'The highest of the low and the lowest of the high,' John says. It should mean that the currents under the pack ice are relatively gentle for our first week walking across the Arctic Ocean. However, in seven days' time the Moon will be full and directly opposite the sun. The gravitational forces set up by this will be enormous and the tide will be the highest of the high and the lowest of the low − a spring tide. After that the polar cap will change considerably.

Rune falls asleep in his canvas bucket seat at the front of the narrow fuselage, but I am thinking of home. I feel like those Nasa astronauts one sees sitting in the van on the way to the Apollo or Space Shuttle launch-pad. Like them, we are going off into the uncharted and unknown; like them, it seems like a death sentence carried out in the full glare of the media. I think back to the first time I came up here to walk to the North Pole. Jim Merritt, the Canadian Twin Otter pilot who dropped me off on that occasion, said to me, 'Dave, this is like camping in your backyard, only bigger.' Although he was joking, he was right. I have to take it a day at a time, slip into a routine and not think of the dangers ahead.

In an ideal world, we would land on the ice-shelf at around 83°05'N on Ward Hunt Island, but if there is a lead I will ask the pilot to head three or four miles further west. The weather closes in again as we approach the top of Ellesmere Island and the pilot tells me we cannot land anywhere else. Instead, he flies a couple of miles out over the ice-cap so that we can assess the conditions. No sign of the Royal Marines – they are too far out for us to see – but we spot Thierry's Canadian-Italian team. They have taken two days to cover two miles.

I am shocked at how broken up the ice appears from the air this year. Last year it was relatively intact. I look around the plane to find everybody staring out of the ice-crystal-speckled windows, with frowns on their faces. Most of the terrain seems to be criss-crossed with grey and black water, a sure sign of fresh leads of open water. The tides are meant to be low at the moment and the ice should be in a good state, but it quite obviously is not. It is very frightening. The only consolation is that there is no sign of Peary's Lead; instead there are many short leads, which we should be able to scout around.

The pilots decide to risk a landing through the low cloud, and consequently the touchdown at 11.22 a.m. is particularly violent. The plane lands on one ski on very bumpy ice and I look around at this godforsaken place. We are back on this tiny cone of land that pokes out of the ocean and is the most accessible point to the North Pole on the Canadian side of the Arctic. Behind us the ice-covered beach stretches up to a Canadian flag, caked in snow and ice, attempting forlornly to fly over a couple of huts and corrugated-iron shelters. Ahead of us the polar ice is as flat, barren and arid as a desert, and with less precipitation than any wasteland on land. The only living things between here and the Pole are seals, Arctic foxes and polar bears, and two other teams of explorers.

We take a couple of pictures and answer a few questions for our last interviews before we set out. With the windchill it is −60°C or below, and the frostbite injuries on my nose are already throbbing. I have already permanently damaged my nose and ought to have an operation, when I can find the time, to put it right. However, I am not the only one struggling with frostbite. While interviewing Rune, Charles Rhodes's nose turns white as the frost nips at his extremities. Rune shouts at him to cover his nose.

'My God,' says Charles, who had not noticed the cold freezing his flesh. 'Thanks.'

'No problem,' says Rune with a big grin on his face, the flaps of his hat thrashing around in the wind, his neck and face uncovered. It seems there is nothing that makes this man feel cold.

After a few more formalities and farewells we clip on our skis, strap on our harnesses, and take the first few steps on our long and agonising trek. As the crow flies – not that any birds fly up here at this dreadful time of year – the Pole is 415 nautical miles away, but despite our best wishes we will not take a direct route. We will have to circumnavigate open leads and will drift east, west and south on the shifting ice. In all our journey is likely to be close to around 600 statute miles, a further distance in a straight line than from London to Berlin or Milan, or from Land's End to John O'Groats.

I feel a bit fed up to be here again after last year when we thought we would do it, and my nose is beginning to hurt. I have slight feelings of dread. The first part is so horrible. It is dark for most of the day and hoarfrost will clamp itself to our faces in our tent and penetrate our sleeping-bags.

At 12.45 p.m. the plane takes off behind us, circles a couple of times so that the photographer and television cameraman can take some pictures from the air, and heads off towards Eureka. Silence returns. It is freezing cold and windy and I am thigh-deep in crusty, decades-old snow. We will be alone for the next fifteen days until our first resupply arrives. At that moment I have only one wish: to be on that plane, headed for civilisation, a warm bed and a decent meal with the journalists. But although it is a dreadful feeling, it feels better than last year. Now Rune and I know each other; we know we can fit in to each other's routines and habits. In 1997 Rune was a friend; now he is more like a brother.

Within an hour of walking we are at Thierry's camp. When we get to his tent I am really shocked. Thierry emerges, looking a mess. He is shot away and I can see in his eyes that he has already given up.

Rune and I can tell straight away that there is a nasty atmosphere surrounding the expedition – Thierry and his partners stand a long way apart, not looking at each other or talking. Thierry says he is very tired and that his sleeping-bag is already iced up. It is a salutary lesson: even the best guys can come unstuck sometimes. I had suspected at Resolute that they would not do it, but I did not for the life of me think they would fail on day one.

A couple of hours later, exhausted by the cold, we pitch camp and climb into our tent. We have managed three miles in one and a half hours, a very good start for us, and we are both extremely pleased. I am excited just to get into it. After a dinner of Irish stew from our thermos flasks, we set up our Argos beacon to beam back the first message of our whereabouts:

```
00165    83.133N      74.138W    1   064/0450Z–064/0520
(3)      −.36211E+2   17    17        00
```

Position: 83°7'58" North; 74°8'16" West
Temperature: −36.2°C (inside tent)
Windchill: −55°C
Hours of sunshine: 3 hours 2 minutes
Nautical miles covered today: 3
Nautical miles so far: 3
Nautical miles to go (*in a straight line*): 412
Status: Everything okay

After dinner I realise I already have my first frostbite wounds on my fingers from filming with the BBC *Video Diaries* camera. I am annoyed because the only frostbite I have previously suffered has been on my nose. I have always managed to protect my fingers and toes on my expeditions. I hope this is not a bad sign.

We decide on a swig of whisky to celebrate our first night on the ice and unpack two hip flasks of single malt given to us by Nigel Bateson. The celebration comes to an abrupt end as soon as we lift the flasks to our mouths and the cold metal sticks to our lips. After pouring the whisky into a cup and sipping it, I wonder what purpose there is to all this. Well, it gets two smelly explorers out of London, and I suppose that has got to be some sort of a benefit to mankind.

Day 2: Friday, 6 March

Position: 83°08'17.5" North; 74°08'45.4" West
Temperature: −36°C
Windchill: −58°C
Hours of sunshine: 2 hours 54 minutes
Nautical miles covered yesterday: 3
Nautical miles covered so far: 3
Nautical miles to go (*in a straight line*): 412
Status: Everything okay

I wake up cold, knowing that there is nowhere we can go to warm up for the next sixty days and aware the relief will come only when we have reached the Pole, a journey fewer men have completed on foot unsupported than have walked on the Moon.

The first night out on the ice is always a monstrous shock to the system. The realisation that you are on your way and now face two months of torture strikes home, but in my case the torture is made slightly worse by Rune's incessant snoring. The solution I found last night was to have several swigs of whisky to celebrate the start of the expedition and to help me beat Rune in the race to fall asleep. Once I am asleep nothing can wake me, but if he beats me to it I am awake all night.

Once we set up the tent, our nightly routine swings into action. Rune lights a couple of candles and we open our thermos of Irish stew. With numb hands and a frozen backside and encased in my lamb's-wool thermal underwear and a layer of fleece, I slip into the plastic vapour barrier bag lining my two sleeping-bags. On my head I have a balaclava and hat. The trick is to leave nothing outside the bag uncovered. At the temperatures we sleep in our flesh will freeze if any is exposed at night. Before we go to sleep we open two embroidered envelopes given to Rune by Ingeweld, a girl he has known since childhood in Norway. They contain some good luck charms and a letter for Rune.

It is so cold in the tent that my teeth chatter and my breath freezes to the inside of the canvas. Worst of all, I have breathed on our video camera which instantly fogged up and looks as if it will be unusable. Once inside my sleeping-bag I soon become warm, probably too warm. The vapour barriers make us sweat profusely, and I am soon very sticky. Two draw-strings hold in all my body warmth and keep out the biting cold as I struggle to breath through the layers of fleece and fabric across my face.

Fortunately it was relatively warm last night – only −30°C in the tent, a pleasant introduction to the ravages of the Arctic – but this worries me. It should be −50°C, so maybe the El Niño weather pattern that has been lurking over the Pacific is now affecting the polar ice-cap. We have deliberately chosen to set off early, when there is little daylight and the temperatures are coldest, because any leads of open water will soon freeze over in the cold. I never thought I would find myself wishing for colder weather, but right now I sincerely hope the temperature soon drops.

So far everything has proceeded better than we could have hoped. At this stage last year we had already made a serious mistake: Rune had forgotten his blue bag and we spent eight days waiting for it to arrive at Ward Hunt Island. This year we have covered three miles in the one and a half hours of daylight that remained after the aircraft departed yesterday. It was a very good start for us – brilliant in fact. All we need now is plenty of luck.

The overriding sense at the moment is one of pressure. We have to reach the Pole by the time Claire, Alicia, my brother Mark and other friends and sponsors fly out to meet us on 27 April. I have worked out a target mileage for each day based largely on my two previous expeditions. Taking storm and rest days into account, I think sixty days is a realistic target, but there is little room for error. I hope I am right. Rune says that he also feels the pressure, but he seems already to have relaxed and settled into the routine of the job.

The morning is the hardest time. Getting out of a warm sleeping-bag is always a struggle on the ice, but crawling out of it after the first night is the worst of all. From the moment I get up I look forward to that time at the end of the day when I can stop walking and can crawl back into the tent, safe in the knowledge that I have a whole night's sleep ahead of me. The Arctic cold is similar to what my wife tells me child birth is like – you soon forget the pain of it but the misery floods back immediately you are once again in the midst of it.

Today the agony of the Arctic is made all the worse by the thought of what lies ahead of us. There is no slow warm-up to ease us into the expedition; walking to the North Pole is like an assault course where the first obstacles are the toughest and the highest. The roughest rubble and the highest pressure ridges cover the first hundred miles. Huge ice sheets, carried by the transpolar drift from Siberia across the Pole, slam into Canada with the momentum of several thousand miles behind them. The force of the collision is immense and the ice floes concertina, creating a succession of ridges like the fences in the Grand National. Some of the ridges descend 150 feet beneath the ice and rise forty feet above it, and to make matters worse the ground between each pressure ridge is filled with a jumbled mess of ice blocks. At its worst it can take a day to cross a few hundred yards of this frozen hell.

Many polar expeditions fear the rubble more than open water and opt to embark from Siberia. The trek from the Russian side is further to the Pole, but it can be easier and ultimately shorter because there are fewer pressure ridges and leads of open water to circumnavigate. A large lead can add tens of miles east- or westwards to the journey, with the result that the eventual distance is closer to 600 miles than the straight-line distance of 415 nautical miles, or 496 statute miles.

It takes us four hours to get going – we are out of practice, it is dark and everything takes twice as long as usual when it is forty below. The last thing I put on is the outer layer of orange windproof trousers and jacket which makes us look like Space Shuttle mechanics as we stumble across the ice. Within an hour of setting off we are fed up. Our skis are difficult to use because the bindings have been mounted too far forward. Rune swears and complains but there is little we can do until the resupply in fifteen to twenty days' time.

Otherwise it is a successful day, marred only by the thought of having to perform a radio broadcast tonight. We dread radio schedules all day because we often struggle to put up the dipole antenna securely. We suspend the aerial from three skis but it is often impossible to embed the ends of the skis in the pack ice, so we have to balance them in place with our ski poles. Tonight is no exception and Rune and I clamber into the tent only to realise that the antenna has fallen down. All this palaver in the dark is not helping the frostbite on my fingers to heal.

At seven p.m. we pick up John Perrins loud and clear on the radio, but our problems are not over yet. We can hear him, but he cannot hear us. Eventually a radio operator in Resolute Bay picks us up clearly and offers to relay all our messages, but it is still a laborious process:

John: British Typhoo. British Typhoo. This is Typhoo Base. Typhoo Base. Over.

David: Typhoo Base, this is British Typhoo receiving you loud and clear. Over.

John: British Typhoo. British Typhoo. This is Typhoo Base. Typhoo Base. Over.

David: Typhoo Base, I am receiving you clearly. Do you receive me? Over.

John: British Typhoo. British Typhoo. This is Typhoo Base. Typhoo Base. Over.

David: John, it seems you cannot hear me. If you can hear me, click your switch twice. Over.

John: British Typhoo. British Typhoo. This is Typhoo Base. You have a very weak signal. Can you tune your radio? Tune your radio. Over.

David: We are tuned to five two eight one point five megahertz.

John: British Typhoo, this is Typhoo Base. You are unreadable. Unreadable. Say again. Over.

David: We are tuned to five two eight one point five. We are receiving you clearly. Over.

First Air: British Typhoo. This is Six Nine Resolute. Go ahead, over.

David: Six Nine Resolute, this is British Typhoo. Can you relay for us? Can you relay our position for us please? Typhoo Base cannot receive us.

First Air: Roger. Go ahead. Over.

David: Our latitude. Our latitude. Eight three point one one. Over.

First Air: Okay. That's eighty-three degrees north. Was that eleven minutes British Typhoo? Over.

David: Roger, roger. That's one-ah one-ah. Over.

First Air: I copy. Roger, roger. Go ahead. Over.

David: Our longitude. Longitude seven four point one three. Over.

First Air: Roger. I copy. Seventy-four degrees and thirteen minutes west. Over.

David: Roger, roger.

First Air: What's the weather like? What was the weather like today? Over.

David: Clear skies. Clear skies. No precipitation. No precipitation. Minus thirty-six. Minus thirty-six. Over.

First Air: Roger. And how's the ice conditions? Over.

David: Very good. Very good. Little rubble and some pressure ridges. Some pressure ridges. Over.

First Air: Okay – that sounds good. Anything else to pass on? Over.

David: Our skis need replacing. The bindings are in the wrong place. Bindings in the wrong place. New skis on resupply. New skis on resupply. Video cameras have iced up. We need new video cameras, they are iced up. Over.

First Air: I missed that David. Repeat the last part again.

David: We need new skis on the resupply and our video cameras have iced up. Over.

First Air: Okay. I think I got that. Over.

David: We need new video cameras on the resupply. Over.

First Air: Roger. Go ahead.

David: We passed Thierry yesterday. Passed Thierry yesterday. He did not look good. Did not look good. Over.

First Air: Okay. Go ahead.

David: Tell John to get new skis from Austria and to ask Peter to fix skins and bindings. Over.

First Air: Roger. Okay. Your skis are on the resupply. Is that right?

David: No. We need, we need new skis to us on resupply. Over.

First Air: And you'd like them to bring two video cameras? Over.

David: Roger, roger. Ours have frozen up. Over.

First Air: Roger. Roger.

David: Tell John to put them on the resupply. Over.

First Air: Roger. Six Nine clear. Have a good day. I will talk to you later.

David: Roger, roger. Standing by.

First Air: Roger. Roger. Six Nine clear.

John: Six Nine Resolute, this is Typhoo Base. Over.

First Air: Yup. Go ahead Typhoo Base.

John: Six Nine Resolute. Can you relay the gist of that message? Over.

First Air: Basically, we got the co-ordinates copied. Eighty-three degrees eleven minutes north, seventy-four degrees thirteen minutes west. Everything is going good. They're taking it easy and getting used to the terrain. They passed the Italians today. And what else? For the resupply they need two video cameras as theirs are frozen over. Over.

John: Six Nine Resolute, this is Typhoo Base. I've got all of that. Can you pass some messages on to them for me? Over.

First Air: Yes. Stand by, I'll see if they're still there. Over. British Typhoo, this is Six Nine. Are you still there? Over.

David: Six Nine, this is British Typhoo. Go ahead.

First Air: Stand by for some messages. Over.

David: Standing by. Over.

First Air: Okay. Go ahead Typhoo Base.

John: This is Typhoo Base. Number one, for David. The skis that he wants can only be delivered from Austria at two zero zero pounds sterling transport costs. Is he prepared to go ahead on this? Please answer yes or no. Question two. Rune left a message to send a cheque to his brother via Rachel. No one understands what it means. Could he clarify? Message number three is about the Canadians – two have gone back to Ward Hunt. They have had a fire in their tent and Carlos has continued on his own. Thierry will stay at Ward Hunt and will then be airlifted out. Over.

First Air: Okay. What was the third request?

John: The third question wasn't a question, it was for information. For information. The Canadian team – Thierry has gone back to Ward Hunt, where he will stay. Carlos has continued on his own and is making a solo attempt. They had a fire in their tent. Over.

First Air: Okay. That sounds good. Is it the skis that will cost two hundred pounds sterling just for the transport costs? Over.

John: Yes, that's the transport costs from Austria. Rachel wants to know if he will confirm yes or no.

First Air: Okay. Stand by. British Typhoo this is Six Nine. Come in. Over.

David: Six Nine, this is British Typhoo. Go ahead, over.

First Air: Okay David. Re: the skis, Rachel wants to know if yes or no. The cost will be two hundred pounds sterling to get them from Austria. Over.

David: Bloody hell! That's a lot. Over.

First Air: Say again please David.

David: I said it is a lot, but we will have to pay it. Over.

First Air: Okay. And the second one is for Rune. Regarding instructions to send a cheque to his brother. Nobody is quite sure what that means. Over.

David: It is the cheque from the BBC that Rachel, my secretary, has. Over.

First Air: Okay, roger. And just regarding the Canadians, two Canadians went back to Ward Hunt Island, and Carlos is going to head out solo on his own to the Pole. Over.

David: Roger that. Over.

First Air: Okay, that's about it. Six Nine to Typhoo Base. Over.

John: Typhoo Base. Go ahead Six Nine. Over.

First Air: Okay, that's a roger for the skis. The cheque that Rune is referring to is from the BBC, if that means anything.

John: Not a lot, but I'll figure it out. Over.

First Air: Okay, and the rest is about done.

John: Yes, roger to that, and look forward to speaking to you again at nineteen hundred, one nine zero zero, on Sunday. Over.

David: Roger, roger. Sunday at nineteen hundred is good. Over.

First Air: Okay, that sounds good. Break British Typhoo, we'll talk again, nineteen hundred on Sunday.

David: Roger that. Over and out.

First Air: Six Nine standing by. Anything else from base?

John: Six Nine Resolute this is Typhoo Base. Is that end of transmission? Over.

First Air: Roger. That's over and out.

John: Thank you Tim, and speak to you again.

It has taken around twenty-five minutes to pass on our position, the weather and a couple of messages, but despite the inconvenience of VHF radio we are pleased to hear a voice from civilisation.

I am surprised at Carlos's decision to continue on his own. His sledge weighed over 400lb when they were a party of three, now he will have to carry the tent, the cooker, his food and all the other equipment on his own. I wish him the best of luck, but he must be a stronger and braver man than I am. It was tragic to see Thierry yesterday. I could see in his eyes that he had lost the dream and I suspected he would not make it when I felt the weight of his sledges, but I did not think it would all be over so quickly.

Now there are just two teams left, us and two British Marines. It amazes me that at the top of this crowded world there is a handful of men trying to reach a common goal, the North Pole, and both of the teams contain Britons. It is quite unique. We often think of the Marines and hope they are doing well. There is no competition between us because we are doing it in different ways and will have a common bond that will unite us, successful or not.

At the end of our first full day on the ice we are three miles closer to the Pole. I am pleased with our progress, particularly with such short daylight hours. We had counted on covering less ground, so for the moment, at least, we are ahead of schedule.

Day 3: Saturday, 7 March

Position: 83°11'00" North; 74°13'04" West
Temperature: −32°C
Windchill: −56°C
Hours of sunshine: 3 hours 54 minutes
Nautical miles covered yesterday: 3
Nautical miles covered so far: 6
Nautical miles to go (*in a straight line*): 409
Status: Everything okay

Good mileage. Thought all day about Thierry going back to Ward Hunt Island. No leads. Hard going. Too cold and too tired to write any more – just want to crawl into my sleeping-bag, draw the hood around my head and lie there shivering. Rune is much fitter – at the end of each day I am exhausted. He has put his Walkman on, is smoking a roll-up and appears not to be feeling any of it. The fourteen years between us makes a big difference. No radio contact scheduled for tonight; we set our position by Argos instead:

```
00165    83.142N      74.333W     3   68/0105Z–64/0133
(3)      −.5053E+2    17     17        00
```

Day 4: Sunday, 8 March

Position: 83°14'10" North; 74°20'00" West
Temperature: −55°C

Windchill: −85°C
Hours of sunshine: 4 hours 43 minutes
Nautical miles covered yesterday: 3
Nautical miles covered so far: 9
Nautical miles to go (*in a straight line*): 406
Status: Everything okay

My God, I wish I was not here. An unpleasant future of physical and mental torture has been dangled ahead of me and I know I have no choice but to survive it. Last night was a hard one. We are not heating the tent because we want to conserve fuel and I was tired and miserable. To make matters worse my imagination was rioting in my head. Every time I heard the ice creak I thought it was a polar bear's footstep and I jumped. Fortunately I was not the only one who was frightened; Rune was just as keyed up as I was and shot out of his sleeping-bag several times. Before it had even sunk in that he had moved he had grabbed the gun and was standing outside. He is the most remarkable man.

'You know David, sometimes I am out of the tent with the gun in my hands before I have registered that I have even heard a sound,' he said to me last night. I tease Rune that it is his Viking heritage that makes him so alert, but he takes my joke quite seriously. 'Oh yes David, you know the Vikings used to eat magic mushrooms to slow themselves down for battle and to make them fearless of pain.' I don't know whether to take him seriously but I certainly feel much safer with my Viking beside me. It is some comfort to have a trained killer with me, especially as I have encountered a polar bear before.

On the sixth night of my solo unsupported trek to the Magnetic North Pole in 1984, I heard a scratching and sniffing sound outside my tent. It was two a.m. and I was exhausted, but the sound instantly brought me to my senses. I did not realise I was not far from Polar Bear Pass, so named because it has the largest concentration of polar bears anywhere in the world, but I did know the sound of an intruder. I unzipped the flap of my tiny one-man tent to find a huge adult polar bear twenty-five yards away, staring straight at me.

I grabbed my gun and fired a warning shot, but the bear appeared not to take any notice. The huge animal had probably not eaten in days and it quite clearly had me in its sights. Compared with a seal, the staple diet of the bears dotted around Cornwallis Island, I was tasty fare and I could see a warning shot was not going to frighten it off its next meal. The bear took a couple of steps away from me, then swivelled and plodded very definitely and menacingly towards me. Although it was happening relatively slowly there was no mistaking the fact that I was being attacked.

I screamed 'You bastard!' at the bear and unleashed a volley of bullets. Back in Resolute, the locals had told me to take careful aim and fire off single, well-aimed shots, but with the countdown ticking I forgot any sensible control and fired every bullet in the gun at the animal. The bear dropped to the ground. Several of my bullets had hit home, but even then I was not taking any chances. Pumped to the eyeballs on adrenalin, I fired a further two shots into the area behind its shoulder, the only access point to its vital organs, then reloaded the rifle with five bullets and emptied them into the bear's huge white carcass. The bear was a mess, but I had survived.

Once I calmed down I felt dreadful. The last thing I had wanted to do when I set out was to kill any of the local wildlife, let alone a beast as magnificent as a polar bear. I had no right to be where I was; I was the intruder, not the other way round, yet the bear had drawn the short straw. Feeling very guilty, I radioed back to Resolute and told them to send a plane.

When the Twin Otter arrived, the pilots were amazed. The bear was lying a matter of feet away from my tent and it was clear that I had experienced a very close escape. With much difficulty they lifted the bear into the plane and ferried it back to Resolute where it was cut up, skinned and ticked off the hamlet's annual quota of polar bear kills. The fell was sold, the meat fed to huskies, and I made the newspapers in England as the first Briton to shoot a polar bear for many years.

Because of our fitful slumber last night, this morning we are both tired and neither of us has much of an appetite. Our metabolisms have not yet adapted to the cold and we are both struggling to digest our 6000-calorie daily rations.

Our main concern has become the cold. Our thermometer measures to −55°C but the needle was off the bottom of the scale this morning. To make matters worse my thermarest inflatable mattress has broken. It is so cold that the layers inside it have delaminated. This vital layer of insulation and cushioning now has a huge bubble between the layers and wobbles like a waterbed. I will be even colder from today until the resupply in two weeks, the period of the expedition when I will need the thermarest most.

I suggest to Rune that he give me his thermarest, but he thinks little of my suggestion. 'Hulashaker David,' he answers, followed by a string of insults in English, all of which he has picked up from me.

I persist in nagging him, insisting that a good friend would forgo his thermarest. No reply. 'Rune, how about we share our thermarest? I sleep with it one night, you the next,' I suggest. No reply. Rune is in the outer tent, puffing on a cigarette while he melts snow and ice to make hot water for our breakfast and hot juice during the day. 'Listen kid, if your thermarest was broken I would share mine with you. You know any good friend would,' I plead.

'Well then I am not that good a friend,' he says, and it appears the matter is closed.

It takes us even longer to get going than yesterday. The difference between −30°C and −55°C is enormous, just as noticeable as the difference between a warm English summer day at 25°C and a near-freezing English winter night. The cold gets right down into your bones and you have got to concentrate.

Just putting my boots on takes me nearly an hour. First we sit fully dressed with our feet in our sleeping-bags while one of us attempts to break the ice off the outside of our boots. Sometimes the ice is half an inch thick. Then, when all four boots are prepared and we are both ready, I quickly lift one foot out of my sleeping-bag while Rune holds the boot in place. With Rune's help I attempt to jam my foot into the boot, which is frozen rigid, like steel. It takes both of us to force the boot on to my foot, then we both stuff our hands into our armpits to warm them – holding the boot has sucked all the warmth from our hands through three pairs of gloves. As our hands warm up from numbness they tingle with pins and needles, an indication that we are on the border of frostbite.

Ten minutes later my hands are warm enough to push the laces through the first two eyes of my boots – two are all I can manage in one go before my fingers are again screaming with pain and seizing up. Again I warm my hands for ten minutes before pulling the laces around another two eyes. In this way it takes at least forty minutes to tie up my laces to the top of my boot, but the agony is not over yet. Within ten minutes of tying the final bow, my feet (which by now have been in the boots for almost an hour) have warmed the canvas uppers sufficiently for them to expand, so I now need to tighten the laces all over again.

Eventually we are ready to get going and it is a beautiful day. A clear sky but bitterly cold. With a twenty-five-knot wind, we work out that the windchill is at least −85°C. It could be colder – the temperature out of the wind does not register on the thermometer all day. We walk with every inch of our bodies covered. At these temperatures skin can freeze in under five seconds if left uncovered.

When we stop it is almost dark and we pitch camp and climb into our sleeping-bags. I remove my boots and socks to find I have frostbite on two toes on my right foot. I have no idea why the flesh at the tip of my toes has frozen but I suspect it is the new boot liners I have been wearing. They are a fraction too small, by only a matter of millimetres but enough to constrict the circulation of blood. I must be more careful. Two toes, two fingers and a thumb is not a good score, especially as up until now I have only ever been frostbitten on my nose, a common injury among mountaineers and explorers. Frostbite on my fingers and toes worries me; we have a long time in front of us to survive and although I do not mind losing the top of a finger or toe, I do not want my injuries to slow us down.

After cooking dinner Rune tends to my injuries. He has completed a medical course in the Norwegian armed forces and is a very know-ledgeable nurse. The skin is hard, white, waxy and cold to the touch, and has no feeling. If only the top layer has frozen I should be all right; it will thaw, blister and heal. But if the blood vessels have frozen I could get gangrene and we will have to amputate. Rune bathes my toes and fingers in warm water to thaw the skin. A burning pain envelops the tips of my reddening toes and fingers, but the damage appears to be only skin deep. Rune cleans the open wounds, then applies antiseptic creams and wraps a bandage around each injured toe, finger and thumb. With his cooking and nursing skills he would make someone a very good wife.

The cold and my frostbite injuries make crawling into my sleeping-bag tonight a particularly painful procedure. It is so cold that it is like getting into a deep-freeze when we first climb into our bags. The plastic vapour barrier bag has frozen and each fold has become a painfully cold, sharp edge. Pushing my throbbing, pus-filled toes against the hard plastic is extremely painful.

At the end of the day, a radio schedule with John. Again it is good to hear another voice in the middle of this empty wilderness. We pass on our new position, 83°19'05" North and 74°27'11" West – five miles a day is a record, even for day four. It took us until day twenty to notch up four miles in a single day last year. According to our schedule we should have taken ten days to reach 83°15' North, but we have already passed this position by four miles. The next twenty miles should be completed by 21 March, a very realistic target at present, although a couple of storm days will soon put us behind schedule.

We also officially left Canadian waters today. Technically Rune and I are a ship because we are carrying a radio on the seas, and we have an appropriate level of insurance for maritime search and rescue. Although Canada lays claim to the pie-slice of ice between its shores all the way to the North Pole, under maritime law we entered international waters when we exceeded a distance of twelve miles from the Canadian coast.

All these high mileages have quite literally gone to our heads; it has been a boozy first few days as each new record warrants a nip of brandy and a cigar for Rune. It is a great feeling.

Day 5: Monday, 9 March

Position: 83°19'05" North; 74°27'11" West
Temperature: below −55°C
Windchill: approximately −85°C
Hours of sunshine: 5 hours 23 minutes
Nautical miles covered yesterday: 5
Nautical miles covered so far: 14
Nautical miles to go (*in a straight line*): 401
Status: David injured – continuing

Bad news as soon as we wake up. Two of the MSR pumps for our stove have failed already, now the third and last one is leaking naphtha fuel at an alarming rate. If this goes on we will not be able to cook or heat the tent and we will asphyxiate on the fumes. Rune cannot understand it. 'These pumps are a disaster, a big disaster,' he says to me as he struggles to get the stove to light before heating the water for breakfast. 'I skied the whole length of Greenland and never had a problem with these pumps in eighty days. All of a sudden we have a problem with all three pumps, and in each case it is the same part, the rubber washer, which is faulty.'

Before we set out we tested all our pumps, including the ones we left behind at Resolute. Each one was stripped down and checked. The pumps, made by the American company Mountain Safety Research, are renowned for their simplicity and reliability, and worked perfectly when we tested them. I have used MSR pumps for years on my South Pole and Magnetic North Pole trips and have never had a single problem. Normally it would be wise to take a spare, but we wanted belt and braces security so we took three. Now, amazingly, we have a problem with all of them.

The pumps connect the one-litre bottles of naphtha fuel (unleaded high-octane petrol) to the stove. Once all the joins are tightened and sealed we pump up the fuel inside the metal bottles so that it vaporises when in the stove's burner jets, but on all three faulty pumps the pressure screw is not held tight into the side of the pump because the rubber washer is damaged.

'Hulashaker. More fuel is coming out of the pressure screw than going through to the burner,' exclaims Rune, who now has spot frostbite on two fingers and a thumb from trying to grip and adjust the metal screw.

Without a functional fuel pump we might as well give up now. Other expeditions have foundered for exactly the same reason. This is a disaster for us, a big disaster. We have faced crises before together and we have always taken the same approach in each case: work through the possibilities and eliminate unlikely explanations.

'Maybe it is the cold. We've never had it this cold before,' I suggest.

'But the first two pumps were not working even when it was minus twenty-eight and minus thirty-two a couple of days ago,' Rune answers.

'Maybe they have changed the design and we are doing something wrong,' I counter.

'No. These are the same pumps we used last year. They worked fine then, they worked perfectly when I checked them in England, and there was nothing wrong with them when I tested them in the garage at Resolute. All I can think is that somebody or something damaged them when we left them lying with the rest of our equipment on the garage floor. People walk in and out of that garage on the way to their rooms or to check their equipment. I cannot think of another explanation.'

Sabotage is an unlikely answer and one we do not want even to contemplate. Accidental damage, such as someone inadvertently stepping on a pump, is a possibility, but it is unlikely to damage all three pumps in exactly the same way.

'Although it would be easy to do, surely nobody would tamper with another expedition's equipment and endanger their lives,' I say to Rune.

Rune agrees that there must be another explanation for the simultaneous failure of all three pumps. 'Maybe we are doing something wrong, or maybe we damaged all of them after we tested them at Resolute,' he suggests. The fact that we have no answer is at the moment irrelevant; we need to work out some way of reducing our fuel use immediately.

We agree to stop heating the tent no matter how cold it gets and to forgo the hot drink we normally have shortly before going to sleep. It is some sacrifice – we both look forward all through the long, cold and dark evenings to a cup of hot chocolate or juice before bed-time, and we will both miss it. We will also instruct John to order some new MSR pumps directly from England, in case any of the other pumps left at Resolute are also faulty, and we will tell him to keep the pumps secure in his room where there is no chance that they will be damaged accidentally. We will also ask him to double the fuel allocation for the next third of the expedition to sixteen litres.

The troubles with the stove have delayed us and again we take a long time to get going. It is almost 10.30 a.m. by the time we are ready to leave. Fortunately the sun has only just risen, which makes me feel less guilty about taking so long to get ready. The sun is up for around thirty-five minutes longer each day; we are aiming to walk for five hours a day at the moment, but will increase it to six as soon as the sun allows.

The sheer beauty of this place never ceases to astound me. At night we see the most spectacular skies; the stars and the Moon are brilliantly clear, but it is nothing in comparison with the spectacle during the daytime. The sun is now up for almost five and a half hours, and speeds across the heavens, struggling to keep above the horizon. There is a very long sunrise, almost no median and then a long sunset because the sun is so low in the sky. While the sun is in its long decline we cross a rare pan of clear ice after struggling through two miles of incessant rubble, and I have to stop to take in the beauty of our surroundings.

It is bitterly cold – at least fifty-five below – and the mountains of Ellesmere Island are behind us, with the pressure ridges of ice lit by a vivid blood-orange light throwing long shadows across the ice pan. A snaky wind is blowing grey rivulets of snow towards us that curl and twist at our feet like trails of cigarette smoke. For once Rune is a few paces behind me; I overtook him when he stopped to light a cigarette, and he stops walking when he draws level with me.

'Look David, you can see where we have been walking,' he says as he points at a mist behind us. It is the most astonishing thing I have ever seen. Stretched behind us is a ghostly spoor, a faint mist like the jet-streams that trail aeroplanes in the sky but slightly more hazy. 'It is because it is so cold and our bodies are so much warmer than the air. It happens only when the wind is still or is blowing lightly into your face,' Rune explains.

I am overwhelmed. 'Christ this is beautiful – the mountains behind, the orange light and seeing our bodily traces. It is absolutely staggering.' We stop to watch our hazy apparitions slowly disappear behind us as the wind takes five minutes or more to dissolve the vapour trails.

At the end of a fabulous day I pull out the GPS to record our mileage. Five miles for the second day running – we are well ahead of schedule and I cannot believe it is going so well. No radio schedule tonight, so we set up the Argos beacon so that John can pick up our position:

00165	83.401N	74.380W	2	69/1150Z–60/0017
(3)	−.5856E+2	17	17	00

Day 6: Tuesday, 10 March

Position: 83°24'02" North; 74°22'47" West
Temperature: below −55°C
Windchill: approximately −85°C
Hours of sunshine: 5 hours 53 minutes
Nautical miles covered yesterday: 5
Nautical miles covered so far: 19
Nautical miles to go (*in a straight line*): 396
Status: Everything okay

Another night of agony. My toes wake me up several times, either throbbing or hurting like a dull toothache. Right now they are numb and Rune is dressing the septic wounds.

Outside the tent it is again a beautiful cold day and I am relieved that the weather is holding. Although I am suffering terribly from cold hands and have a big frostbite blister, I am glad the cold snap proves that all the talk of El Niño may have been misleading. Unseasonably warm temperatures would have hastened the thaw of the ice-cap; we need cold weather to freeze leads of open water.

The mountains are becoming smaller as we walk further from them, and the going is good with less rubble than we expected. We are quickly getting into a routine.

Panic at midday when we see a Twin Otter flying overhead. From the ground we can see it carries the colours of Ken Borek whose air company runs aircraft out of Resolute Bay with the call-sign of Whisky-Papa-Whisky. I worry for a moment that we have accidentally tripped the emergency switch on our Argos beacon and stop to search for the transmitter in my sledge; it is switched off and I realise that the plane has probably come to pick up Thierry's team from Ward Hunt Island. Rune and I wave at the plane as it continues to circle and the pilot responds to our greeting by dipping each wing several times before flying off towards the coast.

Shortly afterwards we come to our first substantial lead, the moment I have dreaded since we set foot on the ice. We have crossed dozens of tiny leads, little cracks between ice floes only inches or a foot wide, but this is the first lead we cannot leap or stride across. Rune is fond of saying that the difference between a good lead and a bad lead is only those couple of inches that are longer than our skis.

'This is where the trouble starts,' I say to Rune, who has stopped ahead of me at the lead's edge. Although not particularly large, it is our first sight of open water and a portent, I feel, of things to come. We have been very lucky so far. To go six days without seeing open water is quite unusual and it seems all the more so after all the warnings we received about wide expanses of broken ice and open water this year. Maybe there will be a lot more to come.

Rune thinks he can see a crossing less than a quarter of a mile to the west and we head off towards it. He is right: there is a section of recently frozen ice that looks thick enough to take the weight of us and our sledges. Crossing leads terrifies me. I am a poor swimmer and frightened of water. I know that any step could plunge me through the ice into the ocean below. Rune does not share my fear of water and the prospect of an icy dip does not faze him in the slightest. Part of his Norwegian commando training involved cutting two holes in an ice-covered lake, diving into the water and swimming below the ice from one hole to the other. It is something that no amount of money could persuade me to do.

Salt water freezes at lower temperatures than pure water so the water at the surface of the Arctic Ocean is −4°C, admittedly much warmer than the air, but you lose heat much more quickly once you get wet. As the surface water freezes it goes through a succession of distinct changes that allow us to gauge whether it is strong enough to take our weight. First small crystals of ice develop and conglomerate to form a thickening mass of frazil ice which looks like a crusty skin floating on the water surface. In time the motion of the water packs the frazil ice together to form small pancakes of ice with upturned edges, still too weak to carry a man or sledge. Within a few hours the pancakes become a thicker, sludgy brown ice like porridge. With a little care and provided you do not stand still for too long, sludgy ice will take a man's weight.

The next stage is the ideal ice on which to pull sledges. It is hard, brown and flat, and is the kind of ice explorers dream of if a recently frozen lead points northwards and they have the courage to follow it along its length. Tracing a newly frozen lead is a game that requires steely nerves; if there is any movement in the ice the freshly frozen surface will be the first to pucker and form a pressure ridge. A sure indication that the ice is sufficiently strong to carry a substantial weight is the sight of white frost flowers on its surface. The whiter the ice, the harder and stronger the surface. One-year-old floe ice is around six to seven feet thick, enough to take the weight of a car. In summer the top will melt and there will be pools of meltwater on the surface, some of which become polynyas, pools that extend right through the ice floe. If the floe survives the summer thaw and refreezes in the winter it then becomes exceptionally strong multi-year ice. This blue ice is strong enough to take the weight of an aeroplane and so tough that most icebreakers cannot crack it apart.

To Rune all this ice science is meaningless. Having grown up in the midst of Norway's harsh winters he has his own tried and tested methods. He steps on to the freshly set ice and stabs it several times with his ski pole.

'If it goes through first time then we look for another crossing point,' he says. 'If the pole breaks the ice on the second poke we will chance it, if it survives three stabs we know it is safe.'

My instincts tell me this is very rough science, but I know from last year that he is right. He prods the ice sharply with his ski pole. It goes through on the third prod, strong enough in Rune's book for us to stop for a picnic on the lead, but it still unnerves me. Rune leads the way and pulls his sledge behind him. I detach myself from my sledge and ski over the lead, holding the sledge ropes so that I can then pull the sledge after me from the other side.

We cross our first lead without mishap. We both know that today is undoubtedly but an appetiser for the main course of hundreds if not thousands of such leads that we will need to breach if we want to reach the Pole. Although I am the one who is afraid of water, I can tell that crossing a challenging lead is just as stressful for Rune. He says he has to look out for me as well as for himself at these times.

'I know how I am going to react David, but I don't know what you are going to do,' he says. 'I worry about you. I am a bachelor, it does not matter if I am injured, but you have a family and so I must be responsible for you too.'

I know I certainly feel more secure with my Viking accompanying me on this expedition. We are a strong team but I think it works because we are so different. We both have strong personalities and if we were more similar we would probably clash. Last time we did not speak a bad word to each other.

At four o'clock, after the sun has set and dusk is falling, we spot a jet-stream high in the sky above. The plane is headed directly for the Pole and is probably on a transcontinental route from Vancouver to Tokyo or London. I think to myself, as I sit at the door of the tent with all my clothes, a hat, balaclava and face mask on, how strange it is that we are sitting here, freezing our nuts off and eating dehydrated food, while up there, nice and warm, are around 300 people watching a film, drinking champagne and eating lobster. 'But you know what makes it even stranger?' I ask Rune. 'The really strange thing is that right now the place I want to be most is right here. And that's because I want to get to the North Pole.'

A radio schedule again with John tonight, and I relay our position to him. Today we managed six miles and I cannot quite believe it; last year it took until day forty to hit six miles a day. After the agony, bad luck and struggle of last year's expedition, this year I feel as if we're on a real roll. We are building up a momentum. We are covering a good distance each day, the sledges are superb and, compared with last year when we had to relay, every step we make at the moment is another step towards the Pole. It makes a fantastic difference and puts us on a real high. I feel now that we are really doing well. It would be foolish even to think of making it to the Pole at this early stage, but I do think this time we have got everything right. We've got a good chance if we keep on like this.

Day 7: Wednesday, 11 March

Position: 83°30'02" North; 74°29'18" West
Temperature: below −55°C
Windchill: approximately −85°C
Hours of sunshine: 6 hours 27 minutes
Nautical miles covered yesterday: 6
Nautical miles covered so far: 25
Nautical miles to go (*in a straight line*): 390
Status: Everything okay

At six o'clock I am woken up by the alarm on my Casio watch tied to the inside of my sleeping-bag and wedged underneath my ear. I look at the cheap plastic timekeeper, given away free at a petrol station, and marvel at its ability to survive extreme temperatures. It must be one of the best travelled watches in the world – I have worn it up Everest, Aconcagua, Vinson, Elbrus and the Carstensz Pyramid. It has kept time at the Geomagnetic North Pole, the Geographic and Magnetic South Poles, and now it is on its second expedition to the North Pole.

I lean over and wake up Rune with a simple prolonged shout: 'Roo-ner!' Then I go back to sleep. Rune is the cook, so he must rise first to struggle with the leaking fuel pumps. He likes the time to himself to listen to music on his Walkman while he boils water, writes in his diary and smokes the first of his never-ending stream of cigarettes.

It is still unbearably cold and the colder it gets the thicker the hoarfrost in the tent. Our tent looks like a steam-room at the best of times as our breath condenses in the gelid air, but when it is particularly cold our breath collects at the top of the tent where it freezes, forming hoarfrost streaks like stalactites. Approximately every hour throughout the night the hoarfrost becomes too long and heavy to support its own weight and a stalactite breaks off. If I am unlucky, it lands directly in my face, a deeply unpleasant shock which instantly wakes me. It is made all the more unpleasant by the ability of the hoarfrost to insinuate itself into the folds of duvet around my face and slide down the gap into my neck. Because of the threat of frostbite from hoarfrost attack I have to wear a full balaclava with only a tiny slit left open so that I can see.

The first routine when it is cold is to rid the tent of hoarfrost. After Rune has lit the stove and finished his first cigarette, I roll over on to my front so that the hood of my sleeping-bag is on top of me, facing the ceiling of the tent with my face buried in my faulty thermarest. Rune then brushes the inside of the tent to remove all the hoarfrost and then the outside of my sleeping-bag to prevent the hoarfrost from melting into the bag and icing it up. I turn over to find myself in a pool of white snow.

After breakfast I reluctantly get dressed. I am aching, cold, tired and desperate for a rest day, and I gasp as I open the zip from the inner to the outer tent, where it is at least ten degrees colder. The difference in temperature is very noticeable and it hits me with a shock every morning. Then there's a second, more acute shock when I unzip the door to the outside and face the full force of the wind. This is always the hardest moment; the temptation to crawl back inside and give up is immense, but we must continue to grind our way northwards. I tell myself that every mile north today is a mile less I will have to walk tomorrow.

My hands are exceptionally cold today. For almost a week we have not been able to measure the temperature on our thermometer. All we know is that it has not lifted above −55°C. It is so cold that the fabric and plastic on the outside of my outer pair of mittens has frozen rigid and I cannot flex my fingers inside to warm them up. The ski poles we are using this year are better and we have put more insulation around them, but they still draw off a lot of heat through three pairs of gloves.

To make matters worse, we stop every hour or so for a hot drink from our thermos flasks. Handling the flasks freezes my hands all the more and it takes the entire hour between drink breaks for my hands to warm up again, by which time I have to stop again for a drink, so once again my hands are cold. There is no solution. We wear three pairs of gloves, which make our hands sweat. The sweat freezes inside the gloves and they ice up, becoming colder as the day goes on. The only way around this conundrum is to wear a pair of inner 'thinny' gloves to wick moisture away from the skin followed by a thicker layer of extremities gloves and then a pair of massive mittens like astronauts' gloves, with a thick spongy layer and a windproof outer layer. But by the end of the day the second layer is thick with ice, and on a bad day the ice can be touching the skin of our hands.

In conditions such as these we have to dig deep. What fails to destroy us only makes us stronger, I keep telling myself, and I console myself with the thought that if successful, this will be my last big polar trip. I cannot do it again, it screws up my body too much, and I certainly do not want to be doing this in my fifties and sixties. I admire men like Sir Ranulph Fiennes, but I could not put myself through the torture he does at his age.

At the end of the day we drag ourselves into our tiny tent only to find that the MSR pump is leaking even more fuel than before. I do not know what we can do to sort this out.

No radio contact, so I set up the Argos to record our position.

According to the GPS we have walked six miles in a day for the second day running. A magnificent achievement. If only the weather would get a little warmer.

```
00165    83.600N       74.497W     2   72/0205Z–72/0310
(3)      –.5578E+2     102   102       00
```

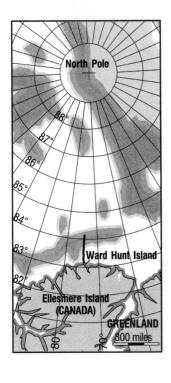

6

Hot Juice and Cold Days

The Second Week

Day 8: Thursday, 12 March

Position: 83°36'00" North; 74°29'55" West
Temperature: below −55°C
Windchill: approximately −85°C
Hours of sunshine: 7 hours
Nautical miles covered yesterday: 6
Nautical miles covered so far: 31
Nautical miles to go (*in a straight line*): 384
Status: Everything okay

Tonight will be the night of reckoning – a full Moon means a spring tide and the ice will shift, buckle and strain under the enormous tidal forces. By tomorrow morning the landscape around us and our route to the Pole are likely to be considerably different.

But first we have to face today, and we are finding that walking to the Pole is quite unlike any other journey. The South Pole had its own unique challenges including crevasses and a steep climb from sea level to almost 10,000 feet, but it is seen as easier to navigate because it is on land and there are maps. At the North Pole we do not know what lies ahead of us; there are no maps to show us the way because we are walking across a frozen ocean where the surface is in a constant state of flux. Every day different leads open up, but if it is cold enough the water can freeze over again within hours, so nobody could ever hope to draw anything resembling an accurate or current map. Sea charts are just as useless; the underwater topography is of little interest beyond an indication of where we are likely to encounter fast-moving currents due to a sudden change in ocean depth. All we can do is head northwards and keep track of our position using a hand-drawn plotting chart marked with the lines of latitude and longitude from Ward Hunt Island to the Pole, and switch to a larger-scale plotting chart for the final five to ten miles around the North Pole.

The simple act of heading northwards is not without its complications. We are north of the Magnetic North Pole and consequently need to walk away from the direction the compass indicates is north. The amount of correction we need to apply to our compass readings, called the magnetic variation, changes from year to year because the Magnetic North Pole is moving slowly northwards. The variation also shifts slightly during the course of a day because the magnetic pole oscillates in an ellipse that can move slowly or very rapidly, depending on the sun's activity. Every year Natural Resources Canada, a government agency, publishes a table of the average magnetic variation values needed to adjust magnetic compasses at various latitudes. I carry a short-list of the figures in the front of my diary, and every few days we have to make a new adjustment to our compass.

At the point where the mountains on Ellesmere Island just disappear from view – 83°30' North and 75° West, or twenty-five miles from Ward Hunt Island – the magnetic variation is −87°. This means we have to take a bearing of 87°, almost directly east according to the compass, to head for the Pole. An alternative method is to subtract 87° from 360°, point the needle of the compass at the outcome – 273°, almost directly west – then walk in the direction the compass indicates is north. To make matters even more complicated, the magnetic variation can move by up to fifteen degrees in a day, which often makes me wonder if it is worth our while getting our compasses out at all. We can check the magnetic variation on our GPS satellite navigation system, but the GPS uses batteries and has to be warmed up before we can use it. Continuing along the 75° West line of longitude, the magnetic variation increases to −90° at 85° North, at 87° North it is −98°, at 88° North it is −99° and sixty miles from the Pole, or 89° North, it is −106°. Beyond the 89th Parallel, the compass points almost directly south when we are heading north.

I am the chief navigator, but Rune likes to be the point man, with only his shadow for company as he leads the way and scouts ahead to find the best way to the Pole. Rune looks for the quickest, most direct and easiest passage through the rubble and pressure ridges, but very often these three factors do not concur. The most direct route might lead us across a particularly high pressure ridge or through a wide lead of open water. Sometimes it is quicker to take a longer route and it is Rune's job to examine all the options; when the route calls for us to cross water or a recently frozen lead, we both make the decision. Rune likes the feeling of solitude, and unsurprisingly he trusts his judgement as to the best route better than mine. I have to admit he is probably better qualified for the job of point man. As a Marinejegerkommando Rune is used to unsupported missions behind enemy lines.

After a couple of hours' skiing this morning I draw level with Rune. He is having a cigarette break and contemplating the best course ahead. With a balaclava, hat and goggles on, all I can see of him are his lips poking out through the hole he has cut in his neoprene mask. There is little to tell us apart when we are fully wrapped up – the only distinguishing feature is the masks that protect our faces from frostbite. Whereas mine is standard issue, with a smattering of small holes punched in the neoprene so that I can breathe, Rune has customised his mask crudely by cutting a square hole in the centre just large enough for him to purse his lips around a cigarette.

'It is not at all easy today,' he said. 'The compass points in a different direction every time I get it out. I think there is a magnetic storm overhead. I am having to navigate by the sun.'

At these high latitudes the sun is generally more reliable than a compass, provided it can be seen. There is a simple formula. At twelve minutes past midday the sun is at its meridian, the highest point of its march across the sky. At this moment the sun is directly south and our shadows point directly north, moving fifteen degrees towards east every hour as the sun passes from east to west. So at six o'clock in the morning our shadows should point directly west, and at six in the evening directly east.

For the solar navigation system to work faultlessly we have to be sure that our watches are set to the correct time zone. When we set out it was our intention to follow the 75° line of longitude to the Pole, a line which is five hours behind Greenwich Mean Time. However, for every fifteen degrees we veer east or west of 75° West, the sun reaches its meridian an hour earlier or later. During the first part of our journey the lines of longitude are relatively far apart and any shift to the east or west will have little effect on our navigation. At 84° North, we would have to walk ninety-four miles west to reach the next time zone, where the sun reaches its meridian an hour later. However, as we walk northwards the lines of longitude squeeze closer together so that at 89° North there are only fifteen miles between time zones. As we approach the Pole it will become even more complicated as the lines of longitude converge and the sun appears never to dip in the sky, circling above our heads always at the same height above the horizon.

Despite Rune's expertise I sometimes wonder if we are really taking the best route north.

'Which way is north Rune?' I shout. 'Are you sure you are headed north?'

We have not had an argument yet on the ice, but I know my nagging about navigation annoys him.

'Don't you trust me David?' he answers. 'Do you want to lead the way? It is very difficult today – the wind is coming from the north and blowing straight into my face. My eyes are freezing over and I cannot focus because the muscles at the edges of my eyes are getting frostnip. You're very welcome to go ahead.'

He knows I am only too happy for him to lead the way. It would be ridiculous for me to go ahead; Rune is twice as fast as I am on skis and he uses his speed to scout around, climbing pressure ridges to see how the ice lies and darting east and west to find the best route. By the time I have caught up with him he has investigated all the options and is waiting for me to arrive so that we can make a joint decision on which route to pursue.

'You can go ahead if you want David. Then you will see what it is like,' Rune says as he unleashes his sledge. He then climbs a pressure ridge beside us to peer into the distance. Rune is looking for big black spots on the horizon. These indicate pans of open ice, the dream surface for a quick route north. From a distance the jumbled surfaces of the rubble reflect the sunlight better than the flat expanse of a large wide pan.

'Bad news David. I can see a lot of white and very little black – there is rubble all around us and no big pans unless we head west a bit and then north. It is a longer route but I think it is easier.'

'How much longer?' I ask

'Difficult to say David, but it will be a lot easier. It is better to walk longer and have a nice think and dream than make life difficult for ourselves by walking through the middle and becoming frustrated, annoyed and angry.'

At times like this it is difficult to analyse why we are here. We are surrounded by hundreds of tons of haphazardly arranged ice rubble and there is little respite in sight. The only enjoyment to be had is from watching our plan work; no matter what happens, at the end of the day we will be closer to the Pole and hopefully still on schedule. Rune leads us off towards the west and I follow, trying to suppress the nagging doubt that he is taking us in the wrong direction.

'Which way is north Rune?' I call after him. It is becoming like a mantra. Rune does not even stop. He simply lifts his right arm and points his ski stick out at an angle. I must stop nagging him.

By the end of the day we have walked nearly six miles. We are doing well, as good as six miles a day for the last two days, and I am amazed at our progress. After last year's struggle through the first hundred miles, we did not think we would clock up such good mileages day in, day out. So far we have not had a single day like last year when we sometimes fought hard to cover 400 yards in a day. The rubble is much less extreme, and I wonder if last year's sledges would have coped a lot better in these conditions.

I hope I do not regret these words by tomorrow morning. With a full Moon above us the tides could change everything in the next few hours. I am worried that we have a full Moon so early in the trip. The ice nearest the shore is the weakest and most susceptible to being broken up. It is bound to be a noisy night; all we can hope for is a few hours' sleep.

A good radio schedule with John tonight. The only bad news is that Swindon Town lost 6–0 to Middlesbrough yesterday.

Day 9: Friday, 13 March

Position: 83°41'47" North; 74°27'40" West
Temperature: −52°C
Windchill: −80°C
Hours of sunshine: 7 hours 38 minutes
Nautical miles covered yesterday: 5¾
Nautical miles covered so far: 36¾
Nautical miles to go (*in a straight line*): 378¼
Status: Everything okay

An appropriate date for our first night of terror on the ice. The full Moon brought a spring tide and with it the titanic forces that create earthquakes at sea. Huge pans of ice, some the size of a dozen football fields, smash and grind against one another as the huge currents of the Arctic Ocean twist, ebb and flow beneath us. At times it sounds as if a hundred dumper trucks have encircled our tent and all have tipped their loads of rock boulders on to a concrete surface at once. Throughout the night, as we lie in our tent, there is a constant crashing and rumbling, and a scraping sound like the rush of a might wind. We can hear huge blocks of ice rubble falling from newly formed pressure ridges, and suddenly a noise like a rifle shot shoots through the ice as it breaks up.

The most frightening element of an icequake is that we do not know where the next movement will be. We pray all night that we have not camped near or on a fault line. In an instant our tent could be overturned and buried in rubble as a pressure ridge is forced thirty feet up, or our pan of ice could split apart while we attempt to sleep, dropping us in our sleeping-bags and tent into the freezing ocean. It is petrifying to be lying in a tent on a pan of ice when the ice starts to move so quickly and the noise builds in a growling crescendo from a creaking rumble to a loud crashing. It could be a quarter of a mile away, but it is very loud and sounds as if it is right beside us.

Worse than the noise are the vibrations. We can feel the ice cracking somewhere near or beneath us, but we never know where the movement or break-up is taking place. At its worst it feels as if the crack is running straight through our bodies. The tent shakes, we shake in our sleeping-bags and the cracking noises shoot through our bodies. It is impossible to sleep. Tucked inside two sleeping-bags and a vapour barrier bag I feel totally helpless – the ice could split open directly beneath the tent and there is nothing I can do. This is the most terrifying part of walking to the Pole. It is better to fall into water in daytime than lie in our sleeping-bags and not know what might happen.

Despite a night of huge upheaval, in the morning the ice is not quite as bad as we feared, but we still spend the morning making up mileage lost overnight. I did not take a position reading this morning but I estimate that during the night we drifted between one and two miles south. The battle against the ocean can be dispiriting. The first two hours are very slow because of new rubble thrown up last night and because it continues to be extremely cold. Two or three times I think my ski pole is about to break as I jam it between two blocks of ice while picking my way through the quarry of ice boulders. To my relief the ice becomes flatter later on.

The front of my boot has split, which does not help my frostbite, and it will no longer clip into my ski binding. I have rigged up a piece of wire that stretches from a second binding clip on the ski around the back of my boot. This is the way old-fashioned bindings worked, but it slows me down.

I do not enjoy today and think of steak and chips the entire time. It is −50°C and my hands are cold from the moment we leave the tent until I crawl into my sleeping-bag. It annoys me because I cannot let my mind wander when my feet or hands are cold. All my thoughts are concentrated on trying to warm them. I try to wiggle my toes while I am walking, but the frostbite and the new binding arrangement makes it difficult to move them in my boot. I hope this is not an indication that my frostbite has penetrated deeper into my toes. My fingers are completely numb with cold. To force the blood to pump through them, I let my hands dangle and drag my ski poles behind me, but I ski at a slower pace when I do not use my poles.

By the end of the day we are six miles further than yesterday, and I suspect we walked further than that to make up lost ground. Still, we are doing exceptionally well – nearly forty-three miles in nine days. We expected to average only two miles a day.

Day 10: Saturday, 14 March

Position: 83°47'49" North; 74°25'04" West
Temperature: −50°C
Windchill: inside tent all day
Hours of sunshine: 8 hours 10 minutes
Nautical miles covered yesterday: 6
Nautical miles covered so far: 42¾
Nautical miles to go (*in a straight line*): 372¼
Status: Storm

After yesterday's sterling performance, not a footstep today. It is blowing a hooley outside and I am stuck inside the tent, frustrated and fidgety. Rune is very happy to stay put. Once we get going he is the driving force, always wanting to walk an extra ten minutes before a break and add another hour on to the end of the day, but he admits he is the lazier one first thing in the morning.

'I think we should take today as a rest day,' he says. 'I am tired, it is minus fifty and it is blowing twenty to thirty knots outside. Let's stay in bed.'

I insist that we review the decision an hour later, but the wind is blowing even stronger then, the visibility stretching no further than eighteen inches. We are a long way ahead of schedule and can afford a rest day. If we keep going at the current rate we will need our resupply earlier than planned, which will mean pulling heavy sledges again sooner than I had hoped. We need more time to build up strength and stamina before we go back to heavy sledges.

A day in the tent is much the same as any other day; we still have to go through the procedures of cooking and tending to our injuries. We wake at six o'clock and Rune gets up to make breakfast. While I go back to sleep, Rune lights a fag, puts on his Walkman and starts heating some water. The first heating is the main heating, around three litres of water using snow from the outer tent to make breakfast drinks and hot juice for the day. If there is insufficient snow we can

At the top of Everest with Natemba on October 9, 1993. (*David Hempleman-Adams*)

South Pole, January 5 1996. The first Briton to make it to the bottom of the world solo and unsupported. (*David Hempleman-Adams*)

January 1998. Dragging my eldest daughter Alicia on a rubber tyre as training for dragging a 200lb sledge across ice for some 600 miles. (*Paul Grover*)

February 1998. Acclimatisation training in the Buxted chickens' deep freeze. (*all pics: Paul Grover*)

right March 2 1998. Testing one of the three stoves whose failure almost ended the expedition. In the garage at Resolute Bay.

below February 1998. The press launch of the expedition at London's South Bank.

Hell on Earth. Resolute Bay in the Canadian High Arctic – on a good day.
(*all pics: Paul Grover*)

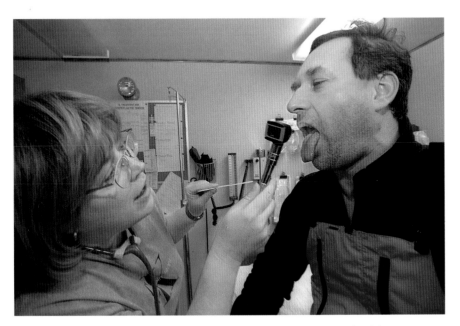

above March 2 1998. Feeling rotten. A health check at Resolute Bay health centre reveals I have high blood pressure and a chest infection.

next page March 3 1998. Rune leaps a crevasse while training on the ice at Resolute Bay.

March 4 1998. The Argos satellite beacon that recorded our daily position and which almost delayed our departure. *(all pics: Paul Grover)*

Our good luck charms and mementoes carried in our blue bags from home.

March 4 1998. A cake to celebrate the last night in civilisation. Our support team (from left) Robert Uhlig and Paul Grover from the *Daily Telegraph*, Rune Gjeldnes, Charles Rhodes from the BBC, base manager John Perrins, David Hempleman-Adams and Nigel Bateson from the BBC.

above March 5 1998. A last picture at Ward Hunt Island before we set out, well-fed and excited. The windchill was -60°C. (*all pics: Paul Grover*)

left March 5 1998. Rune and I shake hands on the beach at Ward Hunt Island before embarking on the 60-day trek northwards.

below March 5 1998. Off into the barren wilderness. Our first steps north from Ward Hunt Island – 415 nautical miles to go.

March 6 1998. First radio contact with John Perrins, our base man, at Resolute Bay. (*Paul Grover*)

One of the rituals on the ice; every evening we positioned the Norwegian and Union flags on the north side of our camp. (*Paul Grover*)

In the tent when the temperature dropped off the bottom of the thermometer. At least -55°C, and nothing to do but lie in our bags and shiver. (*Rune Gjeldnes*

use ice, but we have to be careful to use old ice. New ice contains salt water, but after a year or so the salt filters out. When the water has boiled, Rune mixes up a litre of hot juice for each thermos flask for the day ahead. He then wakes me up with a piece of chocolate and a hot drink. While I am drinking my tea in bed, Rune opens a two-man ration pack and heats the water for our breakfast of muesli, milk powder and vegetable and soya oils. He eats his breakfast first because he likes his muesli only slightly warm, around 30 degrees, whereas I like mine piping hot.

There is no place for manners in the Arctic, particularly as it is so cold that we have to clutch the metal cutlery and plastic cup through a layer of fleece to avoid frostbite. We tried to use plastic spoons last year, but the plastic shattered very quickly in the cold, so this year we have metal spoons. I have to warm the spoon carefully in the muesli otherwise it sticks to the inside of my mouth. The muesli will freeze in minutes if left to stand so I shovel it into my mouth as fast as I can. All the oil mixed in with the muesli makes me gag if it is anything but boiling hot. While I am eating Rune rolls another cigarette and wedges it in the corner of his mouth ready for me to finish. As soon as I am he lights up and starts the washing up by scraping out our plastic cups and any pots he has used.

We spend the first couple of hours after breakfast checking our equipment and tending to injuries. The frostbite on my toes has become septic but my fingers are improving. Once the chores are done it is too cold to do anything much but lie in our sleeping-bags, pull the hoods over our heads, shiver and think of home. We would normally heat the tent on a storm day but the stove pumps are still leaking and we have to conserve fuel.

Rune is listening to his Walkman and I am thinking of my wife and daughters. It is at times like this that I feel guilty about leaving my family on their own. I used to think my children did not worry when I was away from home, but I did not realise the effect my frequent and prolonged absences from home were having until I went last summer to a camp organised by the Mitchemp Trust, a charity I set up with a friend to give disadvantaged children a chance to go rock-climbing, walking and adventuring in the Brecon Beacons, where I started my first Duke of Edinburgh award.

I took my daughters along for a couple of days at the camp and was woken up in the middle of the night by a young girl who had been crying. She was missing her father who had recently died and she asked me to sleep in the tent with her because she was lonely. I knew that for obvious reasons I could not sleep in the same tent as an eight-year-old girl so I called Victoria Riches, one of the camp organisers, to keep the girl company. The young girl soon fell asleep, but seeing her so shaken up by the loss of her father made me realise the effect my expeditions were having on my children. Since they have started school, Camilla and Alicia have met several orphans and have become used to the idea that not every child has a parent. They are now aware that some children have gone through the experience of losing one or both parents and are now much more upset when I leave on an expedition. I don't like that.

In the evening we set up the radio to make a scheduled call to John Perrins in Resolute. Our skis are encrusted with several inches of ice at −50°C and my hands are cold within seconds from handling them. We struggle to fit the dipole aerial clips over the tips of the skis, then return to the tent to speak to John, but he does not come in. We try again at 1915, 1930, 1945 and on the hour, but no joy.

Day 11: Sunday, 15 March

Position: 83°47'48" North; 74°25'11" West
Temperature: below −55°C
Windchill: below −70°C
Hours of sunshine: 9 hours 16 minutes
Nautical miles covered yesterday: 0
Nautical miles covered so far: 42¾
Nautical miles to go (*in a straight line*): 372¼
Status: Storm

At least minus fifty again, but fortunately relatively little wind. Still bloody cold and still a lot of rubble. It is a relief to get out of the tent after our forced confinement, and we are increasing the number of hours walking on the ice from five to six a day from now on.

A lot of cross-leads of open water. Most of them are small, but one of them causes some trouble. It is the fourth or fifth lead we have crossed since this morning and is too wide to leap across. We can see a crossing-point about two hundred yards east and head towards it. The lead turns a corner and Rune finds an area of freshly set ice. He crosses it and then calls to me.

'David, it is very thin but it will hold your weight if you take it quickly,' he shouts from the other side.

There is nothing I hate more than thin ice, especially when I can see the water underneath moving quite quickly, and my fears are confirmed when one of my feet slips through the ice into the water. Fortunately my other foot was already on strong ice on the far side of the lead, and I pull myself to safety as I hear the ice crack. It is a near miss that leaves my knees shaking and my heart pounding.

Otherwise a good day, but still no sign of the pans of ice I was expecting as we approach 84°. Nevertheless, we work up quite a head of steam by the evening, and my whole body is covered in iced sweat by the time we stop.

We are getting into a good routine at the end of the day. It is now working like a dream and for forty minutes we go through it in silence until we are sitting in the tent. Rune is always ahead, chooses the site and direction for the tent, and prepares it by flattening the snow and sweeping away any lumps. He then takes off his harness belt and skis and puts his duvet jacket on to keep warm once he has stopped moving. I then arrive and remove my skis first, followed by my harness. It is my job to put up the tent, but I started to develop pains in my back, so now I get the tent out of my sledge and we unpack it together. Then, while Rune pushes the poles into the tent, I get the tent pegs out and throw a couple to him.

I always use the ski that Alicia painted dinosaurs on to pin down the tent. Both of my skis have been painted by my daughters and, although it sounds stupid, I feel as if the skis are my girls and consequently make sure they are always near the tent. Rune hasn't realised this yet, and he sometimes uses one of my skis to prop up the radio aerial. Whenever he does this I quietly go out and swap it with one of Rune's skis. He must think I am barmy.

Once we have put up the tent, Rune unpacks the sleeping-bags, thermarests and cooking equipment and carries them into the tent while I shove snow around the snow valance. We finish our jobs at around the same time and then we set up the dipole aerial. After that we brush the ice off each other, a procedure that must be undertaken as quickly as possible to avoid frostbite on our chests or legs. I stand with my back to the wind and I ask Rune if he is ready. When he answers I pull down the zip of my jacket and undo my two cuffs. Rune strips my orange windproof jacket off my back, which like my black fleece top beneath is encrusted in an inch of frozen sweat which Rune removes using the snow brush. Every evening we go through the same silly ritual when Rune brushes my chest. As the brush passes over my torso I say, 'Watch my tits,' and Rune laughs. It is a silly routine, but it brings a smile to his face every time. Now we feel superstitious if I do not say it. I then remove my windproof trousers and Rune brushes down my legs. Once this is finished I dive into the tent, followed immediately by Rune who does not seem to ice down as much as me; he probably does not sweat as much. When he is iced up, I brush him down in the outer tent.

The most important thing is to get out of the wind. It has been so cold that we have been icing down very quickly. It builds up all day. After one hour's walking we already have a light frosting of ice; by the end of the day it can be terrible – thick lumps and sheets of ice along our arms and legs. If the wind comes from the east our right sides are worse than our left sides. It is only on the exceptionally cold and windy days, when we have had windchill of −90°C, that we have been totally free of ice because it is too cold for us to sweat significantly.

Once we are inside the tent, the routine continues. I strip off my black fleece layer, tuck my boots in at the back of the tent and fold up my orange waterproof jacket to use as a pillow. I then take my GPS out of a pocket and stuff it between my underpants and long-johns to warm it up, a part of the ritual that always makes me gasp.

Then the cocktail hour starts. I look forward to this moment all day. First a packet of pork scratchings each – high in salt to ward off stomach and leg cramps – followed by two Peperamis which we thaw in our soup or hot juice. Rune thinks the Peperami tastes best thawed in orange juice, particularly after a cigarette. This is the best moment of the day. We are exhausted and ready to sleep, but happy that the work is behind us and we can chat over snacks and drinks. I often suck a liquorice stick, close my eyes to relax for a few minutes and take in the silence which is punctuated only by Rune's munching and the roar of the wind outside.

After forty minutes down the front of my trousers, the GPS is warm enough to measure our position. We look at each other in disbelief when the reading appears. Seven and three-quarter miles today! Hulashaker! Brandy and cigars all round for a new record. We are really surprised to be hitting such mileage so early. We are like two kids, punching the air and whooping with delight.

Day 12: Monday, 16 March

Position: 83°55'26" North; 74°26'42" West
Temperature: below −55°C
Windchill: approximately −85°C
Hours of sunshine: 9 hours 13 minutes
Nautical miles covered yesterday: 7¾
Nautical miles covered so far: 50½
Nautical miles to go (*in a straight line*): 364½
Status: Everything okay

Yesterday I made the mistake of complaining about Rune's cooking. It was only a minor grumble, but he did not take it well. Today I get my comeuppance.

Rune contends that I am never satisfied with his cooking. 'David, if your hot chocolate is eighty-four degrees instead of eighty-five degrees you whinge and complain,' he says.

But I could not let it rest. It seemed to be exceptionally cold yesterday and the fruit juice was only just lukewarm at lunchtime. At the time I vowed not to say anything because it is a thankless task to get up first in the morning to heat the juice, but by the end of the day I could not stop myself. I turned to Rune, who was dozing in his sleeping-bag with a cigarette smouldering between his lips, and said, 'Rune we would have had a better day if that juice was hotter.'

In a flash he sat bolt upright. 'What do you mean hotter?'

'Well . . . just a little bit hotter. I just felt it ruined my day because it was so bloody cold,' I replied.

'What do you mean – cold?' Rune asked.

'Not hot enough for me is what I mean. It was cold at lunchtime and I would have preferred it hotter,' I answered.

There was no reply. Rune glowered on his side of the tent, huffed a few times and then went back to writing in his diary.

It is slightly warmer today and after the first hour and a half's session I stop to have a drink. We don't use cups, we just pull the top off the thermos and take a sip. I take a large mouthful and have to spit it out it is so hot. Rune is a few feet away, on the other side of the sledge.

'Hot enough for you?' he asks.

'Hot? Damn hot,' I reply.

From that moment on a new catchphrase is born, to go with 'Hulashaker' – our multi-purpose all-round exclamation for surprise – 'Old Man' and 'Kid', and 'Dr Livingstone', Rune's nickname for me after I was awarded the Livingstone Medal, which in turn has spawned 'Dr Nansen' for Rune.

Rune agrees now that maybe I was right about the juice yesterday. He is one of those people who takes a long time to be convinced, but once won over concedes defeat very graciously. 'From now on I will measure the outside temperature, listen to the wind and assess the weather forecast before I decide how hot the juice will be,' he says with a smile on his face. 'Hot hot juice for cold cold days. Medium hot juice for medium cold days, and mildly hot juice for mildly cold days.'

By the end of the day we have crossed the 84th Parallel. The first new degree, and in only twelve days. It seems unbelievable, particularly as it took us until day twenty-nine to reach the same point last year. We covered nearly eight miles today, magnificent progress considering there has been no let up in the rubble and it is still below −50°C with a nasty wind.

My hands and toes continue to worry me. They show no sign of improving and the split in my right boot is not helping the frostbite to heal.

A troublesome radio contact with John in Resolute. He doesn't come in at first and we are worried that the radio is broken, then we realise the antenna has fallen down. After that John comes in as clear as a whistle. He tells us that the Marines sent a distress signal to London today. It seems they are in trouble.

Day 13: Tuesday, 17 March

Position: 84°03'14" North; 74°21'17" West
Temperature: −52°C
Windchill: approximately −80°C
Hours of sunshine: 9 hours 44 minutes
Nautical miles covered yesterday: 7¾
Nautical miles covered so far: 58¼
Nautical miles to go (*in a straight line*): 356¾
Status: Everything okay

We need to get to 84°10' North as soon as possible and get the airline companies lined up for an immediate resupply. I have decided that we might as well go for a resupply as soon as possible, while we know the weather is clear. Our fuel will run out in two days and the last thing we want is to spend three or four days hanging around waiting for the plane to come in. There is no point in having a resupply before we reach 84°10' North. We will have heavy sledges again after stocking up on new food rations, so if the resupply comes in any earlier it will defeat its whole purpose.

I budgeted for fifteen days on the first leg, but did not think for a moment we would be so far north by them. According to my initial plan we were scheduled to reach 84°10' on day twenty-four, so we are ahead by around ten days. It is a delicate balance: every mile further north is nearer the Pole before the thaw starts, but the further north we go the more the air companies will charge us for the resupply. We will need to move very fast on the second leg to reach 86°30', another 150 miles, by 15 April. This next third of the trip will be critical.

Our immediate concern is to start looking for a pan for the plane to land on, not an easy feat in the ice conditions we have encountered so far. I really thought the rubble would have ended by now and we would be on a succession of long, wide ice pans, interrupted by the occasional pressure ridge. The ice this year is different to any other I have experienced and my plans are in danger of being shot down.

Even today we do not encounter a single sizeable pan. It is bitterly cold with rubble all the way. It is staggering how we manage to cover six miles with our skis on and off every few minutes. In some spots it takes both of us to lift one sledge through the rubble. For over an hour it is one forty-foot ridge after another. It's a very heavy workout, like doing six hours in the gym; we are really pushing it and I have to grit my teeth and dig deep.

I have a huge frostbite blister on my thumb and my toe is still causing me problems, made worse by the backbreaking conditions. I have now discovered that I also have some small spots of frostbite on my knee, brought on by kneeling down whenever I need to take off my skis, which in these conditions is frequently. My boot is still damaged and is secured to my ski by a length of wire. If my bindings were able to hold my boot I would normally simply push my ski pole down on the binding to release my boot; now I have to kneel down on one knee, pull up the clip and take the wire off the back of the boot. This tedious process makes my hands and left knee very cold, and I have to repeat it when we get to the other side of the rubble or pressure ridge.

We are in the middle of all this crap and I am worried about finding a landing strip – it seems ridiculous. Tonight I will radio for a resupply for tomorrow and hope we can find a landing strip in the meantime. It is a dangerous gamble because we will still have to pay for the flight if the plane has to turn back.

Rune is as brilliant as ever but we are both grumpy today and I know it is best to leave him alone. There is no point in trying to cheer him up, I figure he just needs his own space sometimes. I have a lot on my mind at the moment what with calculating the distance, time and cost of resupplies, which has made me irritable. Maybe Rune did not sleep well last night; if I don't get eight hours' sleep I'm a grumpy shit. Maybe he is worried about the leads and rubble – he sees it as his fault if we encounter a particularly gruelling route – or maybe he is upset simply because John was so curt on the radio.

It can take us ages to get the antenna up, then at least another hour to heat up the batteries in our armpits, followed by another hour or so of nervous anticipation while we wait for John to make contact, hoping all the time that the radio does not become too hot because this will cause condensation to form inside it. We wear woollen gloves to make sure we don't heat the radio with our hands and to protect our fingers from sticking to the metal casing on particularly cold nights. Then after all this hassle we ask John if there is any news or any messages to be passed on from home, only to be met with a swift reply: 'No – bye chaps, I've got other things to do.' That is it, radio schedule over. Rune was certainly extremely irritated. He asked if there were any messages from Norway and, as always, there were none. It is difficult not to become despondent in such circumstances.

At the end of the day we have covered six miles, extremely good considering it was the worst rubble so far on this expedition, and we are only a mile short of 84°10' North. Last year we would have been happy to manage two miles in such conditions. Rune is writing a letter to Ingeweld, the girl who made our embroidered envelopes, smoking a cigarette and telling me of his dreams last night – he was on a fishing trip in the summer with his friend Bjorn up in the north of Norway. That sounds good.

Day 14: Wednesday, 18 March

Position: 84°09'18" North; 74°18'46" West
Temperature: −50°C
Windchill: approximately −80°C
Hours of sunshine: 10 hours 19 minutes
Nautical miles covered yesterday: 6
Nautical miles covered so far: 64¼
Nautical miles to go (*in a straight line*): 350¾
Status: Everything okay

I wake up and it is really cold, −47°C, a cold I can feel on my face as I lie enveloped in my sleeping-bag, but the first thing that goes through my head is that I am really worried about finding a landing strip.

The rubble is just awful, one of those sections that Rune calls an inferno, and there seems to be no abatement. Yesterday we walked all day and did not find anything remotely resembling a stretch of flat ice on which to land a plane. We don't need that much – Twin Otters are remarkable aircraft and the pilots say they need only a hundred feet for a landing, less than the width of a runway. But they need at least 1200 feet to take off, preferably more. The worst thing that could happen if we do not find a landing trip is that the pilots spot a good one and put the plane down a couple of miles away. We will then have to walk there, even if it is behind us. I am reminded of Roald

Amundsen's words from 1925 when he was trying to fly to the North Pole. It hangs in the offices of all the air charter companies that run flights to the polar ice-cap from Resolute Bay: 'Experience showed me that it takes an aviator to express an opinion about landing conditions amidst polar ice, and not an Arctic explorer. What the second considered to be a flat plateau can be absolutely useless in the opinion of the first.'

We climb out of the tent and it is nice weather – blue skies, no cloud, a relief. We are ready much more quickly than we have managed before and walk for a while, with Rune stopping to climb every pressure ridge in search of a suitable pan. After a while he takes off his skis and climbs up on some rubble to take a look at the surroundings. When he climbs back down I say, 'Any pans of ice?'

'Little pan,' he replies

'Is that a helicopter pan, a Concorde pan or a Space Shuttle pan?' I ask.

'A Twin Otter pan,' he replies. 'It is not good enough.'

After about an hour we reach a pressure ridge like a high fence. Rune climbs to the top and whoops. I follow him, and when I get to the top I can see what he is so excited about. On the other side of the pressure ridge is a perfect pan of ice spread out in front of us. I cannot believe our luck. In a perfect world we would walk for six miles and come across this pan at the end of the day, but it seems churlish to complain that we have happened upon it right at the beginning of this day's work. It seems strange but also very lucky that we've had no pans for days and now, suddenly, this immense pan surrounded by very bad rubble materialises. We are still on a roll!

We walk to the middle of the pan and it is clear we are both thinking the same thought. The pan is over a quarter of a mile long and I turn to Rune to say, 'Look Rune, this is it. We are going to lose a day here but I think we should stop.'

'I think you are right,' he answers. 'It's a good pan – a Concorde pan, David.'

'It's a damn good Concorde pan,' I retort, and we stop there and then.

We remove our sledge harnesses and look around carefully to check the pan's suitability. It is ideal. We put up the tent, erect the antenna, unpack everything and put it in the tent, and it looks good. After a hot drink we clamber out of the tent to mark the airstrip with black rubbish bags and check again for leads and cracks. It is a brilliant landing strip and to my great surprise I find it is at 84°10'46" – smack on target.

We return to the tent to mend our kit and sort out the equipment we will exchange or jettison at the resupply. My boots are beyond repair and I desperately want a new pair to protect my toe and end the tiresome practice of using a wire to hold my boots and skis together, a routine that has triggered frostbite on my knee. We heat up the tent to dry our clothing and feet, and Rune checks the frostbite on my toes. There is a big blister on the front tip and behind the nail. It looks bad; I hope it will hang on.

We radio John at seven p.m. He tells us that Jason, the Marines' base manager, has launched a rescue mission to pick up the two Royal Marines. Still no word on why they have abandoned their attempt.

From now on our average speed has to be seven nautical miles a day to stay on schedule to reach the second resupply at 86°30'. Rune says it should not be impossible, and we should also get better ice conditions from now on. We will see.

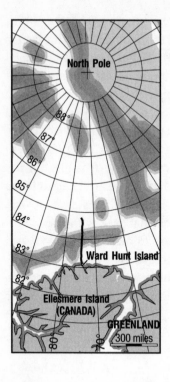

7

Warm at Last

The Third Week

Day 15: Thursday, 19 March

Position: 84°10'46" North; 74°22'53" West
Temperature: −50°C
Windchill: inside tent for most of day
Hours of sunshine: 10 hours 53 minutes
Nautical miles covered yesterday: 1½
Nautical miles covered so far: 65¾
Nautical miles to go (*in a straight line*): 349¼
Status: Everything okay

We wake up early to warm the batteries and set up the radio in time for a weather check with Resolute Bay at 7.30 a.m. We tell the air company that we have found a perfect landing strip and the good weather has held since yesterday, only to be told that a plane is on the way and will be with us in a matter of hours.

The news unleashes a frantic panic. We are far from ready for the drop and need to organise all our equipment into batches – one to go back, one to be exchanged for new supplies and the third to remain with us. Rune and I spend a couple of hours feverishly running about on the ice, shouting at each other as we prepare for the plane's arrival. The last thing we want to do is send back something that is a vital part of equipment.

There is a contingency plan for resupplies: first we take on new fuel, then food, then drinks, then a clean tent, then spare and replacement clothing, and finally videotapes and film. We are then meant to load all our unwanted equipment on to the plane, but what we must avoid is mistakenly putting both tents on to the plane – then we would be in trouble.

While I am making final preparations, Rune is busily filming everything for the BBC programme *Video Diaries* and trying to interview me. We were supposed to shoot about ten tapes by the time of the resupply, but we are behind because we have brought the resupply date forward and because the weather has been so cold. It is chaos.

Towards midday we hear the drone of the approaching propeller plane and the suspense begins: will the pilot land on our strip or will we have to hike a couple of miles to a strip the pilot has chosen himself? I let off a parachute flare just at the moment I hear Rune shout, 'David, David, don't shoot in that direction.' It's too late. With a whoosh the flare shoots into the sky, narrowly missing the Twin Otter circling overhead. 'What are you trying to do – hit the plane, David?' Rune screams.

Above us, the Twin Otter jerks to the left to avoid the flare which shoots past the cockpit, missing the plane by fewer than twenty feet. For a terrible moment I have a vision of the Twin Otter plunging towards us and crashing into the ice with two pilots, John Perrins and all our supplies on board. I look at Rune. He has his head in his hands.

'What is it about you David? Why do you always point the flare at the plane?' he shouts at me.

'I don't know, but I've learnt now not to do it,' I say, feeling exceptionally stupid but also quite exhilarated. 'You'll laugh about this tomorrow.'

The Twin Otter returns and circles above us, inspecting the ice while we wave excitedly below. After five or six circuits, we can see the ski-plane line up for a landing and cruise in over the pressure ridges towards us. There is a massive roar as the skis touch down lightly on the snow and ice – the pilot has gunned the engines and is pulling up the nose. Immediately we think he is not going to land. The Twin Otter climbs several hundred feet, circles above us and then makes a second approach. Again the plane touches down briefly before lifting off the ice and circling around for a third attempt at a landing. Our landing strip is quite clearly not as long and as flat as we had thought. On the third attempt the pilot bangs the plane down on the ice and breaks hard by slamming the reverse-feathered propeller blades up to full power. Our resupply has landed, but it has been a close shave.

It is great to see John, who emerges from the Twin Otter looking like he has crossed the Atlantic in a spin dryer. The first thing he tells us is that we stink to high heaven and look filthy. I am not surprised – we have not washed for over two weeks and have sweated night and day in the same clothes.

Then the bedlam begins. Our disorganisation is soon apparent – there is food, equipment and film all over the place. We race around, emptying and dismantling the tent, and attempting to erect the new tent double-quick. The pilots are in a rush and leave the engines running in case they need to make a quick exit.

John fills us in on the news from Resolute. The Marines have officially pulled out because of a fuel leak. The reason for the demise of their expedition is the same problem we are experiencing, but we have managed to battle through. I am disappointed for them, particularly as I am now the only Briton on half a million square miles of frozen ocean. The pilots tell us that the Marines had walked only twelve miles from Ward Hunt Island. The ice shelf stretches for the first five miles and is totally flat, after that the rubble and pressure ridges start, but they walked only seven miles across the polar ice-cap. Apparently they aborted when the last of their batteries went flat, and they are now walking back to Ward Hunt Island for a pick-up at the weekend.

John dropped off five Norwegians led by Sjur Mørdre – who has already reached the Pole, in 1992 – at Ward Hunt Island on the way up. They are all championship cross-country skiers and are attempting to set a record for the fastest ski to the Pole and should soon catch us up. They are planning to ski for eighteen hours a day in order to reach the Pole in twenty-five days – they must be bionic.

My friend Thierry got into some trouble on his return from Ward Hunt Island because he was carrying a pistol, which is forbidden in the Northwest Territories. He was taken to the courthouse and told that he would be pardoned if he pleaded guilty, filled out some forms and handed over his gun. Apparently it is a very serious offence.

While Rune runs around filming the resupply, John also tells me that the BBC is temporarily putting our *Video Diaries* slot on hold pending more information about the three-minute video we shot for HTV. I was asked to take along a camera by the BBC so they can make a documentary of our trip that will be screened later in the year. If we make it to the Pole, the BBC will have about forty-five hours of tape; by contrast HTV local news, which I cannot imagine is in competition with BBC documentaries, have asked for a couple of minutes of footage to use in an evening bulletin, so I don't think there will be too much of a problem. If anything, the HTV clip might whet the appetites of some viewers. It seems very strange to be thinking about such things when we are thousands of miles from home in the middle of a barren wilderness. The politics of it all!

To complicate matters we now need to book seats for the pick-up planes, but Karrimor, our clothing sponsors, have now decided not to come on the pick-up to the North Pole and as yet there is no commitment from ITN. What a bloody carry-on.

John has brought the replacement skis we requested, but they are fitted with racing langlauf bindings instead of the Rottefella bindings that attach to our custom-made boots. I feel like crying with frustration when I tell John that the skis are useless to us and he will have to take them back to Resolute Bay.

Forty minutes later the weather has closed in and the pilots want to get going. It seems luck was on our side again as Carl, the captain, tells me he would not have landed if they had arrived in the current conditions. John boards the plane, but Rune shouts as I shut the door. He has found in the snow a package of films meant for the *Daily Telegraph* and we hand it in to the pilot through a cockpit window. The plane jolts up and down as it taxis to the end of the landing strip, and then with a roar it takes off. Once again we are alone.

We return to our tent to sort out the new equipment. Almost

immediately I find a bag that should have flown back with John. It contains dirty thinny gloves, outer mitts and shell clothing that need to be de-iced, washed and then returned to us on the next resupply. We will have to dump the bag and ask John to order new clothing from the UK as it makes little sense to carry two sets of gloves and shell clothing to the next resupply. A bloody disaster.

The salami I have been looking forward to getting my teeth into for the last week has not arrived yet in Resolute Bay, so I will have to make do with Peperami. I picked out three Italian salamis in Swindon especially for this trip so I am very disappointed.

Other than these setbacks, the resupply has been a great success – cakes, coffee and fruit in abundance, a newspaper, a new thermometer, clean sleeping-bags, new pumps and stoves, and enough fuel to propel the Saturn V rocket into orbit. Rune and I retire to the tent and make ourselves comfortable.

'I don't care what you think Rune, we've got plenty of fuel now and new pumps so I'm putting the stove on full heat,' I say.

The evening is wonderful – a great moment. We gorge ourselves on Joy's cake, the peanuts and the oranges. For the first ten minutes, as we feel the first heat in two weeks, we are both grinning and purring like cats in front of a fire at the luxury of the warmth. It feels very strange because our skin is not used to the heat and swells up. I look at Rune and ask him if the skin on my face is as taut and puffy as his. With a mouth full of food, all he can do is grin and nod his head.

'Feel that warmth. It's as good as sex,' Rune says as soon as he can talk.

I'm afraid I have to agree. After a fortnight of −50°C I feel as if I have crawled into a cosy, protective womb. For the first time in weeks we are in a tent that is not dripping in hoarfrost and we make the most of it. I push our new sleeping-bags to the bottom end of the tent and we strip off all our clothes and thermals to bask in the heat. Outside it is −50°C and in the outer tent it is −30°C; where we are sitting in the inner tent it is −5°C on the floor but 70°C under the roof of the tent. The warmth is overwhelming, it is like a sauna at the ceiling. We lie with only our woollen underpants on, reading the *Edmonton Mail* and surrounded by food. Rune is smoking a cigar and it all seems very debauched. What a luxury – just wonderful.

This is the first chance we have had to dry out all our clothes, a much overdue necessity as mine are heavily encrusted with ice. We also have new vapour barrier bags to line our sleeping-bags, new liners for our boots, a change of mitts, clean balaclavas and a new thermarest, which will make a big difference.

It is a joy to get my hands on a newspaper after wondering for so long what is going on in the world. For all we know, World War Three might have broken out. I read the paper from cover to cover – news, share prices, international news, features, everything. I am just desperate for news from home and scan the paper for British sports reports – unfortunately no information on Swindon Town's fortunes.

Having a resupply certainly makes the journey more bearable and has allowed us to stock up on luxuries such as brandy and peanuts, both of which are great morale boosters. Some expeditions are very proud that they take no luxuries, but I cannot understand this attitude. It is unpleasant enough up on the ice without making it more miserable than it already is.

There is a lot of contention surrounding supported and unsupported expeditions in terms of definition. Until recently all North Pole expeditions were supported in some way, but it is difficult to know where to draw the line. By modern standards Robert Peary's 1909 expedition was unsupported – he had neither weather reports nor air drops – but he was accompanied by several sledges of supplies, manned by his men and Inuits. For most of the journey, Peary followed the main expedition party like an officer following his troops into battle, and he took the lead only when he was within sixty miles of the Pole. In my book that counts as supported. Some expeditions boast that they do not receive weather reports, but I cannot see that it makes any difference because you have to face the conditions whatever the weather. There is nothing anybody can do if they know that a blizzard and −50°C temperatures are on the way. If you want to be that pure, why not leave your tent and sleeping-bags behind and camp outside, or not take a radio?

In this modern age of adventure we know that there are patterns of water currents under the ice and we know when the weather is best for an expedition. It is different to the days of Shackleton, Scott and Amundsen, who did not know what lay ahead. We know there are radio blackouts and mirages, and that the refractions confused the navigators who came in search of the Northwest Passage. It would be pointless to ignore that knowledge nowadays. One expedition team told me they were taking a GPS satellite position system and an Argos beacon, but they thought it was wrong to take a Walkman so that they could listen to music in their tent at night. I think that attitude is ridiculous. The only reason for leaving anything out that will make the journey more bearable is to keep the weight down.

When I walked to the South Pole I did not take a Walkman because I was solo and unsupported and couldn't justify the extra weight. I took only things which I considered critical. Now I would change my mind because I think a few luxuries are very important and can make the difference between a successful expedition and an aborted bid. For us, a bottle of brandy is essential so that we have something to celebrate with, something to look forward to. Last year we regarded pork scratchings as a luxury and rationed ourselves to a packet between us every five days, but we discovered that the pork scratching calories gave us strength and their salt content reduced the cramps we were suffering in our feet every time we took off our boots and often in our stomachs during the nights. This year we have taken at least a packet a day for each of us, and we have had no cramps whatsoever.

Day 16: Friday, 20 March

Position: 84°10'46" North; 74°22'53" West
Temperature: −43°C
Windchill: −68°C
Hours of sunshine: 11 hours 25 minutes
Nautical miles covered yesterday: 0 (resupply)
Nautical miles covered so far: 65¾
Nautical miles to go (*in a straight line*): 349¼
Status: Everything okay

After the luxuries of yesterday, the hardest day of the expedition so far. We struggle all day through the biggest rubble I have ever seen in conditions of poor visibility and twenty-five-knot winds. For some strange reason we encountered the worst rubble in exactly the same position last year. For once there seems to be some consistency on the Arctic ice, but I am sure it is nothing more than a coincidence.

I am thankful for the new boots which clip directly into my skis. By the time we are through the worst of the rubble I must have taken my skis on and off twenty times. If I had been using the old boots I would almost certainly have frostbite on my knee by now. Rune and I spend most of the day close together, helping each other in the rubble. There are several vertical lifts where we have to haul our sledges up cliff faces of ice up to ten feet high, a task which prompts us to coin nicknames for our sledges. My sledge is 'Fuck' and Rune's is 'Cunt' – not very pleasant names I know, but when you are battling to squeeze and shove a sledge through a gap in the ice with fractions of an inch to spare, swearwords are the only words that come to mind.

Hauling our sledges through the rubble is not made any easier by the fact that they are now heavier than at any time on our trip. We have thirty days' food on them – enough for the next twenty days plus two emergency five-day ration packs – which prompts Rune to dump one of his spare emergency packs, but he won't get rid of all his knick-knacks.

I am paranoid about weight. My blue bag contains just a couple of crosses, some pictures from home, my diary and a set of worry beads given to me by Rajiv Wahi, the managing director of Typhoo. I sent back my goose-down trousers and my World Service radio yesterday and I am already calculating when I can dump my second sleeping-bag. I have given my fleece to Rune and made him hand over his iced-down fleece at the resupply, and now I have cut my toothbrush in half and trimmed bootlaces to the minimum length to cut unnecessary weight. By contrast Rune has two blue bags stuffed to the gills with personal items.

'Stop nagging me about my blue bags, David,' has become a familiar nightly refrain from Rune's side of the tent.

'I just think that it is remarkable that last year you forgot your sole blue bag and were prepared to set off without it, and this year you will not relinquish anything inside the two huge blue bags you have,' I say.

I am so conscious of weight because we are about to increase the number of hours and miles we should be walking a day. Although we have had a honeymoon period – our initial target had been three miles a day but we have managed up to eight on occasions – from now on everything will be completely different. The first part of the expedition was designed to be relatively easy as we had made huge allowances for days lost to bad weather or difficult conditions; now, our sledges are heavier than ever because we are carrying more fuel and food. If the weather closes in we could be twenty-one miles behind target within three days. The second leg is like a second expedition, one in which we cannot afford to lose time if we are to succeed.

One of Rune's blue bags is the size of a rucksack and contains all his video cameras, tapes and batteries. It is also stuffed with excess clothing – in my view much too much. But Rune is extremely strong, and if he wants to carry it I should not moan at him. 'I know how much weight it adds, but I like the extra weight of the video cameras – it gives me something to focus my anger on,' Rune says. He is very grumpy today because he has spent many hours in conditions of −50°C, risking frostbite to shoot footage for *Video Diaries*.

Instead of throwing away the video cameras as at this moment he would like to do, Rune and I agree to dump another five days' food. We are taking a risk, but if all goes to plan we should be resupplied before we run out of rations.

Day 17: Saturday, 21 March

Position: 84°15'51" North; 74°19'17" West
Temperature: −42°C
Windchill: −78°C
Hours of sunshine: 12 hours
Nautical miles covered yesterday: 5
Nautical miles covered so far: 70¾
Nautical miles to go (*in a straight line*): 344¼
Status: Everything okay

A hellish day. Temperatures are on the way up but we are encapsulated in a complete white-out amid ferocious winds from the north. It makes navigation particularly difficult.

'I can see it is a damn hot juice day,' Rune says after poking his head out of the tent at six a.m. Appropriately he is listening to 'Take the Long Way Home' on his Walkman.

Once we set out Rune complains that walking into the wind and snow is like having thousands of insects fly straight into his eyes for hours on end. It is too cold for him to wear his goggles – a layer of ice freezes over them within minutes and they are no help in a white-out. I do not know how Rune manages to find his way through the endless mess of rubble in conditions of almost no visibility. His compass is not working, the sun cannot be seen and there is no point in getting the GPS out as its liquid crystal screen turns black in the cold within seconds.

At one point I consider stopping, but Rune wants to press on. In such conditions, he reverts to Viking and Eskimo practices and uses the sastrugi for orientation. These frozen waves of snow are shaped by the wind and give an indication which way is north. They are a dependable indicator, provided the wind direction is constant. From Ward Hunt Island to 85° North, the wind comes straight from the west and occasionally from the north, creating a criss-cross of sastrugi where the smaller waves point northwards. Beyond 85° North the wind direction will change and Rune will have to re-evaluate the sastrugi, but today the wind is so strong and the white-out so enveloping that even the sastrugi disappear at times. Once again, I am nagging him to check he is sure we are heading north.

'The left side of my nose is colder than the right side, and I can feel the pressure of the wind on the left sides of my legs, so I know we are walking north,' Rune shouts back at me through the impenetrable swirling mist of snow.

I rely heavily on Rune's skills in these conditions. I have walked in white-outs on my own, but never covered the distances that Rune manages, and I soon pitched camp, defeated by the elements and depressed by the struggle. In recognition of our teamwork I promise him I will get him to the top of Everest if we get to the North Pole.

There are a lot of leads today, many of which are just soft snow resting on the water, but we manage to cross them quite quickly and without incident. At midday we stop for lunch – some Mars bar chunks sucked rather than chewed as the cold has shrunk the fillings in our teeth and the sticky chocolate could easily pull out the amalgam. The juice is piping hot and a welcome comfort. I call feel its warmth heating me from within.

After lunch we cut more weight by dumping Rune's fleece and his Rab goose-down boots. His sledge is now eight pounds lighter so I trade some of my fuel with him to lighten my load as well. Then, slightly lighter than before, it is back to the slog against the wind and snow until we stop shortly before six.

In the evening we cook inside the inner tent for the first time and it makes a big difference to the warmth under the canvas. The old leaky pumps forced us to cook in the outer tent, where most of the heat escaped. After weeks of struggling to get the food down, we are now developing raging appetites for our oil-soaked dinners. Rune talks about food all day, detailing what we will eat each night, and once the meal is ready we squabble over the sizes of each portion. The oil even begins to taste good. Our metabolisms have switched into overdrive and we are burning up 12,000 calories a day, but our bodies can absorb only 6000 in twenty-four hours. I can feel my body craving the calories in the oil.

We have walked five and three-quarter miles further north today. It is nothing to write home about, but at least it is further than we managed yesterday and we did walk in a white-out. Unfortunately, we walked a long way west in the process, at least a mile, but we are still almost six miles closer to the Pole.

Although I want to start clocking up some big distances I am conscious that we must not stretch ourselves too early. My biggest worry remains my foot and I wonder how much punishment it can take. I am still firmly of the opinion that this is a marathon and not a sprint, particularly when I hear Rune gasp when he removes the dressing tonight.

'It doesn't look good, there is a big blister on the tip, and behind the nail, where it is very dark red,' he says. 'You will soon lose your nail, I think, and there's a hole at the tip of your big toe. It is totally dark red.'

Rune rubs in some more antibiotic cream but neither of us is entirely sure if it is the right thing to be applying to frostbite. I tell Rune that I do not mind sacrificing my toe, but he insists that we will abandon the expedition if I get gangrene.

After he has bandaged my toe, I play a prank on Rune. Before we left England I wrote to Ingeweld, the Norwegian girl who gave us the embroidered cards, and asked her to send a picture of herself for Rune. I know she and Rune like each other a lot, but both of them are too shy to do anything about it.

'Rune, I have a confession to make,' I say.

'Oh yes David, what is that?' he answers, perking up at the chance of some revelation.

'I have met another woman. I feel very bad about it but I could not help myself. She is very beautiful, with long blonde hair, and she is only nineteen, which makes me feel even worse,' I say.

Rune looks surprised. 'David, I am shocked. What about your wife and children?'

'I don't know what to do. I am besotted with this woman. I first met her when we came to visit you in Norway and I've got to know her better since. She is wonderful and we have the most amazing sex. I don't think I can give her up.'

Rune, who has very traditional values, tells me he does not approve at all.

'Listen, I would not approve if I heard another man might leave his family for a woman twenty years younger than him. But try and understand – maybe I am going through a midlife crisis,' I reply.

He is unimpressed and quiet. I can tell Rune thinks this is not right, so I ask him if he wants to see a picture of my fictitious mistress. He rubs his scraggy beard. I can see he is curious, but he does not approve at all. 'Okay, why not?' he says after a short while. I dig into my bag, pull out the picture of Ingeweld and hand it to Rune.

For a moment he is silent, and then he exclaims 'Hu-la-shaker.' He turns to me with a look of complete bewilderment on his face. 'Where did you get this picture from?'

I explain everything to him and he is soon chuckling, but also concerned that I might have asked Ingeweld too much. I assure him that is not the case and he tells me how much he loves Ingeweld but thinks she is too young for him. 'It is no good being married to an explorer. I will be away from home all the time. She deserves better than that,' he says.

These sentiments remind me that it is Mother's Day in a week's time, so that evening I ask John over the radio to check that flowers have been ordered for Claire and ask him to remind Alicia to write a card. It is a good radio schedule – John is on good form and has plenty of news. The only worry is that Amelia still has not had the operation to examine an unexplained lump in her throat. Apparently she is too ill.

Day 18: Sunday, 22 March

Position: 84°21'37" North; 74°25'24" West
Temperature: −38°C
Windchill: −55°C
Hours of sunshine: 12 hours 35 minutes
Nautical miles covered yesterday: 5¾
Nautical miles covered so far: 76½
Nautical miles to go (*in a straight line*): 338½
Status: Everything okay

From hard rubble yesterday to huge flat pans today, the like of which we have not seen before. We had terrible rubble from 84°02' North and then as suddenly as it started, it stopped at 84°22' North. I hope the flat pans will continue.

However, it is not as easy as it could be. Yesterday's new snow makes the going very heavy and it feels as if we have our heavy sledges from last year. I know it is tough going because for once I manage to keep up with Rune. For the first few days we were never further than thirty feet apart, but we have since found that it is better to be more spread out so that I do not have to grind to a halt when Rune gets to a pressure ridge or a tricky section of rubble. With some distance between us he is through the rubble by the time I get to it and I can keep going. It is better this way; I can just get my head down, slip my skis into Rune's sledge tracks and just think.

But today I am directly behind Rune all the way. I can see it irritates him, but there is nothing we can do about it. All I wish is that I could keep my big mouth shut when I see Rune slip back on a block of ice or fall over on a giant blue ice cube. 'I can do it better than that,' I say. On more than one occasion it spurts out of my mouth before I mean to say it. Brain-before-mouth Hempleman, I repeatedly tell myself, and inevitably I slip in exactly the same way when I get to the rubble where Rune previously stumbled. It happens almost without fail, and I feel stupid for having moaned in the first place.

At long last I am beginning to acclimatise to the temperatures. It is warmer and I have no problems today with my hands or feet. And after two weeks of trouble with my skis, today I have at last got used to them. From the moment we set out from Ward Hunt Island I have been cursing them because they should balance perfectly at the mid-point, but the tips pivot upwards with every step because the bindings are slightly too far forward. We were meant to exchange the skis at the resupply, but the wrong bindings had been fitted. However, today for the first time I realise that fixing the bindings in front of the centre of gravity might have been a brilliant mistake. Our skis drag down at the back and lift at the top instead of balancing perfectly, and although it has taken me two weeks to get used to this strange set-up, now I find it helps me lift the skis over rubble. I tell Rune that I am going to keep my skis as they are, and to my surprise he agrees with me. It is an amazing mistake, but it does actually help us. I suppose you could call it serendipity, but I would call it sod's law.

At the end of the day we have covered nearly seven miles. Rune is disappointed that we have not covered a greater distance, and considering the large pans we had, he is probably right. We are three miles behind schedule but I am not overly concerned. Our sledges are still heavy from the resupply, the snow is thick and we are presently walking only six hours a day. We must pace ourselves, I keep telling myself. This is an endurance event, not a flat-out race.

After dinner we lie in our sleeping-bags, basking in the warmth of the stove and talking. This is the best time of the day, the moment I look forward to. Rune is smoking a cigar and he tells me that he is thinking of his family at home. They will be drinking their Sunday coffee as we speak, he says, and when he thinks of them in their warm home he is proud that we have survived temperatures below −55°C.

'I like the idea of it, but only when it is over,' he says, and he reveals that he has been writing poems in his diary about our expedition.

I tease him about them. It seems surprising to me that a man who boards submarines through their torpedo tubes writes poetry to express his feelings.

'I know a good poem,' I say. 'There was a young girl called Ingeweld, whose main attractions were . . .'

Rune laughs, but I can tell it is best left alone. He is very sensitive at any mention of Ingeweld. Then Rune translates one of his poems from the Norwegian:

I like days with sun,
Where you can just climb up on a big ice block
And where you can scout north.
White and dark areas;
The white areas is the rubble,
The dark is the big pans in the long distance.
I like a lot of dark areas. Big ones.

Again I tease him. 'It doesn't rhyme very well,' I say.
'Don't care,' comes the reply. 'Do you want another poem?'
'Yes, but how about this one first,' I say. 'There was a young woman called Ingeweld, who . . .'
'David, stop,' he snaps. 'Another poem or not?'
I nod.

The landscape is mangled,
So beautiful but so empty of life,
So frigid;
The total silence one moment and then inferno,
The rubble movements and wind.
It's mangled this ice ocean.

'Good poem, kid,' I say. 'Damn good poem.' It won't win any literary prizes but it says it all. He is a remarkable man.

Day 19: Monday, 23 March

Position: 84°28'29" North; 74°25'00" West
Temperature: −39°C
Windchill: −58°C
Hours of sunshine: 13 hours 13 minutes
Nautical miles covered yesterday: 7
Nautical miles covered so far: 83½
Nautical miles to go (*in a straight line*): 331½
Status: Everything okay

A beautiful day, but a cold one. The temperature drops from −39°C in the morning to −48°C in the evening, but not without some consolation. When the sky is clear and the wind drops, the Arctic ice becomes the most beautiful landscape anyone could ever imagine.

But my ruminations on the ice panorama are soon disturbed when I hear Rune shout and swear at me from inside the tent.

'Hulashaker David. *Feltet!*' I hear him scream.

Immediately I know what has happened. The last thing we do before taking down the tent is to take turns to go to the toilet; first me, then Rune. It cannot be the other way round as I have a weak stomach and would be sick at the smell of someone else's business. Now, after weeks of struggling to cope with the rich food, my digestive system has managed to deal with the oil-steeped breakfasts and dinners. I have had the biggest bowel movement for nineteen days and Rune knows all about it – he has stepped in it. He emerges from the tent looking most displeased but I tell him there is nothing I can do about it and that it is my revenge for his attempts to kill me with passive smoking in the tent.

Once out on the ice it is still heavy going with the sledges, particularly as there is a new dusting of snow this morning. We are three and a half miles behind schedule but should pick up mileage in about ten days' time, and we will increase the walking time to six and a half hours a day after tomorrow.

We are both starting to suffer injuries. My arse cheeks are burning sore because I was very overweight when we started out. I am not sure if the lamb's wool long-johns are making it worse, but I can feel the two sides of my backside rubbing together when I am skiing, so I have cut the back pocket off my black thermal fleece and stuffed it between my cheeks. My thighs have been chafed by the friction of skiing, so I have covered them with Lipogel, an ointment cream which looks like goosefat in a tube. It is a familiar injury and always seems to happen to me.

Rune, whose snoring kept me awake all last night and who stretched out of his sleeping-bag for the first time, taking over most of the tent, claims he has a sore left knee which clicks when he walks. 'I had a lot of pain in it in the last hour yesterday,' he says, 'and it kept me awake all night. It feels as if I have stretched something.' Judging from his incessant snoring last night, he had little difficulty sleeping, I tell him. 'No, no. I am not sleeping well at all. I am sweating so much that I am getting bed sores on my hips,' he says, and he pulls down his thermals to show me a massive red area on one side. I cannot believe he did not sleep well after listening to his snoring for most of the night, but I am inclined to accept he is right simply because he is very grumpy all day, in Rune's case a sure sign of a poor night's sleep.

Rune is correct on one matter, however. The vapour barrier bags which have kept our sleeping-bags dry are now becoming increasingly unpleasant to sleep inside. I sweat as much at night, wrapped in plastic, as I do during the day, struggling against the wind and snow. There is very little we can do about it while it is still so cold, but right now I would trade anything for a bath and a good night's sleep in a proper bed.

A radio schedule tonight and John tells us the Marines are now back in Resolute. They lost fourteen litres of fuel, they say. Rune finds it difficult to understand how they lost so much fuel in such a short time. They must have cracked about ten of their four-litre canisters of fuel. John also tells me that we were mentioned in Prime Minister's Questions.

I wonder what the political commentators will make of that as I drift off to sleep to dream of oranges. The ones on the resupply were delicious and I hope John remembers another consignment for the second resupply. With those and Paul Grover's pictures of Ginger Spice we could have a wild time.

Day 20: Tuesday, 24 March

Position: 84°34'52" North; 74°14'32" West
Temperature: −40°C
Windchill: −71°C
Hours of sunshine: 13 hours 49 minutes
Nautical miles covered yesterday: 6½
Nautical miles covered so far: 90
Nautical miles to go (*in a straight line*): 325
Status: Everything okay

My feet are itching like hell. The cheeks of my arse are painfully sore and now my hip is rubbing against my sledge harness. Rune is in an even worse state: his thigh looks raw and he has big blisters on his heels. It will be Lipogel all over tonight.

A tough day: −40°C plus a thirty knot wind all day produces a windchill of −71°C. I keep my head down and think of Everest all day, trying to remember each day on the expedition. By focusing on the places I visited and the people I met at each stage of that eighty-day trip it is easier to come to terms with the monotony and unchanging terrain of walking to the North Pole. Rune asks me how Everest compares with the North Pole but it is an impossible contrast. It is like comparing a Formula One race to Le Mans. Each requires different skills, but I got to the top of Everest on my first attempt whereas this is my third bid for the North Pole, so for me the North Pole must be more difficult.

Rune talks a lot about Sjur Mørdre today. The Norwegian Express is already at 84° North. It took them four days; we covered the same distance in twelve days. 'How do they manage it so quick? How much longer can it last?' he asks. I know Rune is frustrated at our relatively slow progress. Seven or eight miles a day does not seem much to him, particularly as his countrymen are managing double that. 'We have been, and we still are, slow,' he says. 'I know that is the plan but I would still like to get a move on.' We know that the Norwegians are pulling a light sledge each, with a single heavy sledge that they take in turns to haul. They are also all carrying rucksacks. 'Maybe rucksacks are the secret,' Rune says. 'We can walk very easily with ten kilos on our backs, but that will make a big difference to our sledges. Less weight on the sledges is less friction on the snow, so it should be easier.' It is not a bad idea, and we decide to ask John to bring us two Karrimor rucksacks on the next resupply.

The day seems to rocket past. By the time we camp we have covered seven miles and we are getting back on target. Tonight we start on my five-day food pack, thank God. Once we're rid of that and some fuel, my sledge will be 40lb lighter.

Day 21: Wednesday, 25 March

Position: 84°42'08" North; 74°23'06" West
Temperature: −33°C

Windchill: −48°C
Hours of sunshine: 14 hours 31 minutes
Nautical miles covered yesterday: 7
Nautical miles covered so far: 97
Nautical miles to go (*in a straight line*): 318
Status: Everything okay

From today we increase our work-rate. According to our plan we should have walked five hours a day up until yesterday, but we increased the time to six hours as soon as daylight allowed. We then planned to walk six and a half hours from today, but Rune has insisted we walk seven hours now. I think he is right.

The maximum break we can take is three minutes. It is getting warmer so we sweat more, but it is still cold enough for the sweat to freeze and our clothes to ice down within three minutes. That must be avoided; it is the surest route to frostbite and hypothermia.

The extra hour each day will help us counteract the back-drift, which is becoming worse the further north we venture. We drifted back a quarter of a mile overnight and then had to step out into total white-out, rubble and twenty-knot winds. The only saving grace is that the temperature has soared this week. It is in the mid-minus thirties, which feels like the tropics in comparison to the temperatures of −55°C or less we have encountered.

While cursing the white-out, Rune talks all day of his blueberry pie. I tell him I don't believe he can make one so he vows to bake me one as soon as we are back in civilisation. I can't wait. He has also admitted that he is now pleased I wrote to Ingeweld to ask for a picture. He says he wished he had more pictures of her. He is such a sensitive sentimentalist, a fact to which his heavily laden blue bag testifies. 'Looking at the pictures of my nephews and nieces and mama and papa gives me some good thoughts and memories,' he says. 'I must take more next time. When I look at the pictures I forget where I am and it takes me back home. They are good mementoes.'

At the end of the day it appears we have walked a long way west. Rune claims it is a drift whereas I think it is bad navigation. The thought of the wasted mileage in the white-out and winds makes me feel really fed up.

Rune cooks an excellent meal to make up for it. He has a new recipe: spaghetti Bolognese with pieces of Peperami sausage in it. It tastes delicious as long as you don't know how he chops up Peperami. He feeds it from one side of his mouth to the other through his front teeth, chopping as he slides the sausage along like paper through a typewriter. I suppose it is one way to ensure they are bite-size chunks.

As ever, the meal takes ages to cook. I always like mine much sloppier than Rune. He likes his almost lumpy, so he eats first then adds more water, and then I eat mine. To complicate matters, we cannot eat a whole portion in one sitting. The oil-laced food is simply too rich, so Rune cooks up half the rations, we eat, then wait an hour to digest it, then he cooks the second half and we eat the rest. Afterwards I listen to Van Morrison on the Walkman. It is the twenty-first day of the trip and I am allowed the Walkman tonight. Rune listens to it every night, but I ration myself to every seventh day to make it a treat, and because I find warming up the batteries a chore.

We have a great radio schedule with John tonight. He keeps us enthralled with a story of a polar bear that has been rampaging through Resolute Bay. The locals all scrambled out of their houses hoping to shoot it and claim the fur, but apparently it was shot by the shop assistant at the Co-op store as it walked down the middle of the main street.

Rune smokes a cigar, an indulgence he can afford almost every evening since the resupply. Although I tell him he is killing me by passive smoking I am please he is getting through his cigars. Every cigar smoked is a bit less weight we have to haul across the ice.

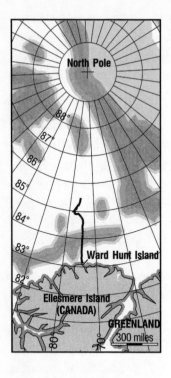

8

The Big Lead and Other Disasters

The Fourth Week

Day 22: Thursday, 26 March

Position: 84°48'54" North; 75°00'00" West
Temperature: −31°C
Windchill: −59°C
Hours of sunshine: 15 hours 15 minutes
Nautical miles covered yesterday: 6
Nautical miles covered so far: 104
Nautical miles to go (*in a straight line*): 311
Status: Everything okay

One of the worst days so far. A total white-out, lots of rubble and twenty-five-knot winds, the strongest we've yet encountered. Despite all this we get out and make good progress. It should be a rest day but we are about four miles behind schedule so we knuckle down and battle our way into the wind. We must want the Pole pretty hard this year.

The wind whistled around our tent all night, so we probably drifted back some distance. I will have to start taking position measurements morning and night so that we can monitor how far south we drift overnight. I had difficulty sleeping. I am worried that we are dropping behind schedule and that the ice conditions do not seem to be improving. The dinner was too heavy. The cod in sour cream knocked me down, but Rune says there is less oil in it than last year. I am also getting too warm in my sleeping-bags. I sweat and itch all night, so maybe it is time to get rid of the inner layer.

The wind is an absolute killer today and there's a lot of rubble. We are walking as if we had white masks over our eyes. We cannot even see our skis. Some of the rubble areas are like city-blocks of ice and it takes a long time to get through them, especially when we cannot see anything. Rune's eyes are freezing over and he has problems focusing. At times he sees double because the wind is blowing straight into his eyes. It is very painful for him.

I am nearly in tears while walking, but for a completely different reason. I keep thinking of Alicia coming to the Pole and when the plane comes in, just seeing her and Claire. It would be lovely to see Alicia all the way up there. Although it is horrible up here, I can still find reasons to remain positive. My skis are covered in pictures of dinosaurs, the sun and flowers painted by my daughters, and each time I look down – the only direction I can look in this white-out – I think it does not matter if I am out here in this horrible weather because even if I make just one mile, I am one mile closer to being reunited with Claire and Alicia.

After walking for four hours we notice that Rune's sledge has broken. There are thin cracks along both sides, and the points where his ropes loop through the carbon fibre are beginning to fray. I hope it holds out until the resupply.

The wind becomes stronger as the day goes on. At one point I overtake Rune to take a picture of him walking through the fog towards me, but I cannot see him. Suddenly he appears out of the icy fog, only three feet away and leaning at forty-five degrees to fight against the wind. While we battle against the wind, almost bent double at times, I think of further items to dump at the resupply. We have to cut more weight.

For the first time since we started out I am thinking of celebrations in Resolute Bay, but I know too well not to dwell on it. I have been scuppered before so I won't think about it until we reach eighty-nine degrees. There is still a long distance to go – we are only a quarter of the way – though not so long in terms of days on the ice. It makes me think of those amazing men such as Peary, Nansen, Scott, Shackleton and Cook who used to go away for three years at a time on expeditions. It amazes me when I realise that I have spent nearly two years up here, but my comparatively short time has been stretched over fifteen years.

At the end of the day we encounter another area of very bad rubble and then stop at an open lead. Because we are being blown west, we decide to head east, but after a couple of miles neither of us can find a crossing point so we decide to camp in the hope that the lead will freeze overnight. Open leads often attract polar bears, which worries me more than usual for some reason. Maybe it is because I have spent the whole day thinking about food. I desperately want a thick juicy steak.

I get out the GPS to discover we have managed six and a half nautical miles, very good considering the number of times we have had to stop to consult the compass, but we have drifted twelve miles west in two days.

Rune changes the dressing on my toes. They still look bad, but I can feel them for the first time since the frostbite set in and they are throbbing a lot. It is a good indication that they are healing. Rune's feet, however, look like a battlefield. The skin is falling off at the top and bottom, which he blames on the vapour barrier bags. He covers his toes with a plaster and a bandage over his heels. The feet are the least of his injuries; his thighs are raw from rubbing and he has some very sore-looking blisters, which he smothers in Lipogel cream.

Afterwards we talk and read. I am reading Kipling, a favourite, and I come across the quotation I always remember on expeditions and that seems so pertinent: 'If you can meet with triumph and disaster/And treat those impostors just the same . . .'

As on many evenings, the talk eventually turns to Ingeweld. Rune tells me he dreams of dancing 'chin to chin' with her when he gets home. It leaves me somewhat confused. 'Why would you want to dance chin to chin?' I ask.

'Because it is nice. It is the normal way in Norway,' he says.

After asking him over twenty questions to find out how and why

Norwegians dance chin to chin, it finally dawns on me.

'You mean cheek to cheek,' I say.

'Cheek to cheek. Chin to chin. Is it not the same thing?' Rune says.

'Chin to chin' is one of the many Rune-isms that have come up on this year's and last year's expeditions, including 'brass monkeys' and, later the same evening, 'girl's ties', which Rune tells me he is very keen on.

'But that narrows your choice a bit doesn't it, Rune?' I say. 'Most women don't wear ties.'

Rune gives me a withering look.

'What do you mean, most women don't wear ties?' he says. 'All women have them, above their knees.'

Again the penny drops for me just a little too late.

Day 23: Friday, 27 March

Position: 84°55'20" North; 76°16'01" West
Temperature: −32°C
Windchill: inside tent all day
Hours of sunshine: 15 hours 33 minutes
Nautical miles covered yesterday: 6½
Nautical miles covered so far: 110½
Nautical miles to go (*in a straight line*): 304½
Status: Storm

Another real blower of a day. The thirty-knot wind is blowing us west at an alarming rate and we are stuck in our tent, in danger of slipping further behind schedule because Rune wants to take a rest day today.

It was very windy all night and I thought I heard a polar bear outside our tent. In an instant I was sitting bolt upright in my bed, and the first thing that went through my mind was, 'Jeez – just wake up Rune and get him out there quick to shoot the bastard.' But trying to wake Rune was like trying to wake the dead. So much for his super-fast reflexes. I soon calmed down and realised that it was just the wind blowing through our antenna, or maybe snow movement near the sledge.

I have been on a knife's edge since Nigel Bateson, the BBC cameraman, said something about polar bears chewing on our shoulders just before we started out onto the ice at Ward Hunt Island. It was the wrong thing to say at the time, along with stories of massacres at crossroads in South Africa, putting tyres around people's necks and lighting them, and shooting children in Sarajevo. These are all things that he has seen in the course of his work, but they were simply the wrong things to say to two people who were about to have a lot of time to think and not that much to think about. I don't think he realised the effect it would have on us.

When I tell Rune in the morning that I thought I heard a polar bear, he just smiles at me. 'Never fear David. If there had been a polar bear I would have heard it,' he says. How can he be so sure, I ask him. 'I have been in those sorts of situations before, when I had to wake up and react immediately. I am confident that everything will be okay,' he says. I press him for further details but he tells me he is not allowed to divulge any more. In spite of Rune's enigmatic reassurances, I make sure the rifle, with its stock sawn off so that it can easily be swung around inside the tent, is close at hand.

In the morning, while Rune smokes a roll-up and shovels ice into a pot on the stove to boil water, I lie in bed with my balaclava and nose-protector on, worrying about the lead we have camped beside. Inside the tent it is still bitterly cold, everything is caked in ice, and Rune does not want to go out today.

We decide to eat breakfast and then reassess the situation. We purposely do not have a leader on this expedition; instead each of us says what he thinks is the best course of action and then the weaker, or more conservative, suggestion always wins. An expedition team is only as strong as its weakest member and there is no point taking risks if one person is unhappy with the decision.

After breakfast I want to get going. Rune is depressed about the lead, so I attempt to buoy him up by pointing out that we made six and a half miles in appalling conditions yesterday, so we will probably do just as well today. 'We are only three miles behind schedule but if we take a rest day now we will be ten miles off target tomorrow morning,' I say. I am also worried about this storm. Bad weather usually passes over within two days in the Arctic, but this is the fourth day so far of this storm. 'There will be more storms ahead of us and they could be worse. We ought to get going now, when we can. We have no idea what might hold us up in the future.'

Rune is still not keen on walking today. He reasons that we are due a rest day in three days' time and he thinks it is better to stay in the tent today. 'In three days the weather could be perfect and we will waste it sitting in the tent. We know the weather is bad now, so why not make today the rest day?' he asks.

The wind is blowing thirty knots outside but I do not think it is a sufficient hindrance to confine us to our tent. The temperatures are now warmer and the sun seems to be up, so the storm could break and then we will regret not moving today. I want to reach 85° North as soon as possible. At the South Pole 85° is the halfway mark, so psychologically half the journey will be over, I say. However, my main concern remains the lead outside our tent. It is the largest we have encountered so far and it could get wider. 'By the time we camped last night, the lead had widened from eight or ten feet to around thirty feet across. If we wait any longer it could become worse,' I say. 'We've got lighter sledges than last year so it won't hurt us to head back west and find a crossing.'

Rune still does not want to move. Once he is out of the tent there is no stopping him, but getting him going on a bad morning is a struggle.

'What I don't want to do is have a rest day today when the sun is up, and tomorrow the lead is huge and we cannot get around it,' I continue. 'We really should get going today.'

Rune is still impassive, and he has a point. As point man he has to brave the worst of the wind searching for a viable route, whereas I can just put my head down and follow his tracks.

'All I can say, Rune, is that once you've been on a few trips in the Arctic and you are an old codger like me, you realise you've got go get up and get out of the tent, because it always sounds worse in the tent. So if you don't want to go, you have to stand up in your sleeping-bag and have a look out of the doorway to be sure that the weather is too bad,' I say. It is my final call.

Rune agrees that we cannot make an informed decision until one of us goes outside to check out the visibility and the lead. I explain to Rune the trick I developed on Antarctica for walking in a sleeping-bag and he clambers to the door of the tent, where he is almost knocked down by the wind. A few minutes later he returns, impressed with my

little trick for walking in a sleeping-bag, and delivers his report. The
lead has widened. It is now over a hundred feet across and stretches
from one horizon to the other.

'It's sunny,' Rune says, 'but the visibility is three hundred metres
because of a lot of snow drift in the air. It is gusting maybe forty knots.
The lead will freeze this afternoon – it already looks frozen but too
dark to cross.' Dark ice is thin ice, so we should not cross it yet. 'I
know you want to go, David, but I am doubtful because I think it is
quite bad; it's possible to walk, but only just. I am much more relaxed
now that I have seen the lead is freezing, and there are some nice white
ice crystals on the top already. A very good sign. We're already late
this morning, and I feel we should stay. Sorry, David, maybe I
am a bit lazy. Maybe in four, five, six hours it is possible to cross the
lead. Maybe we should do that this afternoon, and stay here for
now.'

It's a good call. I want to go because I want the Pole, but Rune has
made a good and sound decision. We're eight days in from our
resupply, so why not take the rest day on a horrible day and hope for
good weather in a couple of days' time when we should be resting?
However, I know Rune regrets not making much of an effort yesterday.

'The lead is now a hundred and fifty feet across,' he says. 'Now I
am asking myself why we didn't go back yesterday and cross it further
west. I'm sure it would have been fine.'

He is right, and it adds to the concerns I already have about drifting
further south. I get out the GPS and take our position. As I had
feared, we have drifted a long way west.

'We are at 84°54'46" North and 76°59'00" West,' I say to Rune when
our position appears on the display.

'Jesus . . . that means that last night we drifted south half a mile, but
we floated forty-three minutes west, which is about five miles.'

We have drifted nearly twenty miles west over the last three days,
almost to the seventy-seven degrees line of longitude. It messes up
our navigation somewhat, because our plans are based on going up
the seventy-five degrees line of longitude. At 77° West we have to take
half an hour difference into consideration when navigating from our
sun shadow.

Decisions, decisions. I don't know what to do. If Rune does not
want to move then we should stay here. He is right – the lead will

freeze over and we can save ourselves a lot of walking if we wait until the section directly in front of us is strong enough to take our weight. We lost half a mile to the south last night, and by tomorrow morning we will have lost another mile, but that's not a big problem. More worrying is that we will have drifted west maybe another six miles. That puts us in a quandary.

Although it is not the first really frustrating day we have had, I am heartened by the fact that everything has gone well so far. We left England a month ago today, and up until now almost everything has worked a dream. If all goes to plan we will be up here for around sixty days, so we have to look after ourselves by putting in rest days and watching our health. So far we have been very careful and we have both adapted well to the cold and recovered from the frostbite on our fingers.

Maybe Rune is right, and I have to admit my frustrations are slightly tempered by the call of my stomach. I have been promising myself some chicken noodle soup on the rest day, and now I can have some today instead of waiting another two days. Rune will have some hot chocolate, because he has been very good, and we'll have chicken noodle soup and a packet of pork scratchings for lunch. After the soup Rune boils up a big pot of coffee which we drink with brandy. It is a very pleasant way to spend the remainder of the rest day. Then Dr Rune takes a look at the frostbite on my toe. It looks pretty foul, with a black spot on the end of my big and second toes and a lot of flaking on the other toes. With a cigarette dangling in his mouth, Rune says, 'I will put something on it to stop you losing it. It looks much better than before, but it looks like it hurts.' He is certainly right about that. My toe sometimes throbs so much at night that it wakes me up. 'I am a very good doctor,' Rune insists, 'and I will put some Scandinavian antiseptic salve and some plaster on your toe.'

'If you're a doctor I can sue you if I lose my toe,' I reply.

'No – don't even try,' Rune replies.

'Thank you, Dr Nansen,' I say.

'No problem. It's a pleasure, Dr Livingstone.'

At times we are like a couple of pantomime dames, camping it up all the way to the North Pole. If anybody could see us now they would be surprised. Rune is sitting in his woollen underpants, which are riddled with holes, fag in mouth, furry hat on his head and surrounded by ointments and pills. I am lying with my foot in his lap, while Rune plays doctor.

Once my toes have been patched up, Rune then prescribes some Ibuprofen for my muscle pain. Like Rune I have a stiff neck and shoulders because I have been using them to try to push my way through the rubble. 'You can have some Tamalgesic if you want, David,' Rune jokes. Tamalgesic is a last resort. It is for when we are on the way out, the last measure before we inject morphine. 'And we have brandy, some sleeping medicine, but that is only for those days we are good and get out of the tent.'

We then write in our diaries. Rune is listening to a tape made for him by his friend Torre, with whom he skied the length of Greenland. All the titles of the songs are meant to be inspirational – songs such as 'See You When You Get There'. His favourite, he has told me, is Lou Reed's 'Perfect Day', something we have not had since we set out. I ask Rune what he is writing and he tells me he is noting down his verdict on our equipment, important notes for our next expeditions. 'And I am writing things about you David – just the positive things,' he teases. 'And at the end I am writing: "We are hoping for a good day tomorrow. And I wish the rest of the world as nice a day as we have had, and goodnight."'

The rest day passes far too quickly. It is a brief respite from the biting wind and the rigours of the Arctic, and as always we end up talking about what we miss most from home.

'Sometimes I just miss the normal life,' Rune says. 'Just taking it easy on a weekend. Waking up and it's not too cold outside. Going downstairs and having a good, hot cup of coffee or tea, and eating my breakfast. Relaxing.'

Day 24: Saturday, 28 March

Position: 84°55'06" North; 77°48'10" West
Temperature: −25°C
Windchill: −61°C
Hours of sunshine: 16 hours 52 minutes
Nautical miles covered yesterday: 0
Nautical miles covered so far: 110

Nautical miles to go (*in a straight line*): 305
Status: Everything okay

I slept dreadfully. Maybe it is all the coffee I drank yesterday. It seems to have a much more profound effect on us up here, although Rune drank a litre of the stuff and slept like a baby. He says he slept better because he has stopped using his vapour barrier bag. It is now warm enough for our sweat not to freeze into the sleeping-bags. Maybe he is right.

We have drifted further north and one and a half degrees west since yesterday morning, at our current latitude another eight miles off track. The storm has abated slightly, but it is still very windy, which means more problems with leads as the wind catches the pressure ridges like sails and blows the ice floes apart. This is our fifth consecutive day with gale-force winds.

We are aiming for seven hours today, but whether we can keep to our target depends on the leads and rubble. We set off in good spirits and at high speed. The lead we camped beside has frozen sufficiently for us to cross it gingerly. We then cross a lot of smaller leads and head north-north-east. It is the same pattern as last year: stray winds are causing open leads, but for some reason it feels quite odd this year, especially as there has been a sudden and rapid increase in temperature.

After two hours out on the ice we are stopped by a rubble field. It is not as bad as some we have come across, but back-breaking nevertheless. Then suddenly we stop dead. 'It is almost as if we have seen the devil himself,' Rune says. The sky and air are dark all around us, but not as dark as the wide lead that stretches out right in front of us. It is the most enormous lead I have ever seen, and very eerie. Rune is right, it appears almost satanic in nature, and the recently unnaturally warm temperatures and swirling winds that have surrounded us for days seem like a mysterious curse.

It is the mother of all leads. It stretches east and west as far as we can see and at places is a mile or more across. Immediately we both think this is it. The end. Our expedition that has so far progressed without a single hitch has been scuppered by El Niño or some other strange weather pattern that has broken up the ice a couple of months too early. No wonder Rune says it seems like the devil's work. We stand at the lead's edge, impressed by the dramatic sight but extremely dejected. The swirling wind is catching the surface and it is the first time I have seen waves on the Arctic Ocean. They are six inches to a foot high.

'We could try crossing it here,' Rune says. 'There is some slightly crusty slushy-porridge ice nearby. I think we will make it.'

'I think you are mad,' I retort. 'I'm not crossing that. I can't swim.'

Rune then suggests strapping our sledges together and paddling across. Again I refuse point-blank.

My fear of water is, I know, most frustrating for Rune. I can see my reticence frustrates him and he feels he has to keep his cool for both of us. My water phobia is doubly difficult for Rune as he has to keep his nerve for both of us and cajole me across – but not this time. The lead is two to three miles wide at places, there is an island floating in it and we can see that the water is flowing fast. To us it appears as unbreachable as the Thames Estuary and we could be stuck here for days. For all we know it will take until next winter for this massive mass of water to freeze over.

For five hours we walk east, following the lead to one crossing point where we see an iceberg drift away at a hell of a speed just as we are about to attempt to traverse a thin sheet of ice on the open water. To make matters worse, the further east we ski the wider the lead becomes, like a funnel. A black cloud hangs over most of the horizon in front of us. It is the water evaporating, but within that black cloud we can see little parcels of white so we head for them, thinking this signifies areas where the lead might have frozen over.

Now I know how Peary felt when confronted by his big lead. We walk and walk and walk, but still no crossing point. Exhausted, we decide to camp near the lead's narrowest point, covered with a thin layer of ice. Hopefully it will freeze in the night. For that to happen we need the wind to drop so the ice stops moving. Even Rune is becoming cautious. 'I will not go out on that lead if the ice starts to move. That would be a real disaster,' he says. 'But our only other option is to continue walking east, and that is not my way to do it.'

We must have been travelling quite fast, or maybe we were just plain angry, because we made nearly four miles in the two hours up to the lead. We both find it very frustrating that we are prevented from carrying on at this rate. I had grand hopes of crossing 85° North today, but we are now at 84°58'57" North and 77°43'21" West – six and a half miles behind schedule and needing to catch up soon – with every chance that we will not be able to advance a single mile northwards tomorrow.

A day from heaven to hell.

Day 25: Sunday, 29 March

Position: 84°59'34" North; 78°14'31" West
Temperature: −30°C
Windchill: −52°C
Hours of sunshine: 17 hours 44 minutes
Nautical miles covered yesterday: 3½
Nautical miles covered so far: 114½
Nautical miles to go (*in a straight line*): 300½
Status: Open water

A tinge of luck seems to have come our way. We woke up this morning to find we had drifted half a mile north overnight. It is Mothering Sunday and unfortunately the mother of all leads is still outside our tent. There is no way that will disappear with a bit of drift.

Last year I got terribly homesick on Mother's Day and wanted to see Claire and the children. Of course I do now as well, but it seems different this year. The journey so far has been very quick because Rune and I know each other, because we are versed in the procedures and with the equipment. It has given us very little time to dwell on our hardships and how much we could be missing home. However, today we think of home, our families and our mothers. I hope Claire's flowers have arrived on time. Stupidly, I have forgotten to send my mother and grandmother flowers and feel a bit of a prat, but wish them Happy Mother's Day in my absence.

Right now, the biggest threat to our return home on time remains the lead. We desperately need a change in fortune. When we were in the same place last year we were held up by a big lead and it was a nightmare. Now we really need some luck because we've been caught in a storm for six days and we've walked and drifted nearly twenty-five miles west of our intended course, so we need to cross this lead as soon as possible to get back on course.

It is still windy outside. This storm shows no sign of blowing itself out, and although it should be our rest day we are going to go out and try to make some headway. Rune hears me muttering under my breath, 'Please, Lady Luck, touch wood. Lady Luck, please be with us today.'

'Lady Luck, what is that?' he asks.

I can see it is not going to be easy to explain this latest English figure of speech to Rune.

'I suppose we say luck is a lady because it is fickle,' I say, tongue in cheek. 'Or at least I think that is the reason. We need that lady to give us a little bit of luck. That's why we say it.'

Rune appears unconvinced and is blunt in his reply.

'Yes we need luck, David. But you also need to take a chance walking over soft ice,' he says.

At times like this I think it is about time I handed the mantle on and gave up this game.

We are half a mile off 85° North. At the South Pole that was halfway, but we are far from halfway up here. The South Pole was hard. Each day was windy and the prevailing wind was always in my face, but I made good mileage. Whatever the weather, I got out and knew I would do at least ten miles. Up here it is so different; we need a lot of luck. A lot of luck.

While we force our disgusting breakfasts down our throats I hear a plane pass overhead and peer out of the door of the tent at the jet-stream. I wonder if it is the plane we saw in the first few days. Like then, I would rather be down here than up there, comfortable, well-fed and warm, because I want more than anything to get to the Pole.

Rune goes outside for a reconnaissance and comes back with bad news: the lead has open water where last night it was frozen; it has stretched wider apart overnight and it is still enshrouded in an ominous black cloud. I feel very despondent. We have to get around or over it, but it is at least thirty miles long and a mile wide where we are camped. There is nothing for it but to keep walking until we find a crossing point. I want to do eight or ten hours a day just to get around this lead.

We set off in a direction where the sky looks whiter, which hopefully means the lead might have closed. We can see some steamy mist, which indicates open water, coming off the area in front of us, but I can see some clear patches further ahead which might mean the lead has frozen over at that point. We walk for several hours until, in the midst of rubble, we spot a crossing. It is a jumbled mass of soft ice, rubble and pools of water, but I think it affords a passage across the water, provided we take the right route through the maze.

We make our way onto an island with rubble about eight feet high. On the far side of the island of rubble I can see that there is just about enough ice to carry us to the far side of the lead. The end of our quest to cross the lead is almost in sight, but for the moment I cannot see a safe route. Above all else, I want to avoid falling in the water. Rune has no qualms. He strides purposefully across the porridge-ice, his ski pole puncturing the surface beside him with each step and his skis bowing ominously into the water, but he does not sink. By moving at speed he manages to walk across the mixture of water and slush to the far side of the lead. I am amazed. I have never seen anything like it. Nobody else would have chanced it and under no circumstances am I going to follow his route.

But the surprises are not over yet. Rune takes off his sledge harness, delves into one of his blue bags and pulls out his video camera, which he sets up on a tripod positioned at the side of the lead. Then, to my complete amazement, he runs back across the slush to me. 'I want to get this crossing on tape, so I will have to do it again with you,' he says.

Even though Rune has crossed the ice twice, I do not like it at all. The state of the surface petrifies me. In normal circumstances, if we had not just walked for two days to find this crossing point, I would have refused to cross here, but this seems our best chance and we should seize it while we can. Rune tries to reassure me, saying he is just as frightened. 'Just keep going David. Cross it fast and you will be okay. This is a safe place,' he says. I tell Rune that I am going to take off my harness and try to cross without my sledge dragging behind me. 'Just keep it loose on you David. Push the sledge towards me,' he says from my right, where he is attempting to cajole me into crossing.

I feel like a little child and I know I am acting like one. Every step I take is accompanied by a moaning exclamation. It must drive Rune insane. 'Move quickly but carefully,' he shouts at me as I edge forward an inch at a time. It is like walking on a precipice. At any moment this ice will give way, I keep telling myself. 'Walk! Walk! Walk! You are safe now,' Rune shouts, but I am frozen to the spot, maybe three feet across the mixture of sludge and water. I do not know how Rune manages to walk so nonchalantly across the flimsy skin of barely formed ice that is flexing under my feet. All around me are pools of water and slush. 'Hang on, I'm coming over,' Rune calls. 'I will show you the way. Now we have to walk in the biggest ice rubbles we have seen for two years.'

The rubble in front of me looks like a giant portion of mashed potato and cauliflower. To me it has as much chance of carrying my weight as the vegetables would. 'Oh fuck,' I say. My language always deteriorates in times of stress, and right now my vocabulary is limited to about ten words, most of them expletives. I inch forward very cautiously.

'Slowly! Don't use too much power on the snow. You are going under,' Rune shouts.

I look around myself – there does not seem to be a safe route to the other side. Where Rune walked before, water is now flowing.

'It's sinking over there,' I shout to Rune, pointing in front of myself.

'Then take it over here,' Rune replies, pointing to my left at an area that seems even more perilous.

'Oh fuck,' I say again.

'Just walk on the bigger-sized rubble. It should be okay. It just goes under a little bit when you walk on it and your feet may get wet, but it should hold,' Rune suggests.

'Oh fuck,' I cry as my feet slip underwater.

Rune shouts to me to pass my harness over to him. 'Throw it over here. You can do it. And I will send the sledge after you.'

'Over there?' I ask, unsure of what Rune has in mind.

'Yes, just don't use too much force on your poles, or you will go under.'

'Oh, you cunt,' I scream at the ice as I try to pull myself forward without pushing my poles through the slush that is barely supporting my weight. The boundary between buoyancy and sinking is a knife-edge. 'Rune, what are we doing here? What the hell are we doing?'

I continue to struggle. It is like some perverse form of the party-game Twister: my legs are splayed between two lumps of rubble and water flows between them; my ski poles poke out around me like supports, attempting to gain a purchase on some morsel of solid ice.

Rune offers to take the sledge off me and I pass my harness back to him. It leaves me free to choose any route around or across the jumbled mass of floating rubble, but Rune insists I take the direct route across to the other side. It is only ten or twelve feet wide, but it is ten or twelve feet of mush that experience tells me will never support my weight.

'There is a big ice rubble. Just walk on the biggest ice rubble; they are moving, but not sinking.'

I follow his advice but I immediately began to sink.

'Whooooah – there is nowhere to go Rune,' I shout.

'David, now walk quickly and carefully,' Rune repeats. 'Come this way, it's safer and easier. Try it straight forward instead of all the way round.'

'Fuck,' I shout and I abandon Rune's instructions. Instead I make a run for it around to the right. I have spotted some thicker ice, and although it is a longer route, I think it will be a safer one.

Eventually I make it round to the other side of the lead and end up at Rune's video camera on its tripod. The relief is immense. It was twenty minutes of complete torture to me. Now it is my turn to instruct Rune.

'Go where I went Rune. Go where I went,' I shout at my Norwegian Viking.

But he ignores my advice and steps purposefully across the section he wanted me to cross. He has already walked across this area twice before and there is nothing left to support his weight. From where I am standing, the slush is at least six inches under flowing water.

'I am going quickly now, and carefully,' Rune shouts. 'David, this is the way to do it.'

He takes a straight line through the water, prodding his ski sticks on either side. With each prod the stick goes right through the ice, but he continues walking. In about twenty seconds he has crossed the strait that I spent twenty minutes circumnavigating. I do not now how he does it.

Our troubles are not quite over yet. We head north-east to get back on course and hopefully to avoid further leads. Nevertheless, we have to cross another six smaller ones, and once again my heart is in my mouth as I follow in Rune's footsteps.

The rest of the day is beautiful with clear skies, and for the first time we can feel the warmth of the sun on our backs. I have to vent my jacket as I am sweating heavily. It does not really bother me as I am just overjoyed to have crossed that mother of all leads.

Towards the end of the day we spot a seal, the first sign of life since we waved goodbye to poor Thierry. The seal sticks his head up through a polynya and then quickly disappears when he sees us watching him. We carry on marching, desperate to make up lost mileage and to get back to 75° West. The sea fog comes in, enshrouding us in its cold vapour, and the temperature drops rapidly. I want to stop and camp, but Rune urges me to continue.

Before we camp we again cross a dangerous lead. I am by now physically exhausted and mentally wrung-out by the tensions of walking on thin ice. Eventually we camp, seven and a half hours after setting off. I feel comfortable with the extra half hour's schlep and proud of our achievements.

Forty-five minutes later the tent is up and we are inside, sipping hot juice. I get the GPS out to find out by how much the leads have held us back. To our amazement it is a double brandy night: we have crossed the 85th Parallel to 85°07'49" North and 77°21'34" West, and it is our best daily mileage yet – eight and a quarter miles. We are ecstatic. I am sure we could have walked ten miles north if we had not had to head east so far this morning.

After the rapid see-saw of despair and elation we have experienced today, I am reminded of Peary's words in 1906 on his first attempt to reach the North Pole: 'What contrasts this country affords. Yesterday hell, today comparative heaven, yet not such a heaven as most would voluntarily choose.' True words indeed.

Day 26: Monday, 30 March

Position: 85°06'43" North; 77°11'03" West
Temperature: −38°C
Windchill: −58°C
Hours of sunshine: 18 hours 52 minutes

Nautical miles covered yesterday: 8¼
Nautical miles covered so far: 121¾
Nautical miles to go (*in a straight line*): 293¼
Status: Everything okay

I wake up feeling dreadful and Rune immediately lets me know that I look as bad as I feel.

'Why is your right eye that baggy? I cannot remember we have been fighting,' he says.

'It's because I'm getting old. I'm past it for this polar lark, Rune. You'll look like this when you're forty-one and exhausted,' I answer.

Rune, as ever, is bright as a spark and raring to go. We do not have a mirror so I cannot see if I look as bad as Rune says. Instead I get Rune to video me for a few seconds, then I look at the footage in the camera's viewfinder. It is a shock to me. He is right, I look dead beat. There are huge rings under my very puffy eyes, I am pale and drawn, and the podgy cheeks I had four weeks ago have disappeared; in their place sunken skin hangs from the cheekbones I forgot I had. Walking to the North Pole is obviously a very effective way of losing weight.

Depressingly, I find we have drifted back a mile overnight and the blue skies of yesterday have disappeared. There is relatively little wind but the low cloud leaves a flat light in which we cannot make out the sky from the ground – in other words, another bloody white-out.

We set off after breakfast and within an hour we encounter disaster. The nightmare that has been haunting me for fourteen years and which stopped recurring only eighteen months ago comes back to torment me, and this time it is real. It is probably the worst single moment I've had in fifteen years of polar exploration.

At the first lead we come to Rune goes ahead with his sledge behind him, and I follow in his tracks. One moment I am crossing what appears to be a solid section of ice, the next I have fallen through the ice into the water with my skis on. In the white-out I had not noticed that a hanging cornice of snow at the edge of a section of fresh ice was only an inch or so thick. Now I am up to my waist in the Arctic Ocean and panicking. As I fall, I rip my ice-spikes from around my neck, attempt to dig the two titanium nails into the nearest piece of white ice I can spot, and shout to Rune, who is about nine feet away and seemingly oblivious. I try to swim, something I find difficult at the best of times, but I cannot move my legs with my skis still attached to my feet. I am sinking, aware that I'll lose strength in the cold water and slip under the ice if I don't do something soon.

Rune has already heard me go, but in the slow-motion world I am enveloped in he has not reacted yet. I have heard that people's lives often flash in front of them shortly before they die, and at this moment it seems as if a brief summary of the last few months is being projected inside my eyes. I see the preparations in Resolute, our departure from Ward Hunt Island and the weeks we have spent together in the tent. Most worryingly, I see the frostbite on my nose, toes and fingers spreading, and this plunge into the Arctic Ocean ending my bid for the North Pole and the Grand Slam. This is it, I think for the second time in three days. The expedition is over. I won't recover from this.

But before I know it the world around me speeds up and Rune is in front of me, hauling me out of the −4°C clutches of the Arctic Ocean. He drags me on to an ice floe, where I lie, gasping for breath, my trouser legs already freezing solid like stovepipes. I want Rune to put up the tent double-quick so that I can get out of my sodden clothing and crawl inside my sleeping-bag, but he advises against it. 'The best thing you can do is to keep walking,' Rune says. 'Then your body warmth will dry out your clothes from the inside.' It sounds unlikely to me. I am terrified that my frostbite will now spread across my entire foot and up my legs. I need to get my clothes off, I insist. 'Trust me David, it has happened to me many times before. If you stop now, the water will freeze into your clothes and you will never get the ice out of them. You must keep walking.'

So we head off northwards again, me with my knees shaking for at least the next two hours. Within a very short time we hit rubble as bad as any we have had on the whole trip, extremely high and no way around it. It takes at least three hours to crawl through only half a mile and it is almost impossible to spot a clear route in the white-out.

At the end of the day we come to yet another frigging lead. We decide that we have to cross it before we set up camp, just in case it widens overnight. It takes us forty minutes to breach the stretch of open water. By the end of the day I am chin-strapped to get in and I collapse inside the tent.

We are amazed to discover we have managed seven miles in the last eight hours. Under the circumstances it is brilliant, and I am sure we would have done ten miles had we had the good visibility and the pans of ice we expect and pray for. We wait in vain, it seems.

This really has been a momentous day. As well as falling into water and tackling cataclysmic rubble in the fifth consecutive day of white-out, we have passed our high point for last year, which was 85°09' North. I remember that we had equally bad rubble at the same spot last year. Please, please, please, big pans tomorrow, I say to myself at the end of the day. I promise to eat all my greens if we get some flat ice. We go to sleep at 85°13'50" North and 76°48'49" West. I hope we are in the same spot or further north in the morning.

Day 27: Tuesday, 31 March

Position: 85°13'10" North; 76°26'20" West
Temperature: −38°C
Windchill: −56°C
Hours of sunshine: 20 hours 50 minutes
Nautical miles covered yesterday: 7
Nautical miles covered so far: 128
Nautical miles to go (*in a straight line*): 287
Status: Man in water – continuing

Predictably enough, given our current run of luck, we have drifted back three-quarters of a mile by morning, and the wind has picked up again.

'Just another day at the office,' Rune says after carrying out a reconnaissance after breakfast.

'It's windy outside. Total white-out. Worse than yesterday.'

'It can't get any worse,' I say. 'What do you suggest?'

'I don't like these weather conditions, walking in a white-out. I hate it, but let's do one more day. That means one less day to the Pole.'

He is right. All I can think is thank goodness we are not waiting for a resupply now; they would never find us. According to my records, we are currently caught in the Beaufort Gyral Stream, an area of huge elliptical currents that, if luck is on our side, will soon carry us northwards after days and days of back-drift. It would be wonderful to have the currents on our side for a change, but I am only too aware that nothing can be counted on in the Arctic.

There is a total white-out on the ice. The winds start from the south, but within an hour they have switched to the west. Again we encounter huge rubble fields, although not as bad as yesterday, but they are followed by an extensive broken-up area of small pans intersected by lots of leads. After yesterday's events I am very careful not to fall in the water again, but at one point I find myself sinking fast, this time up to my knees. Rune comes to the rescue again, pulling me out of the slush. He really is looking after me. Later on, Rune is ahead of me on a lead and I can see him sinking. I shout to him and he hurries across the broken, porridge-like ice that we call steel ice because of its colour. I think we would both have gone through if Rune had not clambered free.

I think all day long about the resupply. We have had only one good day in the last ten, so I think I will call for the plane to come on the twentieth day of this section, in eight days' time. If the weather is bad we will keep walking and aim for the twenty-first or twenty-second day. By then we will be out of food so we may have to just sit and hold on. Running out of food is probably more of a problem for Rune; judging by what he tells me he is thinking about when we walk, ninety per cent of his time is spent fantasising about huge plates of home-cooked food. 'I'm thinking about our place on the coast, down on Molga, eating shrimps, mayonnaise and toast on a sunny summer day. That will be just a perfect day.' Later on: 'Just back to New Year's Eve last year. The lamb steak I ate with some good ingredients. Very nice.'

We are still drifting fast, which I had hoped would stop. This back-drift is terribly demoralising, like trying to run up a down escalator. We have to work so hard for every mile and then some of the fruits of our labours are stolen from us while we sleep.

We end up 85°20'52" North and 75°52'48" West; over seven miles achieved today and we are now nine miles behind schedule. Both of us are suffering badly from aches and pains. First my left knee hurt, now it is my right knee as well; then my crotch was sore and finally my frostbitten toe was painful. I have decided not to use my vapour barrier bag any more. My toe is very swollen and it needs a chance to breathe and dry out.

Each trip you have to have a goal and you have to have a carrot and a stick. My carrot is seeing my wife and daughter at the Pole, and my stick is that I will have to come back and go through this all over again if we do not succeed this time. That is something I desperately do not want to do. I have been floating around on this ocean for more months than I care even to think about. For Rune, his goal is obviously the same as mine, and his carrot is the cigars, brandy and whisky I have brought as rewards for each time we cross a new line of longitude or when we beat our schedule. The only thing I haven't been able to work out is what Rune's stick is. He seems so happy up here that I often think he enjoys this purgatory more than home.

'The only thing I fear is failure,' Rune tells me. 'That's what keeps me going. If we don't do it then my days as an explorer are over and I have big plans over the next four or five years. If I don't succeed on this, I can forget any plans I ever had.'

Day 28: Wednesday, 1 April

Position: 85°20'29" North; 75°31'11" West
Temperature: −37°C
Windchill: −51°C
Hours of sunshine: 24 hours
Nautical miles covered yesterday: 7
Nautical miles covered so far: 135½
Nautical miles to go (*in a straight line*): 279½
Status: Everything okay

Things seem to happen in threes, especially on All Fool's Day (I tried an April Fool on Rune but he immediately saw through it) and the thirteenth day since the resupply. First my laces broke, which is a real bugger in this weather. It is the coldest it's been for many days and repairing my laces is a painful task. Secondly, since I fell into the water my damp boots freeze solid each night and I have to hammer them on to my feet in the morning. Then, once they have warmed up, I have to retie the laces. And thirdly, we are still floating backwards, a third of a mile overnight.

We have had twenty-four-hour daylight for some time now, but today is the first day of twenty-four-hour sunlight. Previously the sun was dipping below the horizon and we had a brief period of dusk; now the sun is always in the sky and just moves in an uncanny circle around us. Although the sun shines all day, it is very cold. It is back to −40°C again. We have had colder conditions, but somehow today seems frostier than any other on the trip. Maybe we are becoming soft to the iciness now. My hands seem to be frozen all day; I suspect it is because my inner gloves do not dry out as thoroughly now that I am not using the vapour barrier bag inside my sleeping-bags. Last night was the first night without the vapour barrier bag, which I discarded in order to try to dry out my toe. It felt fantastic inside two sleeping-bags with no plastic next to my body – warm and comfortable.

Conditions are still far from perfect, although we encounter no big rubble. There is still some scattered rubble and sadly no sign yet of the huge pans we were led to expect by now. For most of the day we walk through a lot of break-up and cross many leads, but fortunately most of the leads are frozen solid in comparison to yesterday's slushy conditions. Nevertheless, very little of our route is in a straight line, and we do a lot of zig-zagging.

In terms of scenery it is at times a stunning day. At one point we are walking into the setting sun, with the wind coming from behind. The snow, streaming in the wind, looks like a river flowing from behind us, and the rubble and pressure ridges look like the trenches at the Somme or on the Eastern Front. They are grey in the setting sun and we trudge along, heads down like Russian soldiers marching home slowly across the steppe. The ice cracks, groans and creaks under our feet and the wind is brutally fierce, which makes the surface of the ice appear to boil with a wispy evaporation of the blowing snow. Later on, the heaven is split in two with dark clouds in the east and blue skies in the west. A magnificent contrast, which is reflected on the ice. Rune repeatedly points out ice sculptures in the pressure ridges and rubble. It is remarkable that when we are struggling through hell, Rune can still pick out the beauty in our surroundings, whereas I am just cursing and hating virtually every moment. Today he points out the shape of a man and a woman with their arms around each other; later on he spots a hand with the index finger wagging, and then the shape of two dogs fighting. The landscape is always in a state of flux.

I help Rune through some rubble, and as he pulls on my ski pole the tip snaps off. It is damage I can do without, but worse is to come.

I snap a tent pole when I tug my sledge after it flips in a lead, ripping the sledge's canopy. The only consolation is that I do not rip the tent, which would have been a disaster. We postpone the repair until we stop for the night, but it takes ages to repair the pole with my cold hands. I am thankful that the wind has at least dropped at the end of the day, although Rune still finds it very cold when he has to run outside with only his underwear on after he left the shotgun outside.

Despite extensive detours we set an all-time mileage record – nine miles, to 85°29'30" North and 75°39'03" West, the furthest we have walked in one day, this year or last. We are now around halfway in terms of days, if not in mileage, and it has been a mixed day: our equipment failures in the cold have been tempered by a record mileage.

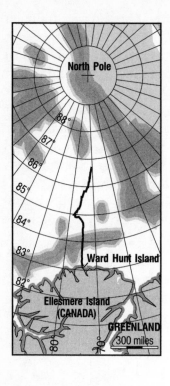

9

Running on Empty

The Fifth Week

Day 29: Thursday, 2 April

Position: 85°29'24" North; 75°39'29" West
Temperature: −32°C
Windchill: −48°C
Hours of sunshine: 24 hours
Nautical miles covered yesterday: 9
Nautical miles covered so far: 144½
Nautical miles to go (*in a straight line*): 270½
Status: Everything okay

Thank God the back-drift appears to be slowing; only one tenth of a mile southwards overnight. An excellent day, even though we walk in white-out all day and have to traverse a very broken-up area. However, the wind is slight, which means less back-drift, and the leads are frozen over nicely, which is a delight.

Leads can be our worst enemy or our best ally when they are frozen over and solid. We cross hundreds today, but still no sign of the big pans I am dreaming of, and there is still a lot of rubble. Some of the rubble is quite beautiful. For several miles we walk through an area of enormous blue ice boulders, some twenty-five to thirty feet high. The enormous ice cubes slow us down because we cannot climb them and have to find a route that weaves through the maze they set, but the grandeur of these enormous monoliths makes up for the extra distance.

At the end of the day we have set a new record – nine and a half miles. We are now four and a half miles behind schedule. Time seems to be merging each day. We have been walking in white-out for over a week and there is little to tell the days apart except when a disaster happens. By the end of each day I feel truly exhausted. We are walking for eight hours a day and my weight is now very low. I have lost at least one and a half stone in the last four weeks, and for the first time in ages I can see my John Thomas again.

The sun is shining but it does not seem to warm us much. Nevertheless, compared with yesterday, when the temperature plummeted, today felt warmer and my hands were not frozen for the first time in weeks. We saw some fox tracks, which could mean a polar bear is nearby. Arctic foxes usually trail the bears, scavenging off the carcasses they leave behind.

The conundrum now is when to call for the resupply. I am sure we can hit ten miles a day if we have some long pans, if the good weather holds so that we can navigate from the sun, and if we dump all our superfluous gear, such as Rune's treasured cigar-cutters. If we continue to walk nine miles a day until the twentieth day of this leg – another six days – we will be between 86°30' and 86°40' North. That would be great news as it would mean lighter sledges and less distance for the third leg, but the price for a resupply flight nearly doubles once the plane has to fly past 86°30' North. It might be best to take the resupply early, accept that our mileage will subsequently go down because of the extra weight and then slog it out to the Pole. Maybe thirty more days, but we don't know for sure. We end today at 85°38'55" North and 75°33'01" West.

A good radio schedule with John tonight. I worry that I have not emphasised the importance of keeping the resupply cost down and keep repeating my demands to John Perrins in Resolute. 'Watch the Charlie Oscar Sierra Tango, John. Watch the cost,' I repeat several times over the radio. John tells me that he might be able to share a flight that will be setting up a fuel cache, but the extra cost will not be known until we know for sure where the resupply is to take place. At least the pound is at its strongest level in ten years, according to some of the news that John passes on to me, so the cost of the resupply will be slightly mitigated and the summer holiday I am dreaming of should be cheaper.

Day 30: Friday, 3 April

Position: 85°38'27" North; 75°09'59" West
Temperature: −38°C
Windchill: −48°C
Hours of sunshine: 24 hours
Nautical miles covered yesterday: 9½
Nautical miles covered so far: 153½
Nautical miles to go (*in a straight line*): 261½
Status: Everything okay

Wha-hey, hulashaker! An amazing day. We set off into heavy rubble, it was slow going and there was a strong wind, but by the end of the day we have covered twelve miles to 85°50'22" North and 74°26'00" West. I can hardly believe it.

It seems as if our fortunes have at last changed. We had half a mile back-drift overnight, but by mid-morning the wind direction changed to come from the south. After being knocked back by the drift day after day, now at last the drift is on our side and I estimate that three or four of the twelve miles we covered was a wind-assisted northerly drift. It's about time it went our way, but I am in no doubt that the Arctic will claw back the four miles before the end. I still cannot believe our luck; this place is such a heaven and hell.

Despite the great advances, it is nevertheless an exceptionally frustrating day. I lose my rag repeatedly as my sledge stops at each bump, catches on ice boulders or tips over. Rune is having similar problems, and all day we can hear each other swearing at our sleds. Being able to curse at the damn plastic things is at times the only way we can stop ourselves from wanting to pulverise them into thousands of little pieces.

How I manage not to break my wrists three times today I will never know. I fall over again and again and again in the rubble. If we were using last year's ski poles I would have snapped three of them today. I have no idea why I am so clumsy today – maybe it is exhaustion and physical weakness.

Towards the end of the afternoon we at last come across the Holy Grail of the Arctic – an immense pan of flat ice. I wish we could have pans all the way to the Pole.

Day 31: Saturday, 4 April

Position: 85°50'37" North; 73°32'18" West
Temperature: −35°C
Windchill: −67°C
Hours of sunshine: 24 hours
Nautical miles covered yesterday: 12
Nautical miles covered so far: 165½
Nautical miles to go (*in a straight line*): 249½
Status: Everything okay

The drift continues to work to our advantage – a quarter of a mile north overnight – but unfortunately so does the storm, which is blowing twenty-five knots, which means a total white-out and −67°C windchill. We would usually camp and let it blow over, but we decide to have a go at walking for an hour. If it is too bad then we will camp up again. Rune is reluctant to go out because he is having trouble with his hands and feet. He does not seem to be able to get them to warm up. 'They are a long way under the comfort limit. They are iced down and I need a long time to heat them up,' he says. So we sit in the tent and listen to the wind while Rune attempts to warm his hands and dry out his gloves. While he is doing this he tells me that he is listening on his Walkman to 'Riders on the Storm' by The Doors – very appropriate.

We climb out of the tent, the thermarest nearly blows away when I am packing it, and it takes both of us to pack up the tent in the high winds. The walking conditions are horrible, but the skiing conditions are very good. The wind has taken the top layer of snow off the ice leaving a flat and hard surface that is ideal. However, a few leads have opened up which take time to cross, and we have to walk several extensive detours.

Rubble, rubble and more rubble – we are still waiting for the promised pans. In the course of the entire day we find only one pan that we could land a plane on. I am worried about the resupply. The weather is dreadful and the ice unsuitable. I hope we don't lose too much time or mileage on the next resupply because it will affect our next section, the most important of the three legs.

As I walk I reflect that it has been the little things that have made this year's expedition so much easier to bear. One of the best improvements this year has been one of the most fundamental: Rune has chosen a tent that, although smaller than last year's model, allows us to have a shit under cover. I was worried when I first saw it because Rune claimed disingenuously that he chose the tent solely for its looks. 'It looks very fashionable. I like the way the tent looks,' he says every evening after we put it up. 'I like my little house on the ice to look smart. I know you wanted a bigger tent, but I don't care. I wanted this one and you will come to see it is best.'

Although for the first couple of days I harboured misgivings that the tent was too small for our purposes, I have to concede now that Rune was right. Last year we waited until the last weeks of the expedition before we crapped in the tent; we would hold our business in for as long as we could before running outside to let it go. That was horrible, and it increased the risk of frostbite. It is often said that more explorers get frostbite on their bum cheeks or on their hands while wiping their backsides after going to the toilet than at any other time during an expedition. Our new tent has a large outer tent, where Rune can cook and where we can go to the toilet just before we take down the tent each morning. It has made a colossal difference to my toilet habits, and I am sure it is one of the many reasons this year's expedition has gone well so far.

Around midday I slip over and jar my back on solid ice. Pains shoot up my spine from my coccyx and straight away I think of the fall I had up here in 1983. This fall is not as bad, but in this rubble we twist ankles and wrists sometimes twice a day. I must concentrate the whole time.

I think of Claire, the kids and Claire's father all day. At the end of a day of misery the fact that we have covered nine miles to arrive at 85°59'20" North and 72°48'24" West lifts my grumpy spirits. At least we will be home sooner.

Day 32: Sunday, 5 April

Position: 85°59'25" North; 72°30'26" West
Temperature: −34°C
Windchill: −46°C
Hours of sunshine: 24 hours
Nautical miles covered yesterday: 9
Nautical miles covered so far: 174½
Nautical miles to go (*in a straight line*): 240½
Status: Everything okay

Another exhausting day. The north drift has abated and last night it was only a tenth of a mile in our favour. Still cold and windy, but Rune is out of the tent like he is off to catch a train. I sweat my socks off trying to keep up with him and have to unzip every vent on my jacket and trousers. There is a fine balance between letting out the sweat so that it does not freeze to me and stopping the cold getting in. Still a lot of rubble too, but I have the feeling there are pans ahead. Hopefully the end of the rubble is approaching. My feet are freezing cold today. I have cracks on the soles of my shoes – I wish it were diamonds.

For the first time I start to think of what it will be like to get to the Pole, but quickly put those dangerous thoughts to one side. There is still a long way to go and a lot of things can happen. For one, Rune's sledge is now well and truly broken and I hope it lasts until the resupply. Sledges obviously have to be very well built to survive a Marinejegerkommando. Secondly, my back is playing up and I am worried it may not last the rest of the trip. After the resupply we will be dragging heavier sledges, which will do my back no good. I am not looking forward to that.

I would kill for fish and chips with salt and vinegar. It is strange that as we lose weight and become weaker I do not want anything sweet; instead I crave savoury food. Hopefully the food will be a bit more varied after the resupply. For some reason all we seem to have at the moment is cod in sour cream and Arctic fish, a stew with tomatoes and meat. I am sick of both of them.

We camp at the end of a large pan and we're both exhausted. We are staying up too late, talking too much and not getting enough sleep. Doctor Rune takes a look at my frostbite. My second toe is clearing up, but my big toe is still very sore. It does not seem to want to clear up and we are running out of treatment ideas. There are many myths surrounding frostbite, the most dangerous of which have decimated armies in the past, so we don't want to do the wrong thing. Warmth, rest and care are the best cures; unfortunately we can afford none of these up here.

My troubles with my toe make me think of Baron Levy, who single-handedly helped the Russians defeat the French Army in 1812. As the French surgeon-general, Baron Levy told Napoleon's troops to rub snow into their frostbitten hands, believing it was best to keep the flesh frozen as the soldiers would freeze their hands while marching and then warm them over their campfires at night. But when flesh freezes, ice crystals form in the spaces between skin cells and the cells dehydrate; if the frozen flesh is warmed too quickly the cells burst and are destroyed, leaving permanent damage. Baron Levy's advice was essentially correct – it was best for the soldiers not to thaw their hands until they could do so slowly and when they were sure the skin would not freeze again – but rubbing snow into frostbite made the injuries worse, encouraging mild frostbite to become severe, deep frostbite and gangrene.

After Rune has applied more salve and a new bandage to my toes I take our position – 86°10'53" North and 72°08'10" West. We have walked eleven and a half miles, and with light sledges and relatively good ice conditions, I am not surprised.

Radio contact is a little fraught tonight. At 2100, the arranged time for our radio schedule, we discover that John has been trying to contact us for the last hour because the clocks went forward an hour in Canada last night and it is now 2200. Of course we did not know this, but decide to keep radio schedules at 2200 to give us extra walking time. Again the bulk of our radio transmission centres on the Charlie Oscar

Sierra Tango. Juggling days, distances, positions and prices for the resupply is giving me a headache and I tell John my concerns over cost are keeping me awake at night. But John has worse news. We want a resupply on Tuesday, or Wednesday at the latest, but he tells us the weather over the ice-cap and the unavailability of planes mean a resupply before next Friday is impossible. By then, I tell him, we will have run out of food.

Day 33: Monday, 6 April

Position: 86°11'00" North; 71°49'33" West
Temperature: −34°C
Windchill: −44°C
Hours of sunshine: 24 hours
Nautical miles covered yesterday: 11½
Nautical miles covered so far: 186
Nautical miles to go (*in a straight line*): 229
Status: Everything okay

A very busy day, full of surprises, strange coincidences and what Rune calls 'hazel'; in other words, hassle.

We lose an hour of sleep because Canada put its clocks forward on Saturday. Six hours is not enough for me so I am grumpy all day, but I am not the only one. Rune is just as grumpy because my sleep-talking keeps him awake. He is very quiet all day, saying he needs to concentrate on skiing. 'Sometimes I'm tired and don't say much. It takes energy out of me just to speak English, so sometimes I would rather not talk,' he says. Neither of us minds this. We have got used to each other and know when the other needs some space.

The first surprise happens about an hour before we are due to camp. Rune stops in front of me and points behind me. 'I looked round to see where you were,' he shouts, 'and instead of one black dot behind me I can see four.' Sure enough, a couple of minutes later the cavalry comes over the hill – it is the Norwegian Express led by Sjur Mørdre, coming over a pressure ridge. They have been following our tracks for the last couple of days and managed twenty miles today.

We set up camp, and after eating Rune and I crawl into the

Norwegian tent for some coffee, some brandy and a chat. It is then we realise the second surprise. Sjur points out that by the strangest of coincidences we have met on the day Robert Peary claimed to have reached the North Pole in 1909, the same date on which Fridtjof Nansen established the furthest point north in 1895. As if that were not enough, we are only a few miles further north than the point at which Nansen turned back. He was at 86°14' North, near Franz-Josef Land; we are at 86°20' North 71°35' West, almost at the same latitude but on the opposite side of the Pole.

It is wonderful to have some new company, especially as they are Norwegians, because Rune and I are striving to end the fierce polar rivalry between our two nations. We get on famously, swapping anecdotes and experiences, comparing notes on survival techniques and equipment, and basking in the shared excitement of a common goal. Much to my embarrassment all three Norwegians speak perfect English, whereas I, like most British people, know only a couple of words of their language. It is another example of our arrogance to go with our competitive, uncooperative approach to exploration, which contrasts poorly with these Norwegians who are only too eager to help out with advice, share their rations and impart their secrets on how they manage to keep the weight of their sledges so low.

Rune is beaming with pride after Sjur and his partners compliment him on his tracks through the rubble and snow.

'Now we will be in your tracks,' I reply, 'following your route north.'

'If you get up early,' Sjur says. 'We haven't had more than six hours' sleep for the last two weeks.'

I tell them I am very impressed, but add that I think they are mad. I cannot survive on six hours. Even Rune agrees.

'Six hours' sleep? That hurts. It's on the limit,' he says.

But Sjur, like Rune and the other Norwegians, seems to be made of something else. He has already walked to the North Pole once before in 1992, now he is back in this hell-hole trying to do it faster than anyone else and starting every morning at three a.m., a time I tell them I think is ball-breaking.

'Six hours' sleep, twelve hours' walking,' Sjur says. 'Then we get to the Pole in under thirty days. This is a horrible place to be; why spend any more time here than we have to?'

They are all extremely fit and do not appear overly exhausted,

The only way to tell us apart – Rune has cut a hole in his mask so that he can still smoke in -80°C windchill. (*all pics: Rune Gjeldnes*)

e-block rubble right outside our tent – the bane and curse of every polar explorer, especially when it the terrain we encounter as soon as we start walking in the morning.

Dinner. Chicken curry swimming in vegetable and soya oil. (*all pics: Rune Gjeldnes*)

My daughters' paintings on my skis; the only things I can see in a total white-out.

right March 10 1998. The temperature has fallen off the bottom of our thermometer, but it does not stop Rune from enjoying a post-dinner fag.

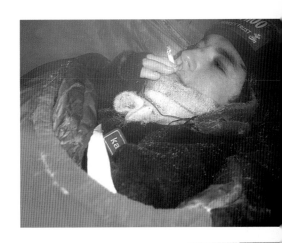

left Another day at the office – battling through rubble.

below Hauling my sledge across a pressure ridge. We crossed thousands on our journey to the North Pole.

White-out – no sky, no foreground, no definition.
Every step is taken with trepidation. (*Rune Gjeldnes*)

March 19 1998. Back to
loneliness – watching the
Twin Otter return to Reso[l]
Bay after the first resuppl[y]
(*all pics: Rune Gjeldnes*)

March 19 1998. Bliss just
after the first re-supply, t[h]
first time we have heated
the tent since setting-off
and a chance to dry our
ice-encrusted clothing.

March 28 1998. Attempti[n]
to find a route across the
mother of all leads. We
wasted two days walking
west on the previous lead[.]

above March 29 1998. After two days' walking we find a precarious route. I hate every step of the treacherous path across the spongy ice which sinks under my weight. (*all pics: Rune Gjeldnes*)

left March 30 1998. Exhausted, fed-up and depressed by a succession of mammoth leads. The lowest point on the expedition.

below Ideal conditions if we can keep our nerve. A recently frozen lead of ice pointing north like a flat, glacial motorway.

Crossing steel-ice on a recently frozen lead, considered ideal conditions even though it creaked and flexed beneath us. (*both pics: Rune Gjeldnes*)

Early March. With less than six hours of daylight, the sun barely rises above the horizon.

although each of them has spots of frostbite and two of their team of five have had to drop out, one with acute frostbite after falling into the water and the other with a muscle injury.

Sjur soon dashes my hopes of any let-up in the ice conditions. He tells me that in 1992 the rubble stretched all the way to the Pole and became far worse the further they walked. We all agree that the North Pole is the toughest challenge any of us has ever faced. I found on my South Pole expedition that although my sledge was twice as heavy as now, I covered a greater distance each day because the terrain was easier, there was no open water to circumnavigate, and because the weather was more dependable.

'It was the same in Greenland,' Sjur says. 'Heavier sledges, but longer distances. On one day we did fifty miles. Here we fight for every step. This is a very easy place to find excuses to go home.'

Strangely, we spend most of the rest of the evening marooned in this Arctic wasteland talking about the best pubs in London and where to get a good curry in Oslo, a discussion that prompts Rune to arrange a meeting with the Norwegians one day in a curry house in London.

After leaving the Norwegians – they need their sleep if they are planning to start skiing at three a.m. tomorrow – we get ready for the radio schedule with John Perrins. It is the last routine of the day, and we lie in our sleeping-bags, ready for bed and with a cup of hot juice each, waiting for John to radio in. It is still cold enough for us to have to cover the radio microphone with a plastic bag, and I have to pick ice off it every time I speak. The news from Resolute is not good:

John: British Typhoo, this is Typhoo Base. Come in. Over.
David: Can you hear us Typhoo Base? Over.
John: Yes, loud and clear. What is your latitude? Over.
David: Position eight six two zero. Over.
John: Eight six two zero. And what is your longitude? Over.
David: Seven one three five. Seven . . . one . . . three . . . five. Over.
John: Was that seven one three five? Over.
David: Seven-ah. One-ah. Three. Five. Over.
John: Seven one three five. Over.
David: Roger. Roger.
John: Go ahead with your temperature. Over.
David: Minus thirty-four. Minus thirty-four. Over.

John: Minus thirty-four. And your weather conditions? Over.

David: Good weather all day. Good weather all day. Sun is out at night now. Sun is out at night now. Good definition. Good definition. Low wind. Low wind. Three octares' blue sky. Three octares' blue sky. No ice crystals. No ice crystals. Over.

John: Received all that. Your weather does not look so good from here. Large low coming in. Low cloud. Low cloud. High winds. High winds. Not looking good for three days. Over.

David: Got that, John. How did it look for today? Over.

John: About right. Looking at your picture, you've now got winds coming over you from the west, from the west. Over.

David: Roger. So, what are you suggesting? Over.

John: The pilots are suggesting they cannot fly in a low cloud situation. The resupply will have to be Friday. Over.

David: Roger that. Do you want a sked in the morning? Over.

John: Tomorrow night. Over.

David: Roger that. We are running low on everything, John. Over.

John: Running low on what? Low on what? Over.

David: Out of food. Out of food. Over.

John: Roger. It looks like Friday is the earliest we can get to you because of flight availability and weather conditions. But we want to reassess it daily. Over.

David: Roger that. What about the cost? The cost? Over.

John: I am looking at it and will keep it down. Over.

David: Roger that. We will keep walking. Keep walking. Over.

John: Are you having a day of rest now? Over.

David: We will walk until Friday and have no food on Friday. Over.

John: Roger that. We will definitely be with you on Friday. Over.

David: We are living on pork scratchings and chicken noodle soup. Over.

John: Roger that. Pork scratchings and chicken noodle soup. I suggest you halve your daily rations. Over.

David: I want the cost split for eight six three zero. I think we will be at eight six five zero, but I want the cost of a flight for eight six three zero, without a fuel cache. Over.

John: I have got a shared flight to Eureka. Over.

David: Yes, but the price goes up substantially at eight six three zero. Keep the Charlie Oscar Sierra Tango down. Over.

John: Yes, I've got that in hand. It looks like two-zero-zero-zero-zero dollars. Over.

David: Roger that. Keep the cost down. Over.

John: Roger. When tomorrow night?

David: Two zero zero zero. Over.

John: I've got three radio schedules. Change to two one zero zero. Over.

David: Roger. Roger. Over.

John: Tell us how you feel. Over.

David: Surviving on half rations is making us weak. Spirits are high. We're ahead of schedule. Doing good mileage, above average. Still lots of rubble, pressure ridges and open water. Over.

John: Roger that.

David: Just get the costs down, John. Over.

John: I'm dealing with that. Over.

David: I can't sleep at night, John. I can't sleep at night. I'm worrying about the cost. Over.

John: How is Rune? Over.

David: He's fine. Hoping for some cherry pie very soon. Out of cigarettes and starting to bite his nails. Over.

The situation is not very good. The air company is telling John that low cloud is heading over the Pole tomorrow, but I do not believe it. I think they have got a problem with aeroplanes. A resupply on Friday means three days' walking, unfortunately, and we are running out of food. I know what it will be like back in Resolute because I have heard Morag Howell, the base manager at First Air, say before that explorers always say the weather is good when they are hungry and want a resupply, but air companies maintain the weather is not suitable for a flight if it does not fit in with their other business. I have also seen them change their minds almost immediately and take off into sup-posedly bad weather conditions.

This uncertainty is very disappointing, not least because I cannot understand how the air company can be so definite about Friday so early in the week. We are paying the air companies a lot of money, including three flights to the Pole at almost $50,000 each, and we booked in this resupply at least two weeks ago, so they have no reason for not having a plane available. They were desperate for our work, but now they've got it they are playing hard to get. I'm pleased John is there. He's a good man, and he's working for us. It's good to talk to him.

Our disappointment is slightly alleviated when we hear John trying to contact Girls on Top, a two-woman expedition of which I agreed to be the patron. Lucy Roberts and Victoria Riches are out on the ice near Resolute Bay, training for a North Pole attempt next year. John does not seem able to get hold of them on the scheduled radio contact. Eventually it is more than I can bear not to chip in with a joke:

David: Never trust a woman to be on time, John. Over.
John: Yes, thanks for that, David. Girls on Top, Girls on Top, this is Resolute Base, Resolute Base. Come in. Over.
David: They've got their battery plugged in the wrong hole. Over.
John: Thanks for that, David. Come again. Over.
David: They've got the battery stuck in the wrong hole. Over.
John: David, go away. Go away. Over.
David: You know what they say about Girls on Top. Over.
John: Yes, I know, David. Go away, David, I just want to speak to them. Over.

Rune and I are giggling like little children. After so long alone it is great to be able to have a laugh with other people, but it does not detract from our concerns about the resupply. The good thing, if there is such a thing, is that we have very lightweight sledges and we are making good progress every day. If the weather is good we can get close to 87°N, which means three days less food when we get the resupply, so our sledges will be a little bit lighter for the third leg. And tomorrow we can follow Sjur Mørdre's tracks and hopefully hit ten miles.

Day 34: Tuesday, 7 April

Position: 86°20'29" North; 71°27'09" West
Temperature: −34°C
Windchill: −48°C
Hours of sunshine: 24 hours

Nautical miles covered yesterday: 9
Nautical miles covered so far: 195½
Nautical miles to go (*in a straight line*): 219½
Status: Need resupply

We wake up at 3.30 a.m. to the sound of the Norwegians leaving. It is strange to hear noise from another tent after all this time alone. We say goodbye to them and wish them well. They have pared their weight down to the bare minimum and do not have a radio, so Sjur asks Rune to send his love to his family and to Lars, the member of their team who pulled out because of frostbite. We will be able to follow their tracks today which will give Rune a rest, although he is sceptical about how direct their route might be. The Norwegians do not have skins on their skis; it means they can ski faster with less effort because there is no friction, but they cannot grip on to ice rubble and will probably go around areas we would go straight through.

Once we get out on the ice, at about 10 a.m., we find it strange to see tracks disappear under rubble which must be just hours old. It is the first day we can take off our masks and we walk for eight hours. I find it much easier than previously, probably because Rune is going at a steadier pace. At one lead we use the sledge to cross the water, which is certainly novel. The lead is only partially frozen, so we cannot cross it. Rune's bright idea is to place one sledge across the water with its ends on the ice, and we then walk across it. It is like a tightrope walk and I expect to be flipped off, but it works. A good idea and very stable.

Rune is nearly out of tobacco so he is not smoking during the day. It must be very hard on him. Following Sjur's ski tracks feels very safe, but they are indeed taking an easier route than we would, going a long way east and then criss-crossing. I think Rune chooses a better route. Sjur's track costs us a mile in distance and we end up at 86°31'52" North and 71°11'35" West. Eleven and a half miles. I am disappointed it is not twelve, considering the light winds, hard ice and large pans we had today, but it is better than a kick in the arse.

In the evening Rune realises that it will be Easter at home next weekend and he tells me he is homesick. 'I miss the mountains,' he says. 'I have not been home for Easter for four years and I have problems remembering what that is like. It would have been nice to have the possibility of sending some Easter eggs to the children at home.'

When he is out on the ice leading the way in a blizzard or telling me his experiences as a special missions commando, entering submarines by their torpedo shoots or blowing up an enemy satellite station, it is difficult to remember that he is a real softie at heart. At the moment he is singing a song he is listening to on his Walkman. 'See You When You Get There' by Coolio, he says.

A good radio schedule with John Perrins and Robert Uhlig from the *Telegraph* tonight. Still no sign of a resupply. They have forty-knot winds in Resolute so it looks like Friday is the resupply. I am resigned to this, but Rune is quite put out about it.

Day 35: Wednesday, 8 April

Position: 86°32'05" North; 71°07'09" West
Temperature: −34°C
Windchill: −40°C
Hours of sunshine: 24 hours
Nautical miles covered yesterday: 11½
Nautical miles covered so far: 207
Nautical miles to go (*in a straight line*): 208
Status: Need resupply

Another perfect weather day with clear skies. We can really feel the warmth of the sun now and we vented out our jackets and trousers for the first time at −34°C. The frustrating thing is that according to the weathermen we should be in the midst of a low pressure zone, covered by heavy, low cloud. The air company guys in Resolute believe the Resolute weathermen before they believe us, yet I would not call in a resupply if I did not think it could land because I am the one who will have to pay for it. We have seven octares' blue sky, no wind and great definition, but no resupply. It's extremely frustrating.

Today is one of the hardest days. It is a beautiful day with a little snow, but our sledges are light. What is hard is that we are running on empty. We have had no breakfast, we don't have any chocolates to keep us going through the day – although we do have some juice – so we are running out of steam. It is hard work on the ice. The pans have ended and we are back into endless rubble, so we are lucky to manage eleven miles.

Then in the tent we have problems with the fuel and stove. Rune refuelled the stove this morning and for some reason it is leaking strongly. The fumes choke me and there are flames everywhere; we cannot get them to go out for some time. It shows what a knife edge we are on: if the stoves do not work we are up the creek very quickly.

Rune and I have settled into a routine and we're a good partnership. Our roles are quite definite: he cooks, I navigate; I put up the tent, he puts everything in it. Up to now, neither of us has had bad words for or thoughts about the other – a remarkable achievement, I think, as countless expeditions end with various team members not speaking to each other. We spend a lot of time larking around, telling jokes and shadow-boxing beside the tent in the morning to warm up, although we stopped the horse-play a couple of days ago when Rune accidentally clipped my knee. In the cold it really hurt, but there were no hard feelings.

I am still always thinking of ways to cut out weight yet remain within the safety boundaries. Simple things such as discarding a personal stereo and the inner sleeping-bags, cutting some of the pages out of a diary, or squeezing out half a tube of toothpaste, or 'teeth pasta' as Rune calls it – I thought he was referring to something he was going to cook – can make such a difference. Cutting weight bit by bit all adds up. By the time we reach the Pole, we should be super-light.

Otherwise, we just get into a groove and try not to think of the outside world too much. The more we think about home, the greater the pressure we feel. We never think of the media and both now feel that this year is different from the last. Last year dragged, this year we have had no time to think. At the moment, our only worry is that we are running low on food, and desperately need a resupply.

I'm thinking of home a lot, about taking the children to the cinema and all the simple things we take for granted. What should I buy Claire for her birthday and where should I take her for dinner? All the time spent skiing makes me feel very guilty. Why didn't I read the children an extra story at night, why didn't I take my wife away for a romantic weekend or say I loved her a couple more times? Each day I walk, I look down at my skis and see my girls' paintings of dinosaurs and flowers on them, and I just think each day is one day less. But as much as I hate this place, I am also addicted to it. The beauty is at times breathtaking and the hard work of survival is very satisfying. On Everest you hope your luck and health will hold out; the South Pole is cruel; but this place has its own magic. I'm also thinking of all the good people, all those people who have helped us get here. I hope we have enough souvenirs for them all.

I often think of Perry and Cook, who tried to get to the Pole. How they must have suffered only to get some stuffed shirt in London or New York saying anyone could do it, or that they failed because they were a few miles short. The one great thing about the Arctic ice is that it is a great leveller, it does not matter who or what you are. It is your skills, intelligence, experience and determination that decide whether you survive or not.

Rune keeps talking about the goodies – cherry pie, sandwiches, peanuts, orange juice, cakes and Irish stew – and how much he is looking forward to seeing Paul and Robert from the *Telegraph*. I just hope the plane comes in before Friday. By then we will have run out of food. We can survive for a few days on hot juice, but it will weaken us and we will lose valuable time. Until then, the long hard grind northwards continues.

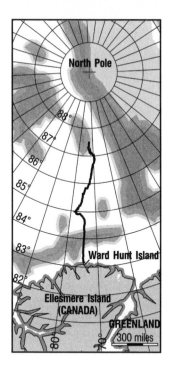

10

The Last Resupply

The Sixth Week

Day 36: Thursday, 9 April

Position: 86°42'59" North; 70°13'56" West
Temperature: −34°C
Windchill: −46°C
Hours of sunshine: 24 hours
Nautical miles covered yesterday: 11
Nautical miles covered so far: 218
Nautical miles to go (*in a straight line*): 197
Status: Everything okay

Last night we had perfect weather. It was a hard slog to the tent, and we camped at the end of a large pan that could serve as a runway. It turns out to be fortuitously good thinking when at 2105 we radio Morag Howell at First Air in Resolute to be told that the resupply aircraft is already on the way and will be with us in two and a half hours.

We are immediately propelled into a mad panic. First the stove will not work for some reason, probably because of condensation in the bottles. While Rune goes out to prepare the landing strip, I write letters furiously to everyone and try to fine Rune's GPS. In my agitation I cannot find it and I hurl some disgusting language in Rune's direction from 300 metres away. I had forgotten that sound travels a long way on the ice, but he is not offended. Eventually we find the GPS, not in his sleeping-bag where it would normally be, but outside in his blue bag.

At 2340 we spot the plane approaching. It is a stunningly beautiful night, like a midsummer's day except that the temperature is −34°C. The sky is blue, the air is still and the midnight sun is shining brightly in the north, throwing long golden shadows across the ice. So much for the weather being too bad for a landing – the visibility is perfect and there are no ice crystals in the air. The Twin Otter circles about a hundred feet above us for several minutes and then comes in and lands first time with an almighty thump. Behind the controls is Russ Bomberry, a Red Indian chief who is nicknamed 'The Cloudsplitter' by other pilots for his incredible ability to find a spot on which to land. His colleagues say the clouds simply part when he turns up.

The doors of the plane open and Robert and Paul from the *Telegraph* tumble out, followed by Nigel and Charles from the BBC and John Perrins. We had not expected the BBC to be on the resupply and we are very pleased to see them. We all hug one another, although I can tell they are holding their breaths. We must stink like sewer rats. If falling through the water and the big lead were the low points of the trip so far, today is certainly the high point. After thirty-five days alone on the ice, it is wonderful to see some friends from civilisation again. The time they are on the ground flashes by as we exchange the tent, Rune's sledge and our sleeping-bags, and take on more fuel and food for twenty-five days.

A requested treat of two cheese sandwiches, a cherry pie and some whisky is immediately carried to the tent for a long-awaited feast as soon as the resupply aircraft leaves to head back to Resolute. Rune accuses John of not supplying enough toilet paper, but John maintains he has brought the amount that was asked for. 'Oh, we will manage. We will use it twice,' Rune answers, much to my amazement. I later realise he means we will use half rations each time we go to the toilet, rather than using the same piece of toilet paper two times.

We exchange news and gossip, and John tells me that Amelia has had her operation on the lump in her throat and everything passed without incident. It is great for my peace of mind and I am very relieved that the biopsy found nothing serious. John says that the resupply flight was not confirmed until the very last minute. First Air had wanted to fly on Friday but Morag changed her mind this afternoon when a storm approached Resolute. The fourteen-seater Twin Otter ski-plane took off in gale-force winds to beat the approaching blizzard and high winds, and they did not know at the time whether it would be able to land on the ice. They have flown for eight hours to reach us, using an astro-compass to locate our position because conventional compasses do not work at this latitude.

After less than an hour on the ice, our five visitors cram back into the plane and once again we are alone, but not before the Twin Otter makes a very uncertain take-off into the early-morning sky. For some reason, The Cloudsplitter does not use the full length of the runway on his first attempt and has to abort the take-off. He pulls the plane round amid a dense fog of snow and ice crystals thrown up by the plane's propellers. He then taxis across the bumpy snow and ice to the far end of the pan of ice and waits for several minutes for the clouds of snow that are now filling the air to settle. Russ then makes a second attempt to take off. He needs at least 1200 feet to take off from perfect, flat ice, but on the bumpy ice and heavy snow of our airstrip 1600 feet is the minimum take-off distance. Rune and I watch with our hearts in our mouths as the Twin Otter accelerates towards a pressure ridge and an area of heavy rubble. At the last moment its nose lifts into the air and the plane rises only ten or fifteen feet before dipping down over the other side of the pressure ridge, levelling off, gathering more speed and then rising into the air. It is a very close thing; from where we are standing it looks as if they missed the pressure ridge by only a couple of feet. Hopefully the next time we see them we will be at the top of the world.

We retire to our new clean tent and once again it is party time. We unpack our supplies to find we are swimming in brandy, whisky, cigars and other goodies. Everybody, including the two Girls on Top, has put in something special as a treat. First we gorge ourselves on the cheese sandwiches, cherry pie and fresh fruit, then we explore the packages like small children at Christmas, whooping and shouting when we find some new surprise. There are Easter cards from my daughters, four chocolate eggs, letters from our families and some photographs of the Spice Girls, the result of a long-standing joke with Robert and Paul. Rune lights up a massive cigar and delights in finding a story in the *Telegraph* about a doctor who claims his research proves passive smoking is actually good for you. All my weeks of moaning that Rune is killing me have been in vain; now he can puff away with impunity. 'I am doing you a favour, David,' he says, dragging on his cigar.

The party goes on until four a.m. For three hours Rune does not stop eating. He quite literally stuffs himself with food, devouring four chocolate Easter eggs in a matter of minutes and having to disappear outside four times to go to the toilet because his digestive system is not used to anything more sophisticated than dehydrated food swamped in vegetable and soya oils. The tent is silent as Rune chomps and we both drink and read the letters and news from home. It is a great moment, and there is nothing we could want for.

For a few hours we forget the severe back pains, frostbite, blisters, aching shoulders, exhaustion and frustrations. Tomorrow we will have to face the Arctic again, dosed up to our eyeballs on some of the 300 pain-killers John has sent us, and continue toiling northwards. Ahead of us is the final and most critical leg of our 600-mile trek. As the thaw progresses, speed is of the essence. We also have to cross the Lomonosov Ridge, where the currents will be fiercer than on any part of the journey. The only way we can cope with the uncertainty and our high expectations is to take each day as it comes.

We take the rest of Thursday as a rest day. We are both tired after waiting up half the night for the resupply and then partying until the early hours, and we need to gather our strength before setting off once again with heavy sledges. In some respects it's harder than last year because of the resupplies. With all the new food and equipment, we are now no lighter than we were when we set out from Ward Hunt Island thirty-six days ago.

Day 37: Friday, 10 April

Position: 86°43'05" North; 70°04'00" West
Temperature: −32°C
Windchill: −40°C
Hours of sunshine: 24 hours
Nautical miles covered yesterday: 0
Nautical miles covered so far: 218
Nautical miles to go (*in a straight line*): 197
Status: Everything okay

I don't want to get out of the tent this morning after our decadent and relaxed rest day. Outside it is snowing and there is a total white-out. Under no circumstances could we have had a resupply today, as the weathermen and Morag had led us to believe. It makes me furious just to think they would not take our weather forecasts seriously.

Rune is having trouble with his eyes. I wake up to him groaning in his sleeping-bag. 'I am almost blind, David,' he says. 'I have double vision and it looks as if I am peering through fog or mist.' My first reaction is that he has snow blindness and I tell him he has to wear his goggles all day. Snow blindness tends to affect the old hat sooner than the novice. Rune has had it before and the eyes of anyone who has suffered it once are more easily affected the next time. Fortunately it is a temporary condition and seldom lasts more than a couple of days, but while it does last it is incapacitating and exceedingly painful. Some say it is worse than the fiercest toothache. 'I don't know if it is snow blindness. There is no pain and the eyes aren't red,' he explains. 'This is a bad thing. It started last night with tears in my eyes and they were burning a lot.' I suggest solutions and remedies, but Rune does not appear to want to take them. 'The pain and double vision is not the worst part of it,' he says. 'The worst is that you are nagging me and giving me a lot of advice on how to get rid of it.'

Fortunately we can follow Sjur's tracks out on the ice, which takes the pressure off Rune. We follow the tracks to the Norwegians' campsite to find that they have dumped one sledge, and we calculate they must have walked for about fourteen hours. Unbelievable. However, their tracks seem to be off course by about 30 per cent and we cannot understand why they do not correct it. They waste some of their hard work and long hours by inefficient navigation. Fortunately they always take the easy route, which helps us with our newly heavy sledges. I am carrying about 16lb in my rucksack and Rune has around 25lb on his back. It will take some getting used to, and it is too early to tell if it is a better method than dragging all the weight on the sledge.

There is a lot of break-up as a result of the full Moon last night. It kept me awake for a couple of hours, listening to the ice floes groaning, grinding and crashing into one another, never knowing if the ice would open up beneath our tent. We are relatively lucky with the leads. No enormous detours, but one lead takes us a mile off course. Considering the white-out and our heavy sledges, and that it is the first day's walking since the resupply, it is a great achievement to do nine miles to 86°52'10" North and 69°04'17" West.

It is Good Friday at home and Rune talks all day of what his parents and family will be doing. 'I am sure they are out on skis,' he says. 'I hope they have good weather and good snow.'

In the evening we have a good radio schedule with John and Robert. They pass on some international news: the Irish Peace Agreement has been signed, George Michael has been caught performing a lewd act in a public toilet in Los Angeles, and Robin Cook got married. Big deal. At the end of the broadcast, Robert adds that it has been announced in Britain that I have been awarded an honorary doctorate by Leicester University. I am obviously very honoured and privileged, but it gives Rune a rich seam of teasing to pick at, particularly as he knows I cannot spell.

Day 38: Saturday, 11 April

Position: 86°52'24" North; 69°05'23" West
Temperature: −37°C
Windchill: −49°C
Hours of sunshine: 24 hours
Nautical miles covered yesterday: 9
Nautical miles covered so far: 227½
Nautical miles to go (*in a straight line*): 187½
Status: Everything okay

We wake up to discover that we have gained a quarter of a mile in drift overnight. With any luck we should reach 87° North today.

I manage to get Rune moving early by tempting him out for an early shit. Once he is up, he is not easy to cajole into swift movement. His eyes seem to be improving, which is one less worry, and he now believes the double vision was brought on by eating too much sugar and chocolate after the resupply. Silly boy.

We follow the Norwegian tracks again, which look like a motorway in parts but veer off course by up to thirty degrees. After an hour and a half we come to our first open lead, which stretches east to west. The tracks show us that Sjur has crossed it, but we decide to go round the water. We head a long way west to a crossing-point where Rune nearly falls in when his sledge slips off some floating rubble into the water. We then head back east to pick up the tracks but come across a second lead, pointing north–south. We are boxed in and there is nothing for it but to head south to find a crossing-point. It is very frustrating and we waste over three hours circumnavigating the two leads.

Eventually we pick up Sjur's tracks, but Rune then veers off north-wards, believing his navigation to be better than the Norwegian Express, and turns up the heat. I am sweating like a pig, trying to keep up. The rucksack makes me sweat all the more, especially as the straps restrict my chest movement, and it is a flat-out sprint across some large ice pans for the last couple of hours.

Late in the afternoon, as we are racing across the open pans, I spot a brown-red splodge of colour on the snow. At first I do not think anything of it, but when I see a second and a third splash of colour, especially after weeks of pure white snow, I am worried, not least because it looks as if Rune might have a digestive problem. We have both been feeling ill at times, and now I fear that Rune has food poisoning or worse, and is bleeding heavily without knowing it. I race to try to catch up with Rune, but find it impossible to draw level. I am drained by the time we come to a stop and the wind is now blowing twenty knots, freezing all my sweat to my thermals and windproof clothing. I mention the mysterious splodges to Rune, but he assures me he is not ill and tells me he does not know the cause. Eventually it dawns upon us: Rune had his chewing-tobacco stock replenished at the resupply, and the splodges are his tobacco-tainted spit.

It takes a long time to pitch camp and brush off our iced-down clothing. Shortly before camping we spot some polar bear footprints, which worries us, particularly as there is little for a bear to eat up here.

Like me, Rune is complaining of exceptionally sore elbows and shoulders. We are using our arms extensively to push our way through rubble, and they do not get a chance to rest and heal at night because we lie in our sleeping-bags with them compressed against our chests. We need time to rest and stretch out our arms. Mine ache all day and I now wish I had spent more time building up shoulder and elbow strength when I was training. Rune says we should have brought stronger pain-killers with us; he nagged me about it in England, and now I am inclined to think he was right.

Amazingly, we have covered nearly nine miles in eight and a half hours and we are a mile beyond 87° at 87°01'05" North and 69°33'31" West. Our only worry is that we are a long way east of our target route. We have to add ninety minutes to any solar navigation calculations – maybe that is what is throwing the Norwegians off course. I am sure we would have done twelve miles if it had not been for the leads, but we can be proud of our work today and we celebrate with some brandy, a cigar for Rune and some of the goodies from the resupply.

Day 39: Sunday, 12 April

Position: 87°00'53" North; 69°57'16" West
Temperature: −34°C
Windchill: −52°C
Hours of sunshine: 24 hours
Nautical miles covered yesterday: 8¾
Nautical miles covered so far: 235¾
Nautical miles to go (*in a straight line*): 179¼
Status: Everything okay

It is Easter Sunday and once again for both of us it is a wrench being away from home. All our thoughts are with our families. It is at times like these – birthdays, anniversaries and family holidays – that the homesickness is most acute. I must strive to be at home for more of them next year. 'My mama and papa will be out skiing on the fjord right now,' Rune says. 'I would like to be there, but I have something else to do.'

We are two and a third miles behind schedule and wake up an hour late. It is the first time we have overslept on the trip, and we cannot understand why. Outside it is a beautiful day, there is not a cloud in the sky, and we have high hopes of a good mileage today.

Almost immediately things go wrong. First the wind picks up and it becomes much colder, then the bindings on my skis, which were mounted in the wrong place, begin to work themselves loose. Whoever fitted the bindings to the skis did not use enough glue, or the glue resin is losing its adhesion in the cold. Every time I stop I have to take off the ski and tighten the screw. It is a tedious business.

We come to our first open lead after only half an hour and walk west until we find a crossing place. Unfortunately it is not a straightforward crossing. Instead of one simple route across we have to negotiate several stretches of open water and leap from one rubble island to another, using them like giant stepping-stones. I am about two thirds of the way across with another fifteen feet to go when Rune starts to drift away from me on an island of rubble that is only nine or ten square feet in area. The danger becomes more acute when the rubble island I am standing on starts to sink. I am very scared, even more than when I fell in the water as I am out of Rune's reach and it will be very difficult for him to rescue me from his island of equally precarious ice. I make a jump for Rune's floe and get my foot wet, but he pulls me to safety. We then cross some porridgy steel-ice to the far side of the lead. I am mightily relieved not to have fallen in.

Within half a mile we come to another lead, so this time we walk west to find a crossing-point. We cross the lead and head east, only to meet another lead after one mile. We then turn south, find a crossing and head northwards again, but within a couple of hundred metres there is yet another lead. These leads are sending us on a wild goose chase. There seems little hope of making any headway northwards. We are walking at sea level and cannot see more than about a quarter of a mile ahead, so it is very difficult to see where the leads lie. I reckon we must have crossed around 500 of them so far.

To make matters worse, we both feel ill. I am swallowing pain-killers like smarties to cope with my back pain and Rune's navigation is off today. He does not know whether it is the compass that is playing up or his solar navigation, but we will have to sort it out tonight.

By the time we pitch camp we are two miles behind schedule and have managed only six miles to 87°06'40" North and 71°00'25" West. It is a shame as I had hoped we could do as well as yesterday, but luck was against us today. Maybe we shouldn't have been walking on Easter Sunday. Rune agrees with me and rustles up a special Easter dinner of lobster paté, sent to us on the resupply by Thierry, and an Easter egg for pudding.

We have a radio schedule with John who tells us that the Girls on Top are having problems after they lost their tent in high winds, and they need to be rescued. All round a terribly depressing day.

Day 40: Monday, 13 April

Position: 87°05'23" North; 71°30'00" West
Temperature: −38°C
Windchill: −73°C
Hours of sunshine: 24 hours
Nautical miles covered yesterday: 6
Nautical miles covered so far: 240½
Nautical miles to go (*in a straight line*): 174½
Status: Everything okay

Another aggravating day. The wind has changed direction and by morning we have drifted back one and a quarter miles, a record so far. Unfortunately, we soon realise that this is the high point of our day when our luck deteriorates once we get out on to the ice.

We are six miles off schedule and desperately need to start notching up some good daily mileages or we will never get to the Pole. We are greeted this morning by a beautiful clear sky, but it is accompanied by twenty-five-knot winds from the north which knock the windchill down to beyond −70°C and push the ice southwards. This back-drift is extremely disheartening and I have started to panic about running out of time.

We camped near a lead last night, hoping that it would freeze overnight so that we could cross it without a deviation. Our mood is low and we were fed up in the tent last night. We are now sleeping only seven hours a night, from eleven until six. We need eight hours to function properly. Although Rune is very religious, I am not, but I have started to pray every morning and evening. I pray for good ice, clear weather and no wind. Please God, stop this wind.

The day starts off well, but very soon the going becomes exceedingly hard. All day we have rubble and leads, many of which buckle under my weight as I cross them. The fact that every step I take could be my last is emphasised when one of the leads cracks open after I have crossed it, but while my sledge is still on the thin ice. We cross dozens of leads, then in the last three hours the terrain starts to open up. We are on old, multi-year ice with humps but little or no rubble. I stumble at least four times, at one point nearly breaking my wrist when I fall straight on to my face, slamming my wrist against some thin ice on a recently frozen lead that is a long step down from an ice floe. Rune comes rushing over to me while I am writhing about on the ground, but I do not get the sympathy I expect.

'Get up, David. Stop lying on the ground,' Rune says in no uncertain terms. 'Get up and get a move on now.' I am in agony, and at least expect a helping hand, but instead Rune shouts more urgently at me. 'David! Get a fucking move on.' It is the only time I have heard Rune swear directly at me. Although he has picked up the worst of my profanities, they are only ever directed at inanimate objects in moments of intense frustration. Sensing his urgency, I ignore the searing pain in my wrist and scarper ten feet across the lead towards him.

As I run, the ice screeches and grinds beneath me, and a crack splinters at my feet. My fall has triggered a fault in the ice-sheet and the floe begins to break apart. 'Come on, David. We cannot stop,' Rune says. Wincing with agony as a stabbing pain shoots through my wrist, I ski behind Rune for five minutes until we are clear of the fissure. It is a narrow escape and for once, I think, my luck holds out. 'It was thin ice – definitely the wrong place to fall down,' Rune says to me after checking my wrist.

But it is not the end of my spell of bad luck today. Later, while climbing through rubble, I slip again and my sledge, balanced at the top of an ice boulder, slams into the small of my back. I scream out in agony and swear for five minutes at the sledge. I already have back trouble; now it hurts at the base, middle and top of my spine.

Eight and a half hours after setting off we come to a stop and have difficulties putting up the tent in the winds. The weather has worsened almost to a white-out and the wind is blowing at least twenty-five knots. I was expecting a good nine or ten miles; instead I am shocked to find we have covered only six and a half to 87°12'01" North and 72°01'38" West. The difference has been lost to back-drift while we were walking. I pray for better weather and less wind tomorrow.

Day 41: Tuesday, 14 April

Position: 87°09'55" North; 72°32'20" West
Temperature: −34°C
Windchill: −49°C
Hours of sunshine: 24 hours
Nautical miles covered yesterday: 6½
Nautical miles covered so far: 245
Nautical miles to go (*in a straight line*): 170
Status: Everything okay

Another bad night's sleep for both of us. We stayed up late using glue and Peperami wrappers to secure the bindings on my skis. We will repair Rune's skis tonight.

Again we are penalised by a disastrous back-drift overnight, over two miles to the south and half a degree west. This is getting ridiculous, but we both suspect it will get worse as we cross the Lomonosov Ridge and approach the Pole. Most of the ice we have walked over so far has been floating on remarkably deep waters. Although the smallest of the major oceans, the Arctic Ocean has a complex seabed and very hazardous currents, primarily because it is a small ocean almost totally landlocked with a narrow deep-water channel near Greenland, whereas other oceans are generally huge areas of water surrounding large land masses.

The Canada Abyssal Plain is over 9000 feet deep and stretches from the coasts of Canada and Alaska almost to the Pole. It is intersected by a relatively small submarine mountain range, the Alpha Ridge, and the Marvin Ridge before the Lomonosov Ridge which, like an underwater Andes or Alps, dominates the relief of the Arctic basin, rising almost 4000 feet from the Abyssal Plain. On the other side of the Lomonosov

Ridge, the seabed plummets into an elongated trough of deep water called the Pole Abyssal Plain, almost directly beneath the North Pole and at around 15,000 feet the deepest point of the ocean.

There are two surface water circulation systems, a clockwise gyre on the Canadian side of the Lomonosov Ridge and a straightforward flow from East Siberia, across the Pole and along the Lomonosov Ridge towards the east coast of Greenland and the Greenland Sea. The Lomonosov Ridge is the most prominent influence on all water movements in the ocean and we are about to cross it. The gyre washes against one side of the ridge and over it to collide with the flow from the Chukchi Sea to the Greenland Sea. As can be imagined, the currents can be colossal and consequently the ice movement is immense in this area. Two and a tenth miles' back-drift is a record so far, but I am certain we will have to battle against even stronger drifts the closer we get to the peaks of the Lomonosov Ridge. This will be our biggest challenge yet.

The day starts in comic fashion. Rune is heating the water in the outer tent, but does not realise the flame has gone out on the stove because he is listening to his Walkman and cannot hear the hiss of escaping naphtha. After a while he notices the smell, but he cannot find a match to reignite the flame. A frantic search begins, in the course of which Rune discovers a pack of pork scratchings. 'Ah, I have been looking for these all last night,' he says to me, and breaks the pack open. By now I am getting quite worried. I remind him that he was looking for some matches. 'Oh yes, you're right. I had forgotten,' he says with a grin on his face. About half a minute later he at last finds a box of matches and attempts to light the stove. There is an almighty whoosh and a flash of flame. 'Hulashaker,' is all I hear from Rune as he emerges from a cloud of black smoke. The stove is lit but we are very lucky to escape without a tent fire.

After his escapade with the stove and a spot of breakfast, Rune does not want to move. For the last couple of days he has seemed very unmotivated, but I persuade him to get going. 'At least we could see something yesterday. Now it is down to zero visibility at times,' he says. Outside it is blowing twenty-five to thirty knots from the north. It will be hardest for Rune because the wind and snow will blow straight into his face. 'I am feeling confident and comfortable with what we have done so far. I don't want to go out,' he adds.

We would both rather stay in the tent. It should be a rest day or a storm day, but with the back-drift we are experiencing I am worried that if we stop now we will soon end up back at Ward Hunt Island. After much discussion and cajoling by me we emerge from the tent into a pea-soup white-out. So much snow has been blown around overnight that we have to dig out the tent.

The recent high tide, the ridge and the wind are conspiring to make it almost impossible for us to make any headway against the drift, and our cause is not made any easier by our navigation problems. We cannot see the sun in the white-out and the compass is playing up. The needle is very sluggish and is dragging against the bottom of the scale. Sometimes our ski poles affect the compass, so I spend much of the day helping Rune by letting him ski away from all our equipment to get a clear reading.

Although the wind is tiresome it has not opened up as many leads as we feared at the beginning of the day, and we have some great pans and a nice frozen lead going north. We have walked over eleven miles, but progress by just under nine miles to 87°18'48" North and 73°23'40" West because of the back-drift. Not bad considering the white-out, our heavy sledges and the currents, but motivation is becoming a problem in this relentless wind and our moods swing from joy to despair all through the day.

Day 42: Wednesday, 15 April

Position: 87°18'58" North; 73°06'31" West
Temperature: −36°C
Windchill: −49°C
Hours of sunshine: 24 hours
Nautical miles covered yesterday: 9
Nautical miles covered so far: 254
Nautical miles to go (*in a straight line*): 161
Status: Everything okay

Another strange day. First the wind starts to calm and, after all the back-drift, now we get a little north drift. I do not understand why it changes so quickly and I am amazed at how powerful the wind can be sometimes. The wind and Moon seem to exert a greater influence on moving the ice around than the currents.

Against my expectations there are blue skies and the sun is out. It is really hot in the tent and we both feel sleepy. I manage to get Rune up and we set off on time, our moods considerably improved by the good weather. However, we are both exhausted by the constant worrying about the weather, the back-drift and how many more days we will last. We also need more sleep – seven hours a night is not enough.

We increase the first session to one and three-quarter hours. It's going well – two large pans in succession – and then we hit rubble and pick up Sjur's tracks. I think at the outset that it will take us ages to get through the rubble, but Rune does well. Nevertheless, some of the rubble is back-breaking. We need two sets of hands for each sledge. I climb to the top of a ten-foot-high ridge of rubble, then Rune helps lift first my sledge then his up a sheer cliff of ice; across the top, down the other side, through an ice gully – again both of us squeezing and shoving each sledge – then up another sheer ice face, this time sixteen feet high. It takes us forty-five minutes to advance just twenty yards.

We head north all day and it seems wonderfully warm. I vent out all my zips and it is the first day my goggles ice down because of the heat. We slow down on the fourth session. My backpack is killing my left arm and shoulder, so I put the pack on my sledge. The backpack is an improvement as it takes the weight out of my sledge, but I am now looking forward to the point at which it might be worth dumping it. For the moment, it makes a big difference to the friction on the sledge.

Rune, who looks quite frightening now that he has stripped off to headband, sunglasses and no face mask, catches some frostbite on his ear during the last hour on the ice. He left the lobe on his left ear uncovered and the wind picked up. 'I stopped to take off my hat and put on other clothing, but I couldn't feel my ear or that I had gripped it,' he says. 'I was wondering what I had got between my fingers. It felt like rubber, but it was my ear.'

We discover we have set a new record by a whisker: 12.05 miles with heavy sledges. Mine is the heaviest I have pulled since leaving Ward Hunt. If everything continues as planned we should be at the Pole within twelve or thirteen days, but, as always, we need to be lucky, and somehow I do not believe our luck can hold that long. Each day is so different. Give me the brandy.

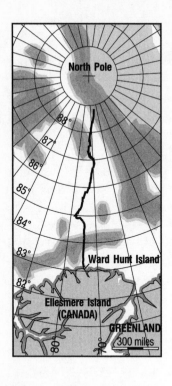

11

Stepping It Up

The Seventh Week

Day 43: Thursday, 16 April

Position: 87°31'05" North; 71°33'00" West
Temperature: −36°C
Windchill: −44°C
Hours of sunshine: 24 hours
Nautical miles covered yesterday: 12
Nautical miles covered so far: 266
Nautical miles to go (*in a straight line*): 149
Status: Everything okay

A great day. At long last the wind has dropped. The temperature has not risen much, but with less wind it feels a lot warmer and there is less back-drift – in fact none at all, except for eighteen minutes' drift east.

I make a big mistake at the beginning of the day. The sky is totally clear, eight octares' blue, so I put some sun-cream on my face. Although it is not as large as the ozone hole over Antarctica, we can certainly feel the effect of the hole above the Arctic and it is important to protect ourselves. However, within a minute of applying the cream to my face I can feel my skin tightening and freezing. The cream contains water, which is turning to ice in the pores of my face. Frightened of frostbite, I rub my skin like fury to keep it warm and prevent the cream from freezing. I manage to remove most of the cream with a cloth and I then cover my face to keep it warm. It is yet another salutary warning that we cannot afford to overlook any eventuality.

Rune is in a very happy mood, humming and singing as we pack up camp. By contrast I am displaying the usual grumpy demeanour I present to the world for the first couple of hours each day, and I cannot help remarking to my Norwegian friend that he is a bundle of fun.

'I am what?' he replies.

'You're a bundle of fun,' I repeat.

'What do you mean, I am a bundle?' Rune asks, and once again my struggles to explain what is to me a perfectly familiar English figure of speech begin.

'Er, bundle of fun. Well, you know what fun is. You know what a bundle is?'

'Erm...'

'Well, if you make a bundle you get a load of things and you tie them all together,' I say.

'Okay.'

'Like you make bundles of straw.'

'Okay.'

'Or you make bundles of ... sticks, for example.'

'Yes, but when are you using it?' Rune demands.

'Well, if you're a bundle of – well, you say, "Go and tie up a bundle of sticks." That's what they used to say on farms,' I say, struggling to describe how something as intangible as fun might be bundled up like a sheaf of corn. 'Or, ahm, you say here's a bundle of papers when you're giving somebody a whole load of papers. So it's something which is big and tied up.'

By the look on Rune's face I can tell I am not making much sense.

'So if you're a bundle of fun then you're a big thing of fun,' I say. 'Basically, it's an affectionate way of saying you're a fun person, you are full of fun.'

By now Rune is even more confused. 'So why do you say it?'

'Well, you can use it sarcastically; if somebody is not much fun you say, "You're a real bundle of fun today." Or if somebody *is* a bundle of fun but you are feeling bad-tempered yourself, then you might say it, again in a slightly sarcastic way to suggest that you are not having as much fun as the other person.'

Rune looks at me with a very bemused expression on his face. 'I will never understand some of these English sayings, but one thing I know is that it is not my fault that I try to be optimistic when you are always pessimistic.'

I regret having ever opened my mouth.

Before we set off, we decide to change the length of each session. Instead of walking an hour and forty-five minutes before the first rest, followed by several ninety-minute sessions, we change to one hour and twenty minutes for all the sessions. It means we have an extra break in the course of the day, but it seems more manageable. Yesterday I was really struggling towards the end of the day. It is a good case in time and motion study, and it gives me encouragement about increasing our working hours to nine and a half after the next rest day.

For the first time since we set out from Ward Hunt Island, we stop for a more substantial lunch than chocolate and hot juice. We have lost a lot of weight – neither of us has ever been this thin – and we chew on a couple of muesli and vegetable oil chunks. The lunch certainly peps us both up, but we find it gives us wind all afternoon. However, flatulence, we decide, is a small price to pay for the extra calories and I am convinced the lunch helps to keep me going faster for longer.

The terrain is fairly good; no huge pans, but several pans with old ice interspersed with a few rubble fields and some big ice sculptures. I find that slipping my rucksack off my shoulders so that most of the weight is held on my waist makes the load on my back seem less and reduces the friction on my shoulders.

We are surprised in the afternoon to cross Sjur's tracks. By now I would have expected him to have advanced much further north.

Surely, we think, he should already be at the Pole, and his tracks should have disappeared or be very faint by now.

'I think Sjur is not as far ahead as we supposed,' Rune says, 'or maybe we are moving faster than we thought we would in this terrain.'

Certainly by the end of the day it seems as if all our hard graft and the new work regime has paid off. We register our best mileage yet, nearly thirteen miles northwards to 87°43'55" North and 72°25'39" West in just under eight hours. We are extremely delighted.

At 2200, John Perrins explains the mystery of the fresh ski tracks to us during a radio schedule. He tells us that Sjur and the Norwegian Express have abandoned their attempt fourteen miles ahead of us and hope to be picked up at the weekend. They have set off the emergency code on their Argos satellite beacon, asking for a pick-up. Nobody yet knows why they have quit, but John Perrins says that Norwegian newspapers are reporting that the Norwegian Express has stopped at a lead of open water ten miles wide and two miles across. If the reports are correct, then our chances of reaching the Pole are very slim. A stretch of open water that wide will not freeze over now that the sun is up twenty-four hours a day. The rumour has apparently been confirmed by a pilot who flew over the Pole recently and reported that the ice is more broken up this year than he can remember.

It is not good news. I am very dejected, but Rune reminds me that the Norwegian Express does not have a radio so it is difficult to work out how anybody could conclude that it has stopped because of open water. As ever, it is best to ignore any reports from the outside world. Up here we have to take each day as it comes and react to the conditions as and when we encounter them.

Nevertheless, I am worried that wide expanses of open water will slow us down considerably and force us to have another resupply. That will be horribly expensive.

Day 44: Friday, 17 April

Position: 87°44'09" North; 72°04'08" West
Temperature: −34°C
Windchill: −49°C
Hours of sunshine: 24 hours

Nautical miles covered yesterday: 13
Nautical miles covered so far: 284¾
Nautical miles to go (*in a straight line*): 135¾
Status: Everything okay

A hard day. My back is getting worse, I am in a lot of pain and I am retching terribly, I suspect because of all the pain-killers I am taking. I ate some breakfast, but probably not enough, and Ibuprofen can really upset an empty stomach. I am on my knees half-way through breakfast, doubled over and regurgitating the scraps that are in my stomach.

After breakfast I tell Rune that Paul and Robert should be back from Yellowknife now. They went there to see the northern lights. It prompts another Rune-ism.

'Oh, Yellowknife, the Billy Butlin of the north,' he says.

'The Billy Butlin? Are you sure that is what you mean?' I ask.

'Yes, of course. The Billy Butlin of the north,' Rune repeats.

'I didn't know you knew about Butlin's in Norway,' I say.

'Of course we know about Butlin's. And we use it in the same way.'

By now I am totally confused. Billy Butlin of the north? Yellowknife is hardly a holiday camp. What can he mean? I explain to Rune who Billy Butlin was and then he realises his malapropism, sparked by a documentary on Billy Butlin that he saw on television shortly before leaving England.

'I mean this,' Rune says, pointing at his stomach.

'That's your bellybutton, not Billy Butlin,' I say.

'Yes, Yellowknife, the bellybutton of the north,' Rune says. 'It means it is nothing special.'

That settled, we get going. I am on the maximum dose of pain-killers and have to stop frequently to be sick in the snow. Leaving pools of vomit on our trail northwards is not a pleasant business, and my empty stomach makes me weak. The pain-killers work, but it is an abhorrent business, particularly as Rune continues skiing, oblivious to much of it. Without the pain-killers, my back, thighs and toes hurt too much for me to be able to make much of an effort. We want and need to start notching up large distances now, and I have resigned myself to the fact that I will have to use anything to help us maintain our daily target distances.

Fortunately, the weather is fantastic. Rune keeps singing 'Perfect Day' by Lou Reed, and he is right. For the moment, at least, conditions are ideal – a clear sun and no wind – which leads me to think that a high-pressure zone must be parked above us. The only drawback is that the warm weather makes me sweat profusely behind my goggles, which soon ice over when my perspiration cools. The only solution is to walk without wearing my goggles, risking frostbite and snow blindness. I have to be very careful and frequently check my cheeks and eye sockets for the first signs of frostnip.

We pass through another area of very broken-up ice. So far so good; there is very little wind to blow the ice pans apart and create more leads. Most of the open water that we do encounter has frozen over and we make good progress, but strange things pass through my mind as I trudge across the ice. In the middle of this barren, frozen wilderness, I am wondering if I will get an upgrade to business class on the flight back to England, how Swindon Town is faring in the First Division, and what my friends and children are doing at home now.

I am ashamed to say that my language has completely deteriorated over the course of the expedition and a string of expletives is unleashed on any encumbrance that dares to block our path. After calling my sledge every name under the sun when it catches on some small rubble, Rune gives me a stern telling-off.

'I don't believe many people are coming up on to the Arctic Ocean without getting a bit religious up here,' he says.

I agree with him. I am not a particularly religious man, but I must admit that I have taken to praying for good weather and wide pans of ice at the beginning and end of every day.

'Yes, you may be praying more David, but only when you can fit it in between all your swearing,' Rune says.

'What do you mean, Rune?'

'I don't like all your swearing, because up here you have to be ... what shall I say?'

'Peaceful?'

'Not peaceful, it's, er ...'

'Placid?'

'Maybe placid. Just ...'

'Chill out a bit?' I suggest.

'Just respectful about all the power around you and just take things as they come. I am getting tired of all this swearing, David.'

I agree with Rune but I still find it difficult not to vent my frustrations in coarse language. Maybe it is a particularly British characteristic to call a stretch of open water a 'buggering, buggering, bastard lead', but at least it makes plain how maddened I am by the obstacles, and I point out to Rune that it has not escaped my notice that he has been quick to adopt several English expletives.

'Yes, but just because I am influenced by you does not mean it is a good influence,' he says, and I vow to attempt to bite my tongue in the future.

Towards the end of the day we spot a tent about a mile west of our tracks, on the other side of a big pan. As we draw closer we recognise it as Sjur's team, and in the light of their bad experience we decide to avoid them. I just want to keep my head down and press on further ahead. We know they are safe and everything is okay because they have sent a message on the Argos system.

At the end of the day we have walked to 87°57'57" North and 71°31'00" West, almost fourteen miles in eight and a half hours. Another new record, and although I am in great pain I am overjoyed at our achievement.

Rune is ruminating over how many days we have left to get to the Pole, but I prefer not to tempt fate by thinking too much about it. If I am optimistic I can see that we could do it within ten days from tomorrow, provided we take no more rest days. Rune thinks that is possible, but I am concerned that we should not overdo it now. 'David, now is not the time to watch our health or conserve energy. The final sprint starts now and we have to go for it. Even if we take a rest day, we must go up to nine and a half hours a day, and I will cut the skins off my skis to reduce the friction and get better speed.'

Rune is obviously very determined to end the torture as soon as possible, but I am still firmly of the opinion that the old cliché of a polar expedition being a marathon and not a sprint is still the case. Even if we have a rest day, we should be able to knock back fourteen miles a day thereafter if the weather and snow conditions remain good. It is important not to let our ambitions run away with us, and we must remember to take each day at a time. That means setting our sights on crossing the 88th Parallel tomorrow. Only then can we consider the 120 miles that remain between us and the North Pole.

Day 45: Saturday, 18 April

Position: 87°58'23" North; 71°05'12" West
Temperature: −32°C
Windchill: −42°C
Hours of sunshine: 24 hours
Nautical miles covered yesterday: 13¾
Nautical miles covered so far: 298½
Nautical miles to go (*in a straight line*): 121½
Status: Everything okay

Once again we think we hear a polar bear near our tent during the night, but unlike last time, Rune thinks he hears it too. He wakes up and says he is convinced we have a visitor outside. I believe I have heard the sound of someone or something walking around and sniffing, and within an instant Rune is outside with the gun, having a look around.

He returns to report a false alarm. The ice to the north-east of us is on the move and the grinding sound could be misleading us. Nevertheless, we play safe and leave a bait of Peperami and a two-man food-ration pack on a sledge about a hundred yards upwind from our tent. If there is a polar bear about, hopefully it will be more interested in a guaranteed meal than two haggard and scrawny explorers in a tent. We are not disturbed again.

In the morning we rejoice that the drift is still on our side, and that we have gained half a mile northwards during the night. Only one and a half miles to 88° North, I tell myself as we set out, but my optimism soon turns sour when we encounter a massive area of break-up an hour or so later. For some strange reason that I cannot fathom the ice is always in a poor state whenever we pass into a new latitude. We spend the majority of the day criss-crossing frozen leads, huge pressure ridges and large rubble fields. I have to take off my skis at least five times and I am really fed up with the ice. When are we going to get the large pans of flat ice we have been led to expect? Maybe Sjur is right; maybe it will be rubble all the way to the Pole. It does not bear thinking about.

At least the weather is good and we can feel spring in the air. The sky is seven octares' blue with some high cloud, which indicates that a cold front is on the way. There is little wind, and −32°C in the sun seems quite warm. The heat of the sun on our backs is a wonderful incentive and it is starting to warm the inside of the tent as well.

Rune is very tired all day and I catch up with him several times. We manage twelve miles, which I consider incredible in such bad ice conditions and certainly better than either of us was expecting.

We are keeping to our plan to up the hours to nine and a half after the rest day. I need to repair my gaiters and boots tomorrow, then I will be ready for the final stretch. We will have to keep to a fast pace to try to beat the break-up and widening leads. I am now so nervous about beating the thaw to the Pole that I have butterflies permanently in the pit of my stomach. Every step we take is a step closer, but it is also a step higher in the stakes of potentially losing out.

A great radio schedule with John and Robert tonight. They say that they think a Czech is attempting to reach the Pole with Borge Ousland from 88° North on the Russian side. Apparently they are the same distance from the Pole as we are. It would be great to meet them there. John also tells us that the Norwegians were picked up today. They were not stopped by open water, as was rumoured, but by equipment failure. Their skis had disintegrated under the almost constant demands of eighteen hours' hard skiing every day. They had used up all their spare skis and their skis were beyond repair. It is a great shame that they have to abandon because of equipment failure, particularly as we are now the only people left on the ice on this side of the Pole.

It will be great to take it easy tomorrow. Both of us need a rest and Rune is complaining that he feels tired and exhausted.

Day 46: Sunday, 19 April

Position: 88°10'26" North; 70°25'26" West
Temperature: −34°C
Windchill: −52°C
Hours of sunshine: 24 hours
Nautical miles covered yesterday: 12
Nautical miles covered so far: 305½
Nautical miles to go (*in a straight line*): 109½
Status: Everything okay

April 6 1998. The meeting on the ice. The Norwegian Express catches us up on a historic polar anniversary at 86° 20' N 71 35' W. (*Rune Gjeldnes*)

April 9 1998. Captain Russ Bomberry and co-pilot Jason Miller use an astrocompass to find us on the ice for the second resupply. (*Paul Grover*)

April 9 1998. The moment the resupply team spotted our tiny home on the ice from the air. (*Paul Grover*)

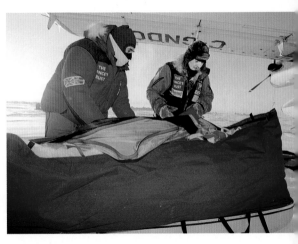

above April 9 1998. Rune and John Perrins rush to exchange tent, sledge, clothes, food and fuel beside the Twin Otter. (*all pics: Paul Grover*)

left Changing my outer clothes in the resupply plane and a rare chance to air my frostbitten toes in relative warmth.

below David Hempleman-Adams briefs Robert Uhlig of the *Telegraph* on the story so far.

April 9 1998. Joy's homemade cherry pie by special order from Resolute Bay and cigars for Rune on the second resupply. (*Paul Grover*)

right March 27 1998: Rune works on his poetry during a storm day confined to the tent. (*David Hempleman-Adams*)

below April 15 1998. Following Sjur Mørdre's tracks north. One of hundreds of tiny leads we often crossed in the course of a single day. (*Rune Gjeldnes*)

above The last week and the rubble has not abated. Still no sign of the wide open pans of flat ice we had been led to expect. (*all pics: Rune Gjeldnes*)

left Crossing a lead of porridge ice and floating rubble. The conditions I hate more than any other. My heart is in my mouth for every step.

right April 23 1998. Only 15 miles to go, the sun is warm on our backs and the end of our torture is in sight. Rune strips off his face-mask to enjoy the heat.

below Mid-April 1998. We encounter more polynyas as we approach the Pole and the thaw accelerates.

April 28 1998. The Pole at last!
Self-portrait at the moment we
reached the top of the world.
(*all pics: Rune Gjeldnes*)

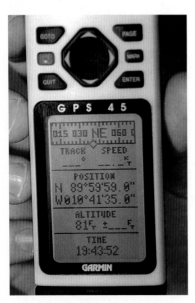

April 28 1998. The smiles say it all. Our mission is over
and the Pole is conquered. We did not know that the
worst 48 hours of the expedition were still to come.

April 28 1998. The final reading at
the North Pole on my GPS. Rune's
GPS measured 89° 59'59.9" N, but
the photograph did not come out
clearly.

above April 28 1998. With Sue Stockdale and Geoff Somers, our drop-in guests at the North Pole. (*Rune Gjeldnes*)

right April 30 1998. Champagne and cigars at the Top of the World party. The first and last cigar I have smoked – it turned me green. (*Paul Grover*)

below April 30 1998. Celebrating the reunion with my wife Claire and eldest daughter Alicia at the North Pole. (*Paul Grover*)

April 30 1998: With Alicia on the plane home.
(*all pics: Paul Grover*)

May 1 1998. Clean after three showers and my clothes fall off me. I have lost four stone in eight weeks.

May 1 1998. Rune brings tears to my eyes when he gives me his treasured Marinejegerkommando beret at the post-Pole party at Resolute Bay.

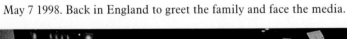

May 7 1998. Back in England to greet the family and face the media.

At last a rest day after four testing days of strength-sapping ice conditions and long walking distances. We sleep until ten o'clock, our first
lie-in on this trip, and spend the day drying out our clothes.

It seems that this is the first warm day in the tent, but our thermometer shows that it is no warmer or colder than over the previous
three or four days. Maybe we are now acclimatised to the cold. I mend
the broken zip on my gaiters by removing the velcro fastening from
the canopy of my sledge and sewing it to the blue material which keeps
snow and ice out of my boots. Rune mends his thermarest and then
we have a relaxed lunch of brandy, soup, chocolate and pork scratchings. Not the healthiest of meals, but packed with the necessary
calories.

We spend the day chatting, and as usual Rune turns up some strange
sayings. While eating lunch, he asks me if I want some more food, to
which I answer, without thinking, 'Do men like sex?'

'But I am not asking you about sex, David,' comes the answer. Once
again, we are off on a long explanation of the subtleties of the English
language, which I make all the more complicated by dropping in the
phrase 'and pigs might fly'.

'No they will not,' says Rune, 'and what have pigs got to do with it?'

The time passes quickly, particularly as we spend a lot of it wondering why all the Norwegians pulled out. If they had used up all their
spare skis, why did one of them not continue on his own, using the
other two team members' skis. They had only just over one hundred
miles to go, and a lone skiier would still have set the record.

All this talking of hypotheticals leads us to talk about what we would
do if one of us was injured or had to go back. Rune has purposely
minimised the amount of information he receives from home so that
he is not tempted to abandon the expedition in the event of an illness
or death in his family. We had already decided that I would turn back
if Amelia's throat condition had worsened. In that event, Rune would
probably have come back with me, but now that we are so close to the
Pole I would not expect him to give up. We decide that if one of us
was to pick up an injury now, the other one would drag him to the
Pole on his sledge. We were each dragging more than our own weights
last year, so it would be possible to drag one person plus tent and
provisions for maybe five or six days. 'If I was seriously injured now
and needed a medical evacuation I would not let you get on the plane,'

I tell Rune. 'There is no way I would let you come this far and not make it to the Pole because of my injury. If necessary, I would break your fingers in the door.'

It is very difficult to know where team loyalties end and personal selfishness begins, but I think we both know that we have come far enough now and struggled sufficiently hard to justify continuing alone if one of us dropped out. Unsurprisingly, Rune does not see it in the same way. He is, as ever, entirely modest and loyal. 'This is your expedition, David, your Grand Slam. If you do not reach the Pole, what is the point of me being here?' he says. I point out to Rune that his Norwegian compatriots carried on after the first two of their team of five dropped out. 'It depends on the injury, and it is very hypothetical to discuss it here,' he replies. I think it is probably all he will say on the matter, but I know that I would pull Rune if he could not continue because of injury or illness and we were within sixty miles of the Pole. And I would expect him to pull me if the situation was reversed. I know it would work because no one could keep up with Rune when he pulled Alan Bywater in his sledge over to the landing strip last year.

We also talk about the first things we will do when we get back to civilisation. 'The first investment will be coffee and cakes for my stomach,' Rune says, cigar and coffee cup in hand. 'After that a bath, and then I will make a phone call home to Mama and Papa.' My intentions are a little different. I crave savoury food, a pint of lager, but most of all I just want to do the simple things that I normally take for granted with my family. Just sitting at home and eating breakfast together, or reading the girls a bedtime story.

In the evening we speak on the radio to a pilot who has just flown to the North Pole. He tells us the ice conditions are good, but we wonder if we can trust his judgement. What looks good from the air can be a jumbled mess at ground level. All I can hope is that we get through this area of heavy rubble quite quickly now.

At the end of the day, the small north drift we had overnight has been swallowed up by a half-mile back-drift during the day. The wind direction has changed and is now against us. Tomorrow we will have to walk into the wind, instead of having it behind us, giving us a gentle push northwards. I cannot help but feel that the change of wind direction is the reward for being too lazy to walk today.

Day 47: Monday, 20 April

Position: 88°09'03" North; 70°26'30" West
Temperature: −32°C
Windchill: −56°C
Hours of sunshine: 24 hours
Nautical miles covered yesterday: 0 (rest day)
Nautical miles covered so far: 304
Nautical miles to go (*in a straight line*): 111
Status: Everything okay

Another mile back-drift overnight, so we have lost one and a half miles in the time we were resting in our camp. It is disheartening, but I do not feel too depressed about it. We needed the rest and I can feel that it has done me good. This is the very last leg now – no more rest days until we get on the plane home, whether we make it to the Pole or not.

The wind has picked up to about fifteen knots, which means around −56°C windchill, and we're back into rubble and break-up. The longer we walk today, the worse the rubble becomes. By mid-afternoon most of the terrain is broken up into leads of sketchy, fresh ice, the kind of conditions I hate more than any other, and I nearly fall into the water at one point.

We walk for nine and a half hours and encounter only one decent pan. It is very disappointing and I hope we soon get some better conditions. It must be the effects of the Lomonosov Ridge, churning all the ice up. We are also drifting east at an unusually high speed, which would also concur with my feeling that we are in an area of fast-moving water, agitated by the sudden change in depth between the deep Abyssal Plain and the ridge. Our only saving grace at present is the sun, which is really imparting some warmth to our bodies now.

However, it is once again a day of injuries. My nose starts to bleed for no reason while we are breaking camp. Although the frostbite from the South Pole left the inside of my nose in a mess, and I need an operation to allow me to breath properly through my nostrils, this is the first time for years I have had a nosebleed. All I can think is that the pressure of our expectations is beginning to affect me, even if I do not consciously notice it. I am also worried that I might have a blood pressure problem, particularly since the nurse at Resolute Bay said my blood pressure was exceptionally high before we set out. I manage to stop my nose bleeding, but it starts again in mid-afternoon, reawakening my fears that there is something else much more serious at the heart of it.

Later in the day I lose my footing while climbing across a pressure ridge, and for the second time my sledge slams into the small of my back, making my already sore and damaged coccyx even worse then before. This time the impact of the sledge almost winds me when the force of it slamming into my back forces me to buckle over on impact.

But the worst injury is my right thumb, which I sprain when I slip on some blue ice. My thumb bends right back to touch the side of my hand. For a while I fear that I have broken it. The pain is intense, and it soon turns blue and swells up to the size of a tennis ball. I am determined to keep going, and try to ski with only my left hand while I strap my right arm to my chest. It proves to be almost impossible, so I revert to skiing with both hands, but gingerly apply all the pressure on my right ski stick by tying the ski pole's strap around my wrist instead of my thumb. It is sensationally painful, but at least we can keep going.

At the end of the day it all seems worthwhile when I get the GPS out. We have reached 88°22'20" North and veered somewhat east to 69°07'00" West. We are thirteen and three-quarter miles closer to our goal and have another seven days to go if we keep up this mileage. A fine achievement considering the ice conditions and bearing in mind that nine and a half miles of our journey was through dense rubble.

Rune immediately attends to my injuries, and we are both alarmed to see how much my thumb has swollen when I take off my glove. We apply heat and ice alternately to reduce the swelling, but it is not an easy procedure. Although there is a plentiful supply of ice, Rune has to warm it up from −35°C to around melting point to ensure that I do not get frostbite from packing my thumb in the ice. Then, to apply heat to my thumb he wraps my hand in a plastic bag and I hold it at the top of the tent, the warmest place we can find, for as long as I can muster. The treatment works; the swelling on my thumb subsides slightly, but I am still very worried that I might have fractured it.

However, as I go to sleep my thoughts revolve around a solitary subject close to my heart: I would kill for a strawberry milkshake and a piece of blueberry pie.

Day 48: Tuesday, 21 April

Position: 88°22'43" North; 68°29'38" West
Temperature: −26°C
Windchill: −38°C
Hours of sunshine: 24 hours
Nautical miles covered yesterday: 13¾
Nautical miles covered so far: 317¾
Nautical miles to go (*in a straight line*): 97¼
Status: Injury David – continuing

My thumb hurts like a bastard. I wake up half-way through the night to take pain-killers and a drink, and cannot get back to sleep afterwards because of the pain. This is the last thing I need; I am getting very tired now and my body has had enough. I need at least eight hours of sleep if I am to function well the next day. Rune is fifteen years younger than me and the age gap makes a big difference, although I know he is now very tired too. It is also his turn to take the lead in illness and injuries today, and he says he has been throwing up all morning because the food did not agree with him last night.

Our routines are now so finely honed that we can break camp in total silence, each of us doing his share of the tasks without needing to speak to the other. We are much quicker than at the beginning of the expedition and we break camp by 9.30. It's a good start, but within sixty feet I have fallen over. We camped right beside rubble and a lead last night, and within a few steps both of the sledges turn over. It is a portent for the day. There is no sun to start with and the conditions are almost a white-out. I am so fatigued by my injuries, by my diminishing body weight and by the interminable slog northwards, that the slightest unevenness is enough to make me stumble and slip up. Sometimes my cack-handed progress seems hopeless and I cannot envisage arriving at the Pole without a swathe of injuries.

The day continues as it began: rubble, a few frozen leads, but no pans whatsoever. I just don't understand it. Where have the big pans of ice gone that other polar explorers have told us about? In the few moments when I can afford to let my mind wander in these conditions, I think of Claire and Alicia, but I try quickly to forget them. We still have a long way to go, it has become very heavy going and thoughts of home make the discomfort of our current predicament all the more galling.

I am concerned that we are still drifting a long way east of our planned route. We are now seven degrees off course, almost half an hour in solar navigation terms, and our struggle against the currents is likely to get worse when we negotiate the peaks of the Lomonosov Ridge. Other explorers have told me that if we get the ridge wrong we will shoot off further eastwards at a rate of twelve miles a day, such are the sub-ocean currents in the area, but there seems to be little we can do about it. Sometimes too much knowledge is a dangerous thing and we have decided to wait until we are over the ridge before heading back west. The further north we venture, the more the lines of longitude squeeze together and the less distance we have to walk to correct our bearing to get back on track. By the time we are near the Pole we will be spinning from one time zone to another every few minutes.

On the penultimate session of the afternoon I climb over a pressure ridge, then ease myself carefully down the other side to a point where I am on a step about a foot above a recently frozen lead. The ice directly in front of the lead looks good; it is blue, flat and solid – several years old, I judge by its appearance. I place my ski pole on the ice, to support my weight while I step down from the ridge. However, before I know it I am lying flat on my face. My arm and shoulder are in the water and my legs are splayed behind me, still on the pressure ridge but snagged in the rubble.

Rune has not realised what has happened. I find it almost impossible to call to him for help as my face is almost entirely in the water and I cannot move it to shout. He is smoking a cigarette and walking nonchalantly towards me, but he cannot see me because I am lying below the level of the surrounding snow and ice. I can see him from the corner of my eye, and notice with some satisfaction the double-take he performs when he spots me. He immediately dives into the water and treads water with his skis on. It is at times like this that I am reminded how immensely strong this young man can be, and I am astonished to find him lifting me out of the water while he is bobbing up and down in the icy Arctic Ocean. With his help I manage to pull myself upright, and then to drag myself on to solid ice. I then give Rune a hand to get out of the water, but only after I have filmed him in the water for our video diary. Rune insists that I film him and he seems completely unfazed by the whole experience. I think it is extraordinary that we have both been in the water at the same time today, but our reactions to the experience are so remarkably different.

We walk hard all day to drive the damp out of our sodden clothes and in the late afternoon the clouds break and the sun comes out. It is wonderfully warm, and for the first time I walk the final session without my black Karrimor fleece trousers on. At the end of the day we have reached 88°36'07" North and 66°17'09" West, a long way off the right edge of my plotting chart but thirteen and a half miles further north. A good distance. We are both looking forward to ending this trip; we are sick and tired of zig-zagging our way to the top of the globe.

Day 49: Wednesday, 22 April

Position: 88°36'45" North; 65°33'00" West
Temperature: −34°C
Windchill: −47°C
Hours of sunshine: 24 hours
Nautical miles covered yesterday: 13½
Nautical miles covered so far: 331¾
Nautical miles to go (*in a straight line*): 83¼
Status: Man in water – continuing

We wake up to two problems: firstly, the radio seems not to be working, and secondly, every mouthful of food I eat seems to contain a hair. I do not know where the hair is coming from, but it is infesting my rations. At first I think it is the fur from the edge of my jacket hood, then I think I must be losing my own hair from the top of my head, but in both cases a quick examination reveals that there is no sign of hair loss due to stress-induced alopecia. It is not of vital importance, but the frequent tickle at the back of my throat while I am eating is driving me to distraction. I have to stop ten or fifteen times each meal to pluck a stray hair from between my teeth or the roof of my mouth, and it is driving me insane.

The failure of the radio is, of course, a much more serious matter. We were meant to have a radio schedule with John last night, but he did not come in. We try again at 0700 in the morning, our scheduled back-up time, but again we pick up not the faintest trace of a signal. Rune checks the antenna several times and I look the radio over. It seems to be functioning correctly and there is no explanation for its silence.

I worry about the radio all day. My biggest concern is that John could panic and send an aeroplane, which is the last thing we want him to do. God forbid. I hope that he will realise from our Argos satellite beacon readings that we are still making good progress, and assume that all is still okay.

Things seem to occur in threes, it is said, and the events of today are no exception. Following my troubles with rogue hairs and a non-conformist radio, I snap one of the tent poles while packing up the tent. It shatters like glass in the cold, but fortunately we have a spare female tent pole that we can use to patch up between the two broken pieces. Without it we would have been in dire straits.

At last we come across some decent pans of ice, and manage two or three good sessions interspersed with some break-up and rubble. It turns out to be a good day, with a gusting wind from the south-west that could cause some trouble with the leads over the next few days. For the moment the leads are frozen over, but that could all change very soon if the wind continues. We accomplish our highest mileage yet – three seconds short of fifteen nautical miles, which takes us to 88°51'42" North and 64°25'50" West. As we sip our celebratory brandies tonight, I allow myself to contemplate for the first time the possibility that we could make it to the Pole, provided our luck holds out.

In the evening I take the radio apart to check there is not a loose lead inside, but everything seems to be working normally. I do not understand why we are not picking up John. Maybe the high latitude and curvature of the Earth cuts off radio transmissions? It seems unlikely.

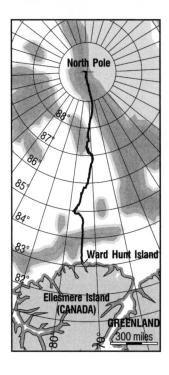

12

Top of the World

The Eighth Week

'The pole at last ... My dream and goal for twenty years! Mine at last! I cannot bring myself to realise it. It all seems so simple and commonplace. As Bartlett said when turning back, when speaking of his being in these exclusive regions which no mortal has ever penetrated before, 'It's just like every day.'

– Captain Robert Peary on reaching the North Pole in 1909

Day 50: Thursday, 23 April

Position: 88°51'53" North; 64°08'07" West
Temperature: −30°C
Windchill: −36°C
Hours of sunshine: 24 hours
Nautical miles covered yesterday: 15
Nautical miles covered so far: 347

Nautical miles to go (*in a straight line*): 68
Status: Everything okay

We are both quiet and tired this morning after staying awake almost to midnight, trying to get the radio to work. I am worried that John and Robert in Resolute Bay will think we are purposely not calling in because we want to manipulate the story over the last few days. Nothing could be further from the truth; it is right now that we want to keep them briefed precisely to ensure that everything is ready for the pick-up.

I could do with another hour in bed, and I think Rune feels the same. We both eat our breakfast quietly; the only conversation to break the silence is another moan from me about yet another hair in my food. Where the hell are they coming from? Nevertheless, I scoff down my entire breakfast, yet I am still hungry afterwards. I am longing for the time when we can eat some proper food without having to then walk it off all day every day.

Fortunately, the going is relatively easy. The sky is almost cloudless, the wind has dropped to a light breeze and there are several small pans of flat ice. As it gets warmer through the day we both strip off, until Rune has only his head-band and sunglasses on his head. He looks very mean with his goatee beard and mirrored shades.

Towards the end of the day, just before our fifth rest stop, we see two seals ahead of us. The sight of these two animals scares us both. It can mean only one thing – open water. Five minutes later we are in front of a large lead, the first we have seen in days, and it is an inauspicious sight. We both know that the only thing that can keep us from the Pole is open water, and now we are confronted by a huge stretch of broken ice. Injury is no longer a worry – even if one of us is injured, I think we would both make it to the Pole – but open water is one handicap we cannot banish simply with hard work and determination. It is a particularly dangerous lead too, with a lot of floating ice, but we manage to cross it, and carry on to pass the 89th Parallel. Hulashaker, we are now in the final straight, and the Pole is within grasp. I can hardly believe it.

Half a mile beyond the lead we run into a lot of rubble and old pack ice, probably as much as we have encountered at any time. It is depressing still to be struggling against the rubble we thought we would leave 300 miles behind us. We stop at a particularly large pressure ridge and put up the tent.

As on every night since we left Ward Hunt Island, I call us both to attention when I stick the Norwegian and Union flags in the ice at the northernmost point of our camp. Rune is inside the tent when I give the salute: 'God save your King.' He scurries out of the tent, stands up and returns the tribute: 'And God save your Queen.' We then go back to our business of preparing for the night on the ice. I do not know why such rituals have become so important to both of us, but I suspect they keep up morale and give us focal points in each day. Without the little ceremonies and procedures with which we dot each day, maybe our sentence on the ice would stretch into a disheartening, unstructured miasma of events.

I take out the GPS to measure our position – 89°06'27" North and 64°59'00" West. Fourteen and a half miles, which warrants two packets of pork scratchings and two nips of brandy tonight, because we've passed into a new latitude. From now on each step we take will be a perceptible one closer to home, but I am still aware that we cannot take anything for granted. Sjur Mørdre is a very experienced man, yet he failed only seven days from the Pole. We are still encountering a lot of rubble, and either one of us could easily break an arm or a leg in these conditions.

We want to push hard, but we are faced by a dilemma. We could increase our walking time to ten or twelve hours a day, but then we will arrive at the Pole too early. Claire and Alicia arrive in Resolute Bay on Tuesday, so it makes little sense to reach the Pole before then. There is no point in sitting at the Pole for three days, particularly as the drift will push us off it and we will have to keep walking each day to stay close. Still, we are both looking forward to enjoying the last few miles up to the Pole. After seven weeks on the ice, now is the time we ought to savour the last steps and moments.

Day 51: Friday, 24 April

Position: 89°06'26" North; 65°09'40" West
Temperature: −35°C
Windchill: −44°C

Hours of sunshine: 24 hours
Nautical miles covered yesterday: 14½
Nautical miles covered so far: 361½
Nautical miles to go (*in a straight line*): 53½
Status: Everything okay

It was as if I were having a nightmare. In the middle of the night I am woken by the sound of a bird screeching. This cannot be right, a bird so far north, I think as I awake. But I am wrong – a lone snowbird has spotted our tent and is inside, picking at crumbs near the door.

Rune is all for cooking the little bastard that has broken our much-needed sleep. 'There is only enough meat on him for two mouthfuls,' he says, 'but it would make a nice appetiser for tonight, David.' I tell him we have our freedom so the bird should have its too. He gets up, groaning that it is four o'clock in the morning, and tries to catch the tiny bird. It is quicker than the Norwegian Marinejegerkommando, and manages to evade every attempt to ensnare him, so Rune lays a track of rolled oats back out of the tent door. Eventually, the bird falls for Rune's bait and he manages to grab the tiny creature without injuring it. He then carries the bird outside, where he releases it. 'A very confused bird, I think,' Rune says. 'Wherever it is coming from, I don't think the way home is over the Pole.'

Tired by yesterday's exertions and drained by our nightly struggles to make the radio work, we went to bed earlier than usual last night. The extra hour we had to sleep makes a big difference, despite the early-morning wake-up call by the snowbird.

I still feel very apprehensive. I am scared to think that we might actually do it, now that we are within spitting distance. I keep telling Rune not to become complacent. 'On Everest, most people fail on the way down. They make it to the top, but are then exhausted and careless on the descent, because they think the hard work is over. That is when they slip and fall.'

'Don't be so negative David. We will get there now. Do not worry,' Rune replies, although I know he is less optimistic than he is pretending to be. I can sense his nerves from his grumpy behaviour.

'Rune, if we keep going so far off track, we are never going to get there,' I say at one point when we seem to be veering off course.

'Oh, listen to you. Aren't you clever now,' he replies.

'We'll never make ten miles today if we don't keep on course,' I insist.

'Wait until the end of the day, then we will see how far we've gone and who is right.'

I know better than to push it. We are both anxious now that the end is in sight. We are just as likely to injure ourselves now, or face an equipment failure, as on any of the previous fifty days, only now the stakes are higher. Having walked all this way, it would be a tragedy if we failed with only a few days to go.

The ice is a mixed challenge today; some large flat pans, but also a lot of rubble. We are lucky with leads; there is a lot of open water, but we manage to find good crossing-points whenever we come to a gap in the ice. Today, it seems luck is on our side for once. Hopefully, three good days will get us to the pole, or within a couple of miles of it. All I can think about now is the food we will be able to eat when we get home. My body is craving a proper meal – beef sandwiches, a steak and a baked potato, fish and chips, and a pint of Stella. I can almost taste it now. Rune is dreaming of a huge omelette when we get back to England, which he says he plans to eat while watching *Pulp Fiction*, followed by a big cigar. It does not take much to keep us happy.

Around midday we cross a pressure ridge, and I can tell that Rune is disorientated. He is heading too far east and his shadow is on his left. The closer we get to the Pole, the more wayward Rune's compass becomes, and I suspect that his ski poles are affecting the magnetic variation, which is almost 180 degrees now. I am tempted to say something straight away, but I hold off to see if he corrects himself. A point-man will always turn into the wind when confused; it is a natural thing to do. But after five minutes Rune is still heading east and I have to correct him, tactfully this time. 'When I was at the South Pole, and I had my ski poles too close to my compass, it would give me a wrong reading,' I venture. 'Now I don't know if that's the reason, but it seems to me that we're a bit off course.'

Rune stops and glowers at me. He gets out his compass and looks at his watch to take a solar reading for comparison. Without speaking he then turns and heads off at a right angle. It is one of the few slip-ups he has made. His navigation has been excellent and he has done a brilliant job. If Sjur Mørdre's team had followed Rune's tracks all the way, they may well have got to the Pole, or at least very close. We found they added a third to their distance just by going up to forty-five degrees off course at times.

There is so much that can go wrong now as we try to juggle ice conditions, schedules and the needs of the television crews and newspapers. If we push it, we could be at the Pole on Monday, but we have agreed that we will aim for Tuesday because the BBC and ITN crews do not arrive until then. It would not be fair on Charles Rhodes if he was to depart from Heathrow already knowing that we have reached the Pole. We will slow down so that he is not offended.

My other concern is that there is still a lot of rubble in front of us, and we are both worried that we will not be able to find a flat enough pan for the planes to land near the Pole. However, our main concern remains open water. The lead we crossed yesterday frightened both of us. It is an indication that our final sprint for the Pole is not as straightforward as we had assumed. A big lead, like the one that took us several days to circumnavigate a couple of weeks ago, could put us back a few days. Even worse, we could come within a mile or so of the Pole only to find that the whole area is broken up, or that the Pole is in the middle of a large pond of open water.

I tell Rune that we should not count our chickens before they have hatched. Inevitably the remark prompts a long explanation of yet another English proverb that does not seem to translate well into Norwegian, but eventually he understands what I mean and agrees.

We manage fourteen and three-quarter miles. Another good day, especially considering the ice conditions. It is Friday evening and our families at home should be able to see that we are very near to our goal. I wonder what they are feeling. Rune says he hopes his mama and papa will be proud of him.

Day 52: Saturday, 25 April

Position: 89°21'05" North; 68°24'14" West
Temperature: −36°C
Windchill: −58°C
Hours of sunshine: 24 hours
Nautical miles covered yesterday: 14¾
Nautical miles covered so far: 376

Nautical miles to go (*in a straight line*): 39
Status: Everything okay

A lot of rubble today and two big leads, which take a long time to walk around. At one point I have a horrible feeling that we are not going to find a crossing-point on the second lead, but after walking for forty-five minutes we find a stretch of very spongy ice that we chance our arms on. Two or three weeks ago I would have refused to cross ice like this, but now I want the Pole so much that I am going for anything that looks as if it will take my weight.

The weather is not on our side. The sun is hidden behind thick cloud and we are in the midst of what is almost a white-out. Then, between the fourth and fifth sessions, we are plunged into darkness. I would never have believed it if I had not seen it for myself and can only assume that some particularly thick clouds have moved across the sun. It is as if someone has switched the light and heating off. Almost instantly it is much colder and darker, and it is very hard to keep going. The temperature plummets to −36°C and the wind picks up. It reminds me of the day we happened upon the big lead and felt we were looking at some satanic nether world.

In the semi-darkness, picking our way through the rubble becomes much more difficult and we struggle to find a clear route ahead. The wind moves round to the north, straight into our faces, and we decide we have had enough, so we camp for the night. The northerly wind will push us back overnight, but I feel we are close enough not to need to push ourselves to the limit. We have walked thirteen miles today to 89°34'22" North and 68°49'40" West. A very satisfactory mileage.

All I hope is that the weather will clear by Wednesday, when we want the planes to pick us up. For the first time I realise that I am planning the final days and beyond, and I tell Rune that now only one thing matters: the Pole.

Day 53: Sunday, 26 April

Position: 89°34'20" North; 71°17'36" West
Temperature: −30°C
Windchill: −49°C

Hours of sunshine: 24 hours
Nautical miles covered yesterday: 13
Nautical miles covered so far: 389½
Nautical miles to go (*in a straight line*): 25½
Status: Everything okay

A day of contrasts. I am quite scared of getting out of the tent first thing in the morning as I am worried about everything – the weather, the ice conditions; you name it, it frightens me. I felt the same way on the last few days of the South Pole and on the day before the summit at Everest. I have to find some way of keeping my mind busy with matters other than worrying about the logistics and likelihood of making it to the Pole.

The total white-out and bitterly cold wind at the beginning of the day soon take my mind off the matters that have been tormenting me for the last couple of days. To make matters worse, we come across the most dreadful break-up in the ice I have seen so far. I am surprised to see it this far north, especially as we are well past the Lomonosov Ridge now. I struggle to think of one good pan we have walked across the whole time we have been up here. I cannot think of any, which does not bode well for finding a pan suitable to land three fully laden aircraft later this week.

The first, second and third sessions of walking are exceptionally slow with a lot of rubble, but we keep plugging away, hoping that the ice and weather will improve. Rune is very quiet; I think it is tiredness, but I know he is also brooding about the possibility of failing so far into the expedition. Then, in the early afternoon, the weather changes from the west. I can occasionally see the sun near the horizon, and it helps to lift our dour moods, to fire our motivation and to make navigation much easier.

Again we encounter a lot of leads, but this time we are much luckier and they are either frozen or the crossings are easy. Some have started to open up a little, a condition I feared once the wind moved round to the north, but they appear to be relatively stable. On the last session we come across an open lead that heads north. We follow it, hoping that it will bear west, away from the north, or that we will find somewhere to cross. For once our wishes come true and we are rewarded with an open vista as the lead bends away from us and the landscape opens up towards the northern horizon. Ahead of us we can see a shift of light, almost as if the Pole is lit by a spotlight, and it seems tantalisingly close. It entices us to keep walking and we add on an extra forty minutes to our normal workload.

A short while later we see some Arctic fox tracks in the snow. Although it could mean that polar bears are nearby, at least it indicates that we are not the only living things all the way up here. We are not alone, and it seems like a good omen. Hopefully, with a little sun tomorrow, we will make it to the Pole. Our adventure is nearly over, and frankly I am relieved that we will soon be going home. I am bored of walking across this hellish landscape every day. We have seen great changes in climate, terrain and our fortunes, but I have had enough. I want to get it done and get it over with. With any luck, a fifteen-year battle with this unpleasant and awful yet strangely beautiful and tranquil place will soon be over.

Shortly before stopping I nearly castrate myself with my left ski. The bindings are still loose, and because it keeps coming off I have named my left ski 'Bastard', to join the two sledges, 'Fuck' and 'Cunt', and my rucksack, 'Shit'. As I push my left foot out in front of me while crossing some rubble, the ski lifts up and I stumble across it; in my desperate effort to keep my testicles out of harm's way, I impale the cheek of my bottom, tearing a large hole in the backside of my windproof trousers. It could have been much worse I suppose, but it is still very uncomfortable and my arse is getting very cold.

We have walked thirteen and a half miles to 89°47'49" North and 80°20'25" West. Provided we do not float too far back overnight, we have 12.2 miles left to walk.

Day 54: Monday, 27 April

Position: 89°48'08" North; 88°53'00" West
Temperature: −32°C
Windchill: −64°C
Hours of sunshine: 24 hours
Nautical miles covered yesterday: 13½
Nautical miles covered so far: 403
Nautical miles to go (*in a straight line*): 12

Status: Everything okay

It has become obvious that the conditions are going to become tougher and harder the closer we get to the bitter end. We wake up to a gale outside and a complete white-out. Thank God we put the hours in yesterday and notched up a decent mileage, because there seems to be scant likelihood of achieving much today.

We cannot navigate by the sun, and the wild variation of the magnetic compass makes it next to useless so close to the Pole, so we have to depend on the GPS system. However, the closer we get the more worried and confused I become. Navigating is becoming very difficult because at this latitude the GPS gives vastly different bearings for the North Pole depending on the longitude of the way-point. I would have thought the bearing would be the same irrespective of the longitude setting as all lines of longitude meet at the Pole, but obviously not, according to my GPS receiver.

While we try to work out how to navigate the last stretch, I ponder all the conundrums facing us. Should we walk beyond the Pole, some way towards Russia, to get eastings to prove that we have walked across the Pole? Did Claire, Alicia and all the others catch the plane or not? Should we stop as soon as we find a decent landing strip? Will this weather clear and will planes be able to land on Wednesday? Will our plans fit in with the schedules of Borek Air and First Air? If not, will our food and fuel last until the planes arrive? Why is our radio still not working? There are dozens of imponderables and no simple answers. This is a great place to get an ulcer.

We start walking into the wind, which soon veers to become a westerly wind, generating a lot of back and west drift, slowing our progress considerably. I am too tired to continue battling against this wind and wish it would stop. It is a terrible day; a lot of rubble, huge mounds of pack ice and the wind blowing constantly like some demented spirit that is trying to keep us away from our goal. I am particularly cold because of the rip in my trousers, which I cannot be bothered to mend properly now that the end is in sight. Right now, we need this kind of final challenge like we need a hole in the head. It is enough to drive anyone insane.

After eight hours we have both had enough, and we camp two miles from the Pole. We are at 89°58'01" North and 120°12'00" West, about ten miles closer to the Pole than this morning, but we have walked a greater distance because of the back-drift. I hope it is not a mistake to stop so close to our target. We have stopped for one simple reason: Charles Rhodes and the BBC. After supporting us for the last three years, it would be disloyal to reach the Pole today while Charles is in the air, flying from England to Canada, but I hope our decision does not prove to be a mistake. It is pure arrogance to stop so close to our goal and I fear we are courting disaster. We could have continued to the Pole tonight, but after a lengthy discussion we have decided to wait. Rune is not pleased with the decision and believes we should keep walking while there is such a strong back-drift. It will be a hard push tomorrow, but if all goes well we should get the Pole and the T-shirt.

Day 55: Tuesday, 28 April

Position: 89°56'20" North; 169°46'00" West
Temperature: −34°C
Windchill: −47°C
Hours of sunshine: 24 hours
Nautical miles covered yesterday: 10
Nautical miles covered so far: 411½ ‾
Nautical miles to go (*in a straight line*): 3½
Status: Everything okay

I wake up early at five a.m., anxious to get down to complete the task that we failed exactly a year ago. On Monday, 28 April 1997, Rune's sledge finally collapsed and we lost the Pole. Now it is exactly a year later and the Pole is tantalisingly close. We could not have planned it better if we had tried.

However, the top of the world is not quite as close as it was last night. The currents and wind are ferocious, and we have drifted back overnight to about three and a half miles from the Pole. For some reason, possibly because we feel the weight of expectation on our shoulders, it takes us longer to get going, and we are nearly an hour behind schedule when we start off. It is still very windy and almost a white-out, making navigation by the sun almost impossible. Rune

switches the Argos beacon on and secures it inside his backpack so
that we can register an ongoing track of our route to the Pole. We also
both clip radio microphones to our jacket lapels so that we can record
our commentary as we approach the end.

We walk for an hour and then stop to take a position on the GPS.
I get my enlarged chart out ready to plot the last stretch, which will be
the most difficult part to navigate, while we sit down to eat some
chocolate, drink some juice and wait for the GPS to register our
position. It usually takes around thirty seconds for our position to
appear on its LCD screen, but this time there is no reading, even after
five minutes. I panic; this is the worst possible moment for this grey
box of navigational electronics to fail. Fortunately Rune has a spare
GPS, so he digs into his sledge and pulls it out. We hunch over it,
waiting for a positional reading to appear. Again, no reading, even
after five minutes.

I break out in a cold sweat. This is a nightmare. With neither of our
GPS receivers working we cannot possibly find the North Pole. We
could use a sextant and calculate our position, as I did to some extent
on my first North Pole attempt in 1983, but we have not brought a
sextant with us. Rune and I look at each other, speechless. Why after
all this time have both GPS receivers failed?

'Check the batteries,' Rune suggests.

'They're warm and fresh this morning. I kept them especially for
the last few miles,' I reply.

'Then we must be doing something different. There is no reason
why they should both fail at the same time,' he says.

I cannot think of anything we have done differently. I go through
the well-practised routine of calibrating the GPS and then leaving it
to pick up several satellites to work out our position by triangulation.
There are more satellites within sight of the Pole than at most other
locations on the planet, so the reading should be more accurate here
than anywhere else, but we are not getting a reading at all. Normally,
a series of dots appears on the screen, indicating each of the satellites
that has been detected. Each satellite carries an atomic clock, and the
receiver works out its position by comparing the difference between
the time signals from each of the satellites within range. At the moment
it appears not to be detecting any satellites or time signals at all.

'You don't think they have turned the satellites off, do you?' I ask Rune.

'The last time they did that was the Gulf War. Surely we would have heard something about it by now,' Rune says.

It then strikes me that we have not been able to speak over the radio for almost a week. All sorts of doomsday scenarios flash through my mind. Maybe war has broken out and all unnecessary radio broadcasts have been terminated. It is not only John Perrins who has been silent, we haven't heard anything from any other radio transmitters. It seems an unlikely event, but when you are in the middle of nowhere and have not seen civilisation for two months, almost anything seems a possibility. We left home as the stand-off between Saddam Hussein and the Western world was coming to a head again over the chemical weapons inspections; maybe the crisis has escalated and a second Gulf War has broken out, I think.

While my guts are churning with nerves and my thoughts are running away with me, Rune is taking a much more practical approach. 'Start at the beginning of today and think what you did step by step, then we will probably find something that is stopping the GPS receivers from working.' I mentally re-enact the events of the last couple of hours, but I can think of nothing that is different. Then it dawns on me: we are both wearing radio microphones for the first time. Maybe they are interfering with the GPS.

I switch off my microphone and walk away from Rune to avoid interference from his microphone, then I switch on the GPS receiver. To my immense relief, a series of dots appears on the first screen, and then a position: 89°57'24" North and 169°46'00" West. We are a mile closer to the Pole, and with a large smile on my face I plot our latest co-ordinates on my enlarged chart. Thank God, I think, and for the second time today I pray that we will make it all the way without any more mishaps.

We walk for another hour, and again I take our position. Now we are at 89°58'52" North and 175°24'00" West, just over a mile from the Pole. It is a strange feeling to be so close to the goal I have striven for since 1983, and the sensation is made all the more curious by the behaviour of the sun. The clouds have cleared partially and it is above us, but by my reckoning in the wrong part of the sky. It is evident we cannot rely on solar navigation for this last stretch and I have to improvise on a bearing for the Pole.

I am enjoying every minute now. It is like some bizarre orienteering puzzle – how do you find your way to the place where everything points to? We become quite cold as I keep stopping to check our bearing and refer to the chart. The conditions are not too bad; a little rubble and some pressure ridges, but no open water yet. Rune is in a good mood and at last we both feel safe in the assumption that we are going to make it.

We walk for another half an hour, which flies by in the excitement of the occasion. We stop, film and photograph ourselves, and take another reading. It is 1.12 p.m. and we are at 89°59'30" North and 154°35'00" West, exactly half a mile from the Pole. I can hardly believe my own words when I say, as much for my own benefit as for Rune's, 'Somewhere out there, within sight, but I don't know in which direction, is the North Pole.'

The plotting chart is a godsend. The GPS gives us our position, but it does not give us a visual indication of our location relative to the Pole. I had debated the merits of the small-scale plotting chart when I was trying to cut weight to a minimum, but now I am relieved I did not dump it.

We walk for another fifteen minutes and then take another reading. I am very excited. It feels a little like the final few hundred feet up to the summit of Everest, from the south summit up to Hillary's Step and then along the ridge to the top of the mountain. At 1.44 p.m. we are at 89°59'51" North and 166°04'00" West, less than 300 yards from the Pole. Our goal is so incredibly close, but still I cannot relax. If we do not get our navigation right we could miss the Pole altogether, either by walking away from it or directly parallel to it.

Rune paces out the steps to the next stop while I film the countdown. It is a great feeling as we notch off the final feet to our target. At 1.56 p.m. we stop again and take our position – 89°59'54.5" North and 133° West. The GPS is becoming confused and will not give a longitude reading to any accuracy greater than a degree. We are less than 150 yards from the Pole.

At this crucial moment, we have our first disagreement. Rune insists that I lead the way, whereas I want him to go ahead.

'This is your Grand Slam, David. You should go ahead,' he insists.

'No Rune, you got us here. You have led all the way and it is right that you should lead the last few steps as well,' I say.

In the end we reach a compromise. We walk together, side by side, and with the GPS in my hand we count down the last hundred feet to the North Pole.

The sun is breaking through the clouds and we are in the midst of a rubble field, but it is the greatest few minutes of my adventuring life. We finally reach 89°59'59.4" North and decide it is as close to the North Pole as we will be able to get. According to the GPS we are within fifty-five feet of the Pole. It is as close as dammit, taking the accuracy limitations of the GPS into account. It is impossible to navigate any closer now, so we turn to each other and hug.

'Hulashaker! We have done it!' I say as I embrace Rune.

'This feels very strange,' Rune says. 'I have never hugged a man with any emotion before. Well done David. Congratulations on reaching the North Pole, congratulations on completing the Grand Slam and thank you very much for a wonderful trip.'

A year ago Rune had seen me break down in tears when the 1997 North Pole expedition ended, now he is about to see me cry again, this time with joy at finally reaching the top of the world.

'Congratulations to you, Rune,' I reply with the tears freezing in my eyes. 'I would never have done this without you. This is your triumph. You got us here.'

'And I would not have done it without you,' Rune says. 'Without you I would not be here.'

Then Rune, who thinks he is the seventh Norwegian to reach the Pole on foot, adds in his mother tongue: 'Polen er náad. Alt vel. It means "the Pole is reached. All well".' Rune explains that this Norwegian phrase was what Roald Amundsen uttered when he reached the South Pole ahead of Captain Robert Scott in 1911. It has become a household expression in Norway.

We look around us. It seems startlingly mundane. The North Pole looks no different to any of the other stretches of ice, snow and rubble we have crossed in the last eight weeks. Rune cheers and whoops, and hugs me again for good measure. Then he turns to me and repeats the mantra that has become a ritual every time we pitch camp.

'God save your Queen,' he says, and salutes me.

'And God save your King,' I reply.

By now we are both getting dangerously cold, and we walk about twenty yards away from the 'Pole' to pitch camp. We get the tent up double-quick and crawl inside for a late lunch and a mighty celebration. While he gets the stove ready, Rune takes one last GPS reading and I hear a whoop from the outer tent. 'Look David,' he shouts, holding up his GPS for me to see. In the time we have been standing at the Pole and then lying in the tent we have drifted closer to the Pole, and according to his GPS we are now at 89°59'59.9" North, within ten feet of the Pole and as close as is humanly measurable to the top of the world. It is 2.20 p.m. precisely, and for a minute or so the world is quite literally revolving around our tent. We capture the reading on film, then toast ourselves with brandy and a cigar as the ice floe we are camped on floats off the Pole again. In all, we probably spent no more than a minute or two right on the North Pole.

It is a brilliant and intensely emotional time. I think of Claire and Alicia flying today from Edmonton to Resolute Bay. By the time they arrive in the High Arctic they should have heard the news that we have reached the Pole. I am now feeling cock-a-hoop and taking it very easy. 'We've earned a rest and I have every intention of doing absolutely nothing now,' I tell Rune.

After eating some lunch, drinking a coffee and warming up, we abandon our plans to continue walking towards Russia to record some eastings. We have spent the last two years fighting to get to this strange place where all directions point south and decide it would be stupid to carry on. Again we try to get the radio to work, but to no avail as the weather is worsening and a storm is on the way. The winds buffet the antenna and we cannot get a signal. I am relieved that we made it to the Pole before the storm came in.

We lie back in our sleeping-bags and stretch out our weary limbs. This is the moment I have waited so long for, the moment when I can relax, safe in the knowledge that I have at last overcome my personal Achilles' heel. But within a few minutes my self-indulgent reverie is broken by what is to me a very unfamiliar thudding sound. 'That's a Russian M1.8 Hip helicopter,' Rune says. He says he can recognise any type of helicopter by the sound of its rotors. He peers out of the tent to see the chopper pass near us and then fly away. We both wonder what it is doing so far north, and why it has not landed at the Pole. Half an hour later we get our answer when it returns and lands.

To my utter amazement, Mikhail Malakhov, Viktor Boyoski, Geoff Somers and Sue Stockdale step out. It seems utterly surreal to be meeting these people at the North Pole. I know Geoff and Sue from past expeditions but have never met Malakhov or Boyoski. It is quite a thrill to meet these two Russian legends of polar exploration and they tell me they have heard about our expedition in Russia. I tell them we are immensely proud to be the first successful joint British-Norwegian polar expedition and they say they are impressed that we have done something towards softening the intense rivalry that has existed between Britain and Norway for the best part of a century.

We stand outside our tent for ten minutes, chatting and taking souvenir photographs. They tell us they have walked the last sixty miles to the North Pole and ask us if we need anything. I am tempted to ask for chocolate, but our overriding need is fuel, so we ask for some naphtha to heat the tent. They give us some fuel and then, as suddenly as they arrived, they disappear again into the white-out of the sky.

We talk all evening. I now feel disorientated; the mission has been accomplished and we do not know what we are doing here any more. Now I just want to get it all over, see Claire and Alicia, and go home. 'At home they are sleeping and tomorrow they will get the message that we reached the Pole and they won't have to worry any more,' Rune says. 'I am looking forward to telling Mama and Papa on the telephone. It will be good to hear their voices and even better to see them at Oslo airport, but right now I hope they will raise the flag tomorrow and have a small party.'

Before I go to sleep I reflect that our helicopter visitors will be in a warm hotel by now. I wish I was with them, but we still have to find a landing strip and wait for good weather. We have reached the Pole, now we must pray that we do not drift too far away from it overnight.

13

Long Walk Home

Family Reunion

Days 56 and 57: Wednesday, 29 April and Thursday, 30 April

After the excitement of reaching the Pole and the surprise of the unexpected helicopter visit yesterday, another revelation today. As usual we try the radio first thing in the morning, hoping to pick up John in Resolute to tell him to fly up here to pick us up as soon as possible. We warm the batteries under our arms and then I call out in the usual way to John and to First Air in Resolute Bay: 'Typhoo Base. Typhoo Base. Six Nine Resolute. Six Nine Resolute. This is British Typhoo, can you hear me?' Immediately, a voice replies, as loud and clear as if it was in the tent with us: 'British Typhoo, this is Polar Cache. Come in. Over.'

Rune and I are astounded. After a week of silence, a mystery voice is coming in five-five. Radio signals do not get any better than this.

'Polar Cache, it's great to hear you. Who and where the hell are you? Over.'

'British Typhoo. I am at eighty-six degrees north, guarding the fuel cache dumped here to refuel the planes that are picking you up. Over.'

'So they know we have made it to the Pole? Over.'

'Yes. I heard your radio call on Monday and relayed the news that you were a mile from the Pole then. Over.'

'Great news. So who are you? Over.'

'I'm Clarke Marcino. I've been here for over two weeks, camped on the ice with my Eskimo dog Manitou. Over.'

It is wonderful to hear another voice, and such a charming one too. Clarke passes on congratulations and tells us that three planes are leaving Resolute today, bound for Eureka, where Claire, Alicia, the media, the sponsors and some friends will overnight before collecting us tomorrow. We send a message back to Resolute via Clarke, asking for some sandwiches and orange juice to be brought to the pick-up, and sending our love to our families at home.

Outside the winds are very strong, gusting up to thirty knots, and there is still a complete white-out. The planes will not be able to land if this weather does not break tomorrow. However, our biggest problems are that we have now drifted over four miles away from the Pole to 89°55'57" North and 157°06' East, and that we do not have a suitable landing strip. Clarke tells us that another polar flight is due to come in tonight, bringing a group of polar historians to the Pole. If they can find a suitable landing strip they will radio us with its position and we will head for it in time for our three flights tomorrow. But if the weather is too bad, the historians will stay at Eureka and our three flights will stack up behind their flight, waiting for an opportunity to fly up on to the ice. At $350 a night per person for accommodation at Eureka, a delay is the last thing we need. Fortunately we have enough food and fuel to last us five or six days, but by then the expedition will be overdrawn.

We decide that we are not going to venture out into the white-out. We have done enough walking in driving winds, and it is time to take it easy, I say to Rune. He agrees, and we spend the day drinking juice and coffee and chatting. For once we are not exhausted, but Rune is like a bull in a china shop – a phrase which again takes some time to explain to him – excitedly charging around the tent, filming and photographing us.

We continue to drift backwards during the day until we are eight miles from the Pole, and eventually it dawns on me that we could be more than ten miles away by the time the planes arrive if we do not get out of the tent and start walking soon.

'Rune, I want us to be on or near the Pole when the planes come in so that Claire, Alicia and all the others can also say they have been to the North Pole,' I say.

Rune does not like this suggestion. 'I am tired and I have had enough. Why do we have to keep walking for the benefit of the media and your sponsors?'

He is right, but I think it is only correct that we should be as close to the Pole as possible when everyone arrives. 'We might as well get going because we need to find a decent landing strip. We'll stop when we find somewhere to land,' I say.

Reluctantly we break camp at about six p.m., and pack up our sledges for what I hope will be the last time. We are both drained of energy and now that the adrenalin has ebbed, every footstep is heavy work. Fortunately the weather clears in the early evening and the going is not as tough as it could be, although there is a lot of rubble and still some open water.

We walk and we soon find a strip, around seven miles from the Pole. We pitch camp and put up the radio to speak to the flight coming in with the historians on board. We then pace the strip and mark it with plastic bags so that the pilot has somewhere to aim for.

An hour or so later we hear the plane approaching. As usual it circles above us and then passes low to drop a package containing the sandwiches and oranges we requested. Carl, the pilot, radios to tell us that our landing strip is too short and that he has spotted a better strip one mile from the Pole at 89°58'74" North and 77°19'70" West. We are furious – our strip is easily long enough.

We crawl back into the tent to consider our options and eat the oranges. The last thing we want to do is go through the commotion of trying to navigate close to the Pole all over again, but we have no choice. When it comes to landing on the ice, the pilots always trust their own instincts before those of others, and we decide that we would ideally like to be waiting at the airstrip, ready to greet Claire and Alicia when the three planes land. We decide it is better to get going now, instead of sleeping. The ice is moving at some speed, and our task could be even more arduous tomorrow. However, it means breaking camp once again and walking through the night to find a strip which for all we know is no better than the one we are using.

Once we get going I remember why I always say never plan for anything in the Arctic. The terrain is stunning and it is a beautiful night, probably one of the best I have ever seen in the Arctic, but we are beyond exhaustion. I strain to keep my eyes open while I am walking and several times I nod off while I am skiing, waking with a start, suddenly aware that I have not seen the last ten feet I have covered because I was unconscious. We walk and walk and walk, making more and more mistakes in our exhaustion. I fall repeatedly and soon give up looking at my watch because clock-watching only seems to make our desperation worse. All I am aware of is that we have been walking for at least eight hours when we come to a couple of leads, one of which is only just covered with brown ice. I am so desperate to find the pilot's landing strip that I agree to venture across the most skittish ice I have ever attempted to pass over.

It is a big mistake to attempt to cross such fragile ice. We would never have countenanced crossing such a thin crust before we reached the Pole, and now we are making silly mistakes because we are tired, just like the mountaineers who injure themselves or die on the way down from Everest. My worst fears come true when I slip through the ice with one leg, drenching my boot and trouser leg up to my knee. Fortunately, Rune does not hesitate in coming to my rescue and jumps into the water with his skis on. Much to my alarm, he immediately disappears below the surface for a couple of seconds and emerges from the black water, spitting ice-cubes and treading water with his skis still attached to his feet. He seems totally unfazed by the experience, but I am frightened senseless for him. As usual, Rune is a star and helps me across the lead, insisting afterwards that he should keep walking so that his body heat can force the dampness out of his frozen clothes. He keeps his frigid clothes on because, he says, he fears that he will run out of time to prepare a landing strip if we stop.

We continue to make good progress up to the position Carl gave us. The sweat is pouring off us but we cannot find his damn landing strip. Once again, the way-points do not make any sense on the GPS. We head off in a different direction each time we take a new reading, and gradually our enthusiasm for finding the strip turns to desperation. Rune is so tired that he falls on ice he would normally have skipped across, and I become worried that one of us is going to do himself a serious injury. 'We should never have crossed that lead when we did,' I say to him, referring to the lead where we both took a dip in the water. 'We should have camped there and said to the pilots: enough is enough, you come and get us.'

Rune is equally fed-up and tells me that he has lost any feeling in his feet since plunging into the water. We both know he is close to frostbite. 'This is the best weather we have had since we started. Clear sky, no wind and it is warm, but it is the worst day of the expedition. I want to stop,' he says. 'We should have relaxed after reaching the Pole. Instead we are having the most tiring time of the expedition.'

But we keep going. The ice conditions become worse: one pressure ridge after another in quick succession, interspersed by large rubble fields. I thought I had seen the last of this a couple of days ago. I sweat profusely and my glasses steam up so much that I repeatedly trip over my skis, twisting my knee as I stumble on in search of the landing strip.

We keep walking for fifteen hours, searching for the pilot's landing strip. Eventually we come to the co-ordinates he gave us, but we are in the midst of a large area of break-up. The strip must have drifted at least two miles from the position we have been given. I stop while Rune performs a sector search, dividing our immediate environment into nine sectors, each of which he walks across and climbs to the highest point to scan the horizon for a sign of what now seems to be a mythical large pan, but to no avail.

I am absolutely furious. This could really screw up our plans of having three planes come in to land. The pilots might abandon our plans, I think, and land only one plane to pick us up, while the other two planes circle overhead. We have walked so far into an area of break-up that I cannot envisage the planes landing anywhere near us. They could set down a couple of miles away and then we will have to walk to them, which will give us no time to celebrate and film at the Pole. What a bloody mess.

Eventually, at around eleven a.m., seventeen hours after we started to walk and thirty hours since we last slept, we decide we have had enough. 'We could keep walking for another six hours and still not find the strip,' I say to Rune. He agrees, and we pitch camp and set up the radio antenna. Clarke comes in loud and clear again, and is a great help. Three planes, he tells us, are already in the air and about to land at the fuel cache he is guarding. It will take them around forty minutes to refuel and then another two to two and a half hours to reach us. I pass on a new plan to Clarke. We will make a strip on our ice floe and all three planes should land at Carl's strip at the Pole. Then one empty plane should pick us up and take us back to the Pole party.

'Good luck,' Clarke says, 'and I'll see you when you stop off on the way back to Eureka.'

Once again it is a panic. Rune is determined to do the job properly and insists on preparing a strip on our ice floe. He races around flattening the snow and marking the strip with black plastic bags and a flare. Meanwhile, I scribble the last entry in my diary and prepare to see my wife and eldest daughter again.

It is exactly nine weeks since I kissed Claire, Amelia, Camilla and Alicia goodbye in the hall of our house in Wiltshire. It was very difficult to leave home on that cold morning in late February, particularly as I did not know what lay ahead of me. I thought back then that we had a good chance, but more than anything I feared failing the North Pole for the third time. Now it is all over, and in some strange way I do not want to leave. For eight weeks we have had this massive wilderness to ourselves, except for a few brief incursions, and I have come to love its harsh beauty. It will be very difficult to return home to the school run, to days spent behind a desk in an office and evenings in the pub with my brother Mark and our friends, or at home with my family. For two months I have fought against the elements and faced a mental battle against the unknown ahead of us, but it has been an escape from the reality of having to pay the bills and deal with the monotony of mundane matters. It is something I am very reluctant to give up.

It is quite a bizarre experience to see the planes arrive shortly after midday. We hear the first one above us and we wave, wondering if Claire and Alicia are on board and hoping they can see us. The plane circles for a couple of minutes and then it heads off. We speak to the pilot on the radio and he tells us he is going to land on the fabled landing strip we strove so long to find. A minute or so later the second plane arrives, and again it circles around us before heading off. This time we can see it descending to land, around two to three miles away from us. The third plane does not circle for as long before it also heads off to land. For about ten minutes there is utter silence. Rune and I look at each other, now aware that our little world is about to be invaded in a massive way.

'Well that's it, Dr Nansen,' I say. 'It will all be over soon.'

'Not until we see everybody else, Dr Livingstone,' Rune replies. 'I won't feel it is over until I see Claire, Alicia, Nigel, Charles, Paul, Robert and all the rest. Then it will be over and we can go home.'

The silence is broken by the buzz of one of the three planes coming to collect us. We bustle around the tent, gathering the goods and chattels that have kept us alive and in relatively good spirits for so long, and a minute or so later the plane thumps down on our ice floe.

We drag our sledges over to the door and open it to find Rob Bowles, an ITN cameraman inside. He and the same pilots who picked up Alan Bywater from us last year congratulate us and then help us load our equipment into the Twin Otter. Ten minutes later we are in the air for a brief three-minute flight to the landing strip. It is a perfect place to land, the longest pan of ice we have seen in the entire eight weeks we have been on the ice-cap. I am disappointed only by the fact that we were so close to it, yet failed to find it.

Robert Uhlig is the first person we see after the plane lands. He opens the door and immediately Michael Nicholson, the ITN reporter, sticks his head into the plane and congratulates us on our achievement. We climb out to find a camera crew outside and my family and friends waiting at the edge of the landing strip.

We walk across to where Claire and Alicia are waiting, beside a Norwegian and a Union flag on a barber pole stuck into a mound of snow, and we all embrace. It is a very emotional moment for all of us, but it is made somewhat odd by the fact that we are being watched by a dozen or so people, all toting cameras. It seems to be a very British celebration. To a chorus of cheers and hoorays, we both kiss and hug Claire and Alicia, then take off our skis. It is not until I feel my body enveloped in the arms of my wife that I realise how emaciated I am. My clothes are hanging off me, I smell like somebody who has been sleeping on the streets for two months and my face is grimed with greasy dirt.

'That's the last time I do that,' I say as I unclip the harness that has kept me attached to my sledge for the last fifty-seven days.

'That's what you said last time, dear,' Claire answers straight away, with a massive smile on her face.

Rune, standing beside me, immediately pipes in, 'Well, for this year at least then.'

Alicia seems quite taken aback. She has not seen me like this before. By the time I have returned home from the previous trips I have shaved and had several good meals. I can tell she is shocked. She hands me two cups of snow she has been holding as presents, and having overcome her initial shyness, she hugs me tightly.

Michael Nicholson cracks open a bottle of Champagne and sprays it all over Rune and me. After the weeks of silence and solitude, the hullabaloo is bewildering, but at last I begin to feel that the task is over, although what we have achieved has not quite sunk in yet. The time spins past in a mêlée of interviews and pictures, while I attempt to greet all my friends who have come so far to meet me. I feel very privileged to have all these people come to pick me up, and even more fortunate to have had the luck of meeting Rune, without whose assistance I would not be standing here. I feel very protective towards Rune, the man who has kept me sane, saved my life at least once and who has driven me on when I wanted to give up, until we both reached the Pole.

It is lovely to see all these people, although I do not recognise some of them at first, such as Peter McPhillips, who does not have his glasses on. Many of the people standing around me on the ice have helped me get to where I am now standing, either through sponsorship or by encouragement, and I am overjoyed that their investment has at last paid off. Many people knock explorers such as me who use corporate sponsorship to fund expeditions, but in my mind it is better than using taxpayers' or military money for what is a private indulgence, and I have no qualms that several of the people standing beside me at the North Pole are here to represent a business interest.

After about an hour the pilots call us over to the planes. There is a long flight ahead of us and we have to take off soon. I climb into a plane with Claire and Alicia, while Rune sits in another plane with Robert and some of my friends from home. The third plane carries the media on ahead to file their stories back to London.

As soon as we take off I find I can no longer speak to the people around me and I have to look out of the window. From the air the ice looks like a powder-white version of the English countryside. The ice floes are like fields, intersected by pressure ridges instead of hedges. The leads of open water are like trunk roads cutting through the farmland. It looks very picturesque and gives little impression of the conditions on the ground Already it is easy to forget what we have been through, but I am shocked to see the state of the ice behind us. There are huge expanses of open water and I am convinced that we would not have made it had we crossed the last two degrees a week later.

A couple of hours later we land at the Polar Cache and meet Clarke and his dog. They climb aboard the plane, their eighteen-day stint on the ice over now that we have been picked up.

By early evening we reach Eureka. I think back to the last time we arrived at this remote weather station from the ice, and the dreadful sense of failure we felt then. Now we return as victors, and although it is difficult to come to terms with the conventions of civilisation after our time away, it is great to be returning with a job well done.

We miss the minibus shuttle that has carried Claire, Alicia and the rest of our troupe from the airstrip down to the bunkhouses at the weather station, so I walk with Rune and Robert down the hill to this strange outpost and talk about the fact that I started the Grand Slam in 1980, the year I met Claire.

'This is the last big one,' I say as we stroll in the evening sun. 'I am too old for this and my grandmother keeps asking me when I am going to grow up and become responsible. Now, I think, is the time.'

I have reached all five poles and climbed the highest summits in each of the seven continents, but in all this time spent largely in my own company, or with one or two carefully chosen companions, I have not been able to work out why I am driven to such extremes of endurance. All I can think is that it is a drive that is simply born inside some people. There are people who will strive to reach the pinnacle of their careers or to play an instrument like a virtuoso; there are others who will want to climb mountains or overcome the worst that the natural environment can throw at them.

There is something wonderful about knowing that Rune and I are part of a group of very few people ever to have walked to the North Pole. For that reason I will continue always to look for the next big challenge, and against my better judgement give in to that driving force inside me that makes me persist in putting my body, mind and resolve through torture in pursuit of a dream that to many other people might seem meaningless, but to me is the most important thing in the world. It has been a stressful and gruelling couple of months, and I am pleased to be going home. Yet I know the worst is still ahead of me. It is when I leave that I miss it most.

Appendices

As published in the *Daily Telegraph*, 30 April 1998, 2 May 1998.

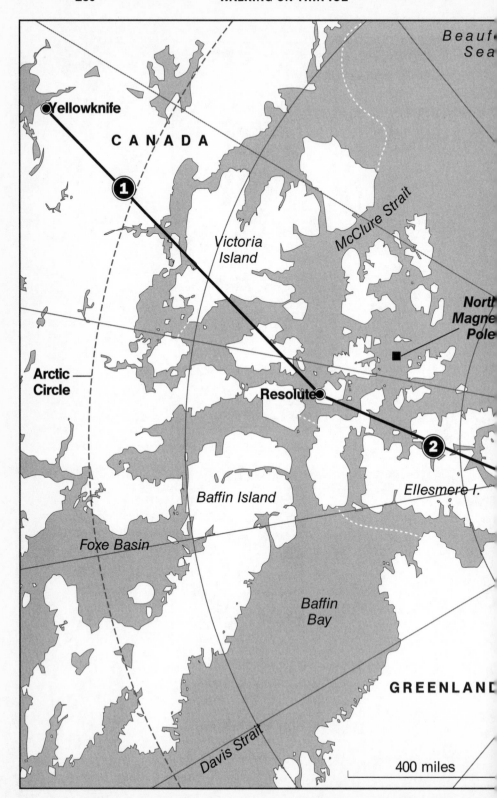

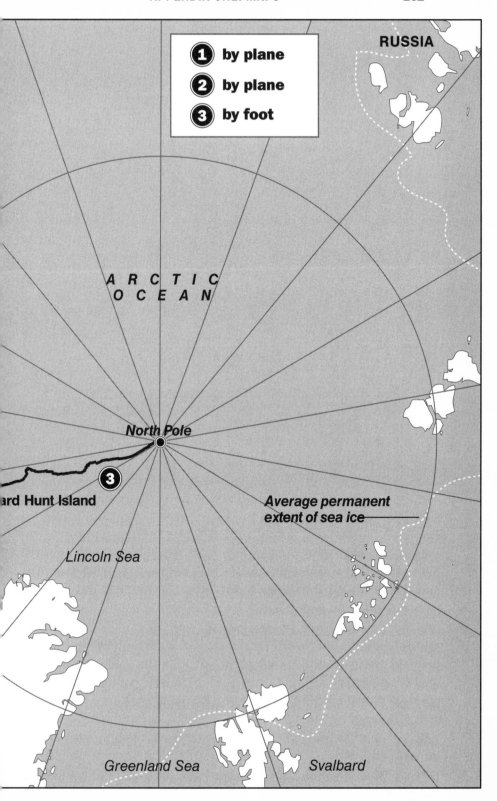

RUSSIA

1 by plane
2 by plane
3 by foot

A R C T I C
O C E A N

North Pole

3

ard Hunt Island

Average permanent
extent of sea ice

Lincoln Sea

Greenland Sea   *Svalbard*

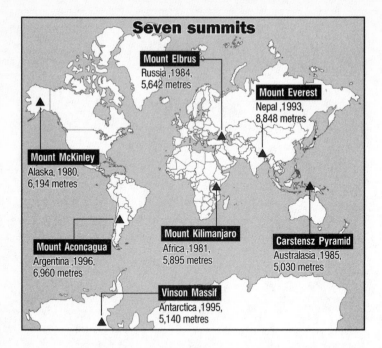

The Seven Summits: August 1980 – May 1995

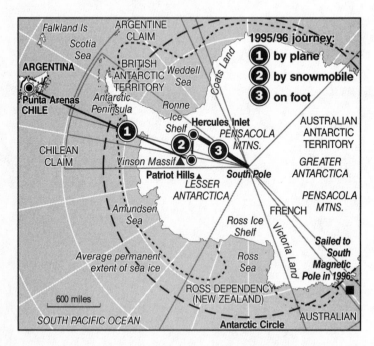

Route to the South Pole: Solo and unsupported.
November 1995 – January 1996

Appendix Two

Positions

THE READINGS FOR the first 22 days are the positions reached at the end of a day's walking. In the text, the readings correspond to those at the beginning of the following day, as we did not take positional readings each morning. From day 23 onwards, when we realised we were drifting back substantially overnight, there are separate readings for each morning and evening. In some cases, such as on rest or storm days, there are midday readings as well.

The information is presented in the following order: Day, Date, Latitude, Longitude, Distance covered that day, temperature, wind-chill, and hours of sunlight. There are no windchill figures for days we spent cooped-up inside the tent.

Ward Hunt Island 83°05'00"N; 74°07"W
Day 1 Thursday March 5; 83°08'17.5"N; 74°08'45.4"W; 3 miles; −38°C; −58°C; 3hrs 7mins
Day 2 Friday March 6; 83°11'00"N; 74°13'04"W; 3 miles; −36°C; −58°C; 2hrs 54mins

Day 3 Saturday March 7; 83°14'10"N; 74°20'00"W; 3 miles; −32°C; −56°C; 3hrs 54mins

Day 4 Sunday March 8; 83°19'05"N; 74°27'11"W; 5 miles; −55°C; −85°C; 4hrs 43mins

Day 5 Monday March 9; 83°24'02"N; 74°22'47"W; 5 miles; below −55°C; below −85°C; 5hrs 23mins

Day 6 Tuesday March 10; 83°30'02"N; 74°29'18"W; 6 miles; below −55°C; below −85°C; 5hrs 53mins

Day 7 Wednesday March 11; 83°36'00"N; 74°29'55"W; 6 miles; below −55°C; below −85°C; 6hrs 27mins

Day 8 Thursday March 12; 83°41'47"N; 74°27'40"W; 5¾ miles; below −55°C; below −85°C; 7hrs 0mins

Day 9 Friday March 13; 83°47'49"N; 74°25'04.7"W; 6 miles; −52°C; −80°C; 7hrs 38mins

Day 10 Saturday March 14; 83°47'48"N; 74°25'11"W; 0 miles; −50°C inside tent; 8hrs 10mins

Day 11 Sunday March 15; 83°55'26"N; 74°26'42"W; 7¾ miles; below −55°C; below −70°C; 9hrs 16mins

Day 12 Monday March 16; 84°03'14"N; 74°21'17"W; 8 miles; below −55°C; below −85°C; 9hrs 13mins

Day 13 Tuesday March 17; 84°09'18"N; 74°18'46"W; 6 miles; −52°C; approx −80°C; 9hrs 44mins

Day 14 Wednesday March 18; 84°10'46"N; 74°22'53"W; 1½ miles (prepared for resupply); −50°C; approx −80°C; 10hrs 19mins

Day 15 Thursday March 19; 84°10'46"N; 74°22'53"W; 0 miles (resupply); −50°C inside tent; 10hrs 53mins

Day 16 Friday March 20; 84°15'51"N; 74°19'17"W; 5 miles; −43°C; −68°C; 11hrs 25mins

Day 17 Saturday March 21; 84°21'37"N; 74°25'24"W; 5¾ miles; −42°C; −78°C; 12hrs

Day 18 Sunday March 22; 84°28'29"N; 74°25'00"W; 7 miles; −38°C; −55°C; 12hrs 35mins

Day 19 Monday March 23; 84°34'52"N; 74°14'32"W; 6½ miles; −39°C; −58°C; 13hrs 13mins

Day 20 Tuesday March 24; 84°42'08"N; 74°23'06"W; 7 miles; −40°C; −71°C; 13hrs 49mins

Day 21 Wednesday March 25; 84°48'54"N; 75°00'00"W; 6 miles; −33°C; −48°C; 14hrs 31mins

Day 22 Thursday March 26; 84°55'20"N; 76°16'01"W; 6½ miles; −31°C; −59°C; 15hrs 15mins

Day 23 Friday March 27; 84°54'46"N; 76°59'00"W; ½ mile back drift by morning (rest day)

Day 23 Friday March 27; 84°54'54"N; 77°25'06"W; ⅙ mile north drift by 5pm (rest day); −32°C inside tent; 15hrs 33mins

Day 24 Saturday March 28; 84°55'06"N; 77°48'10"W; ⅕ mile north drift by morning

Day 24 Saturday March 28; 84°58'57"N; 77°43'21"W; 3½ miles; −25°C; −61°C; 16hrs 52mins

Day 25 Sunday March 29; 84°59'34"N; 78°14'31"W; ½ mile north drift by morning

Day 25 Sunday March 29; 85°07'49"N; 77°21'34"W; 8¼ miles; −30°C; −52°C; 17hrs 44mins

Day 26 Monday March 30; 85°06'43"N; 77°11'03"W; 1 mile back drift by morning

Day 26 Monday March 30; 85°13'50"N; 76°48'49"W; 7 miles; −38°C; −58°C; 18hrs 52mins

Day 27 Tuesday March 31; 85°13'10"N; 76°26'20"W; ¾ mile back drift by morning

Day 27 Tuesday March 31; 85°20'52"N; 75°52'48"W; 7 miles; −38°C; −56°C; 20hrs 50mins

Day 28 Wednesday April 1; 85°20'29"N; 75°31'11"W; ⅓ mile back drift by morning

Day 28 Wednesday April 1; 85°29'30"N; 75°39'03"W; 9 miles; −37°C; −51°C; 24hrs

Day 29 Thursday April 2; 85°29'24"N; 75°39'29"W; ⅒ mile back drift by morning

Day 29 Thursday April 2; 85°38'55"N; 75°33'01"W; 9½ miles; −32°C; −48°C; 24hrs

Day 30 Friday April 3; 85°38'27"N; 75°09'59"W; ½ mile back drift by morning

Day 30 Friday April 3; 85°50'22"N; 74°26'00"W; 12 miles; −38°C; −48°C; 24hrs

Day 31 Saturday April 4; 85°50'37"N; 73°32'18"W; ¼ mile north drift by morning

Day 31 Saturday April 4; 85°59'20"N; 72°48'24"W; 9 miles; −35°C; −67°C; 24hrs

Day 32   Sunday April 5; 85°59'25"N; 72°30'26"W; $\frac{1}{10}$ mile north drift by morning

Day 32   Sunday April 5; 86°10'53"N; 72°08'10"W; 11½ miles; −34°C; −46°C; 24hrs

Day 33   Monday April 6; 86°11'00"N; 71°49'33"W; $\frac{1}{10}$ mile north drift by morning

Day 33   Monday April 6; 86°20'22"N; 71°35'54"W; 9 miles; −34°C; −44°C; 24hrs

Day 34   Tuesday April 7; 86°20'29"N; 71°27'09"W; $\frac{1}{10}$ mile north drift by morning

Day 34   Tuesday April 7; 86°31'52"N; 71°11'35"W; 11½ miles; −34°C; −48°C; 24hrs

Day 35   Wednesday April 8; 86°32'05"N; 71°07'09"W; ¼ mile north drift by morning

Day 35   Wednesday April 8; 86°43'05"N; 70°21'53"W; 11 miles; −34°C; −40°C; 24hrs

Day 36   Thursday April 9; 86°42'59"N; 70°13'56"W; $\frac{1}{10}$ mile back drift by morning

Day 36   Thursday April 9; 86°42'59"N; 70°13'56"W; resupply day; −34°C; −46°C; 24hrs

Day 37   Friday April 10; 86°43'05"N; 70°04'00"W; $\frac{1}{10}$ mile north drift by morning

Day 37   Friday April 10; 86°52'10"N; 69°04'17"W; 9 miles; −32°C; −40°C; 24hrs

Day 38   Saturday April 11; 86°52'24"N; 69°05'23"W; ¼ mile north drift by morning

Day 38   Saturday April 11; 87°01'05"N; 69°33'31"W; 8¾ miles; −37°C; −49°C; 24hrs

Day 39   Sunday April 12; 87°00'53"N; 69°57'16"W; $\frac{1}{5}$ mile north drift by morning

Day 39   Sunday April 12; 87°06'40"N; 71°00'25"W; 6 miles; −34°C; −52°C; 24hrs

Day 40   Monday April 13; 87°05'23"N; 71°30'00"W; 1¼ miles back drift by morning

Day 40   Monday April 13; 87°12'01"N; 72°01'38"W; 6½ miles; −38°C; −73°C; 24hrs

Day 41   Tuesday April 14; 87°09'55"N; 72°32'20"W; 2 miles back drift by morning

Day 41 Tuesday April 14; 87°18'48"N; 73°23'40"W; 9 miles; −34°C; −49°C; 24hrs

Day 42 Wednesday April 15; 87°18'58"N; 73°06'31"W; ⅙ mile north drift by morning

Day 42 Wednesday April 15; 87°31'03"N; 72°51'08"W; 12 miles; −36°C; −49°C; 24hrs

Day 43 Thursday April 16; 87°31'05"N; 71°33'00"W

Day 43 Thursday April 16; 87°43'55"N; 72°25'39"W; 13 miles; −36°C; −44°C; 24hrs

Day 44 Friday April 17; 87°44'09"N; 72°04'08"W; ¼ mile north drift by morning

Day 44 Friday April 17; 87°57'57"N; 71°31'00"W; 13¾ miles; −34°C; −49°C; 24hrs

Day 45 Saturday April 18; 87°58'23"N; 71°05'12"W; ½ mile north drift by morning

Day 45 Saturday April 18; 88°10'22"N; 70°30'47"W; 12 miles; −32°C; −42°C; 24hrs

Day 46 Sunday April 19; 88°10'26"N; 70°25'26"W; ¹⁄₁₅ mile north drift by morning

Day 46 Sunday April 19; 88°09'58"N; 70°36'00"W; ½ mile back drift by evening (rest day); −34°C; −52°C; 24 hrs

Day 47 Monday April 20; 88°09'03"N; 70°26'30"W; 1 mile back drift by morning

Day 47 Monday April 20; 88°22'20"N; 69°07'00"W; 13¾ miles; −32°C; −56°C; 24hrs

Day 48 Tuesday April 21; 88°22'43"N; 68°29'38"W; ⅓ mile north drift by morning

Day 48 Tuesday April 21; 88°36'07"N; 66°17'09"W; 13½ miles; −26°C; −38°C; 24hrs

Day 49 Wednesday April 22; 88°36'45"N; 65°33'00"W; ⅔ mile north drift by morning

Day 49 Wednesday April 22; 88°51'42"N; 64°25'50"W; 15 miles; −34°C; −47°C; 24hrs

Day 50 Thursday April 23; 88°51'53"N; 64°08'07"W; ⅙ mile north drift by morning

Day 50 Thursday April 23; 89°06'27"N; 64°59'00"W; 14½ miles; −30°C; −36°C; 24hrs

Day 51 Friday April 24; 89°06'26"N; 65°09'40"W

Day 51 Friday April 24; 89°21'12"N; 66°55'09"W; 14¾ miles; −35°C; −44°C; 24hrs

Day 52 Saturday April 25; 89°21'05"N; 68°24'14"W; ⅙ mile back drift by morning

Day 52 Saturday April 25; 89°34'22"N; 68°49'40"W; 13 miles; −36°C; −58°C; 24hrs

Day 53 Sunday April 26; 89°34'20"N; 71°17'36"W

Day 53 Sunday April 26; 89°47'49"N; 80°20'25"W; 13½ miles; −30°C; −49°C; 24hrs

Day 54 Monday April 27; 89°48'08"N; 88°53'00"W; ¼ mile north drift by morning

Day 54 Monday April 27; 89°58'01"N; 120°12'00"W; 10 miles; −32°C; −64°C; 24hrs

Day 55 Tuesday April 28; 89°56'20"N; 169°46'00"W; 1⅔ miles back drift by morning

Day 55 Tuesday April 28; 89°57'24"N; 169°46'00"W; 1 mile north after one hour

Day 55 Tuesday April 28; 89°58'52"N; 175°24'00"W; 1½ miles further north after another hour

Day 55 Tuesday April 28; 89°59'30"N; 154°35'00"W at 1.12pm

Day 55 Tuesday April 28; 89°59'51"N; 166°04'00"W at 1.44pm

Day 55 Tuesday April 28; 89°59'54.5"N; 133°W at 1.56pm

Day 55 Tuesday April 28; 89°59'59.9"N at 2.20pm NORTH POLE; −34°C; −47°C; 24hrs

Appendix Three

Equipment

Clothing

Karrimor Polartec 100 top – two pieces
Karrimor Polartec 100 tights – two pieces
Karrimor Polartec 300 fleece jacket – two pieces
Karrimor windproof jacket – two pieces
Karrimor windproof salopettes – two pieces
Rab expedition goose-down jacket – two pieces
Rab expedition goose-down vest – two pieces
Lanullva untreated lamb's-wool long-sleeved vest – two pieces
Lanullva untreated lamb's-wool long underpants – two pieces
Lanullva untreated lamb's-wool windproof underpants – two pieces
Lanullva untreated lamb's-wool head-over – two pieces
Lanullva untreated lamb's-wool balaclava – two pieces
Karrimor Polartec balaclava – two pieces
Lanullva untreated lamb's-wool socks (not worn for walking) – two pairs
Extremities thinny socks (first layer on foot) – four pairs

Plastic bags (second layer on foot) – four
Polypropylene-cotton socks (third layer on foot) – four pairs
Katangaer (wool shoes, strengthened – wool linings for Alfa boots) –
two pairs
Alfa polar boots Mørdre Extreme – two pairs
BF cap (black furry cap with flaps to cover ears) – two pieces
Karrimor balaclava fleece hat – two pieces
Wind protection mask – two pieces
Pulse-warmer – four pairs
Extremities thinny gloves – five pairs
Thick wool mittens – four pairs
Extremities windproof gloves – four pairs

Expedition
Arctic Acapulco sledges – two pieces
Elastic ropes – two pieces
Sledge harness (Norwegian Army) – two pieces
Karrimor Condor backpack – two pieces
Spare parts (quick lock) – six pieces
Garmin GPS satellite navigation receiver – two pieces
Silvia compass – two pieces
Astro-compass and tripod – one piece
Argos position, temperature and emergency-code satellite beacon –
one piece
High frequency radio – one piece
Dipole antenna – one piece
Radio batteries – twenty AA-size alkaline
Maps, ocean charts and hand-drawn progress chart
Vapour-barrier inner layer to sleeping-bags (thick plastic) – two pieces
Helsport lightweight first-layer sleeping-bag (synthetic mixture) – two
pieces
Helsport Sleeping-bag Baffin Special (goose down with hood) – two
pieces
Karrimat (ridged mat; allows air to circulate under sleeping-bags) –
three pieces
Thermarest inflatable insulated ground bed – two pieces
Helsport Svalbard expedition tent – one piece

Helsport tent pegs (standard, serrated ice anchors, 1" × 8") – ten pieces

Snow spade (collapsible) – one piece

Flare – two pieces

Ice hooks – two pieces

Fisher 99 Europe skis – two pairs

Rottefella ski bindings – two pairs

Swix Expedition ski-poles – three pairs

Ski skins – two pairs

Customised rifle – one piece

Ammunition (Winchester Super-X 12 gauge 2¾" 1oz rifled hollow-point expanding slugs) – two twelve-packs

Nylon 5mm rope – two × fifty metres

Ice axe – one piece

Repair kit (contains Swiss Army knife, helicopter ties, screws, rope, sewing equipment, drill, binding, ski tips, spare kit for the stove) – weighs two pounds

Leatherman pocket-sized pen knife/pliers/toolkit – one piece

UKE torch (tiny torch, hooks on to sleeping-bag) – one piece

Toilet paper – enough

Walkman – two pieces

Revo glacier spectacles – two pieces

Revo sunglasses – two pieces

Thermometer – two pieces

Scissors – one piece

Diary book – two pieces

Pencils – four pieces

Equipment bags (large & lightweight) – eight pieces

Breitling emergency transmitter watch – one piece

Signal pen flare – two pieces

Signal patrons red/white refills – eight pieces

Flags: Union flag and Norwegian – four pieces

Toothbrush – two pieces

Toothpaste – one tube

First aid kit: various grades of pain-killer from Ibuprofen to morphine, sticking plaster, gauze, antibiotics

Food and cooking

Mountain Safety Research XGK II fuel pump – three pieces
Mountain Safety Research stove plate – one piece
Mountain Safety Research one-litre gas bottles – six pieces
Mountain Safety Research spare parts kit
FFI cooking system (one-burner cooker) – one piece
Matches and disposable lighters
Breakfast (muesli with milk powder, vegetable, soya and olive oils) – 24lb in eighty sachets
Lunch (muesli with raisins, oils and nuts) and chocolate chunks
Dinner (freeze-dried choice of Arctic fish, spaghetti Bolognese, beef stroganoff, chicken curry, cod in sour cream, chicken and noodles; Mars bars for pudding) – eighty sachets
Peperami – eighty packets
Pork scratchings – eighty packets
Chocolate (for lunch and in snack bags) – 40lb
Olive oil and soya oil – seven litres
Butter – 2lb
Sugar – 2.5lb
Milk powder – 1.5lb
Typhoo tea and coffee
Confecta soft drinks – eighty sachets
Thermos one-litre Isotherm – three pieces
Thermos cups – two small, two large
Spoon – two pieces
Food bags – ten pieces
Romeo & Juliet cigars
Drum tobacco – sixteen large packets
Cigarette papers
Courvoisier Cognac – one litre

Base station equipment

Panasonic ruggedised laptop computer for e-mail and faxes – two pieces
Spare sealed food sachets for breakfast, lunch and dinner for twenty extra days
High frequency radio receiver

First resupply
Twenty days' food in five-day packages
Twenty-five days' drinks in five-day packages – tea, coffee, hot chocolate, orange and apple
Two inner and two outer sleeping-bags
Fifteen litres naphtha fuel
Replacement tent and thermarest
Two Mountain Safety Research pumps
One services Mountain Safety Research cooker
Six packets tobacco and ten cigars
New batteries for GPS
Exchanged video camera and lithium batteries
Matches and disposable lighters
Change of outer windproof clothing
Four boxes of Smarties
Fresh fruit
One flask coffee, one flask tea, one flask Irish stew
Half a pint of brandy

David and Rune wanted change of skis but did not take them because wrong type of bindings fixed to replacement skis. David sent back to base: films, videotapes, letter to wife and daughters, letter to Robert Uhlig, and exchanged Karrimor windproof for fur to be fitted to hood. Rune sent back to base camp: thermarest, UKE torch.

Second resupply
Twenty-five days' food and drinks in five-day packages
Complete change of clothing (except underwear), i.e. new socks, gloves (inner and outer), Polartec clothing, Rab vests, windproof outer layer. David had a new pair of boots and replaced his Karrimor windproof with the jacket exchanged at the first resupply, now with fur attached to the hood.
Two inner and outer sleeping-bags
Replacement tent
Fifteen litres naphtha fuel
Foot powder
One flask coffee, two flasks Irish stew
Additional empty thermos flask

Cheese sandwiches
Cherry pie
Easter eggs
Small bottle of whisky and half a pint of brandy
Photographs and newspapers
Easter cards from daughters
Change of skis supplied (this time with right bindings) but David and Rune did not want them because they had become used to the shorter skis. David and Rune sent back to base: letters to David's wife and daughters, letters to Charles Rhodes and Robert Uhlig, spare Mountain Safety Research pumps and cooker, extra batteries for GPS, HF radio and the video camera, clean inner sleeping-bag, Sony Walkman, Sony radio, outer mittens (frozen and not wanted).

Appendix Four

The Roll Call

Special thanks to my main sponsors:

Rajiv Wahi, managing director of Typhoo.
Peter McPhillips, managing director of Buxted.

Thanks to my other sponsors, friends and associates:
Aase Inger Kroken; Adrian Cornwell; Adrian Van Klaveren; Amir and Glen; Andrew Adams; Andrew Stafford; Anne Kershaw; Barry Mason; Beth Vaughan; Bill Tidy; Bjørn Loe; Bob Long; Bob Sheard; Borge Ousland; Charles Rhodes; Chris Stone; Chris Thomas; Christian Muri; Colin Hill; David Heyes; David Munro; Emma Cooper; Eric and Eileen Rose; Gudmund Kaarvatn; Harald and Mrs Loe; Harald Kenneth Loe; Heidi Woods; Hilary Curtis; Ian Stafford; Ingeweld Kaarvatn; Jack Culley; Jane Lyons; Jeremy Lang; Jim Bradley; Joe Marney; John Hunt; John Nelligan; John Perrins; Joy Rochen; Julia Drown M.P.; Keith Rugg; Kelvin Ogunjimi; Kjell Oestbye; Lars Arne Gjeldnes and The Gjeldnes Family; Lillian Sullivan; Lucy Roberts; Lynn Orr; Mac; Maggie Coomb; Margaret Setters; Mark Hempleman-

Adams; Malcolm Wallace; Matt; Michael Ancram M.P.; Michael Jermey; Mike Boon; Mike Pope; Morag Howell; Neill Williams; Nigel Bateson; Norman Smith; Paul Grover; Peter McPhillips; Peter Robinson; Pippa Rees; Rachel Clarke; Rachel Foster; Richard Bull; Richard Mitchell; Richard Wood; Rikki Hunt; Robert Uhlig; Rune Gjeldnes; Sjur Mørdre; Steffen Bang; Stein Helliksen; Steve Pinfield; Steve Pollocks; Steve Vincent; Stuart Wilson; Sue Clark; Sue Godfrey; Sue Harding; Susannah Charlton; Terry Jesudsson; Tom Shebbeare; Tony Rolls; Torre Larsen; Ulv Skaffle; Victoria Riches.

Advantek; Alfa Skofabrik; Arkells Beer; Barbary Shooting School; Bath Chronicle; BBC News, Video Diaries and World Service; BCB; Breitling England; Bristol Batteries; Britannia Music; British Midland; Buxted Foods; Café Nicole & Son; Canadian Air; Cascade Designs; Chilprufe; Confecta; Cuprinol; Daily Telegraph; Denplan; Drytech; Duracell Batteries; EUA International; Europrint; Extremities Clothing; First Air; Fuji Photo Film; Gjeldnes Data; Global Resins; Helsport; HTV; ITN; Jaeger Clothing; Janet Senneck; Kaarvatn Fjellustyr; Karrimor; Kenn Borek; Mast-co; Nacls; National Westminster; Nimbus; Orion Books; Panasonic Norway; Peperami; Pheasant Pub; Pork Scratchings; Rab; Revo; Robnor; Royal Scottish Geographic Society; Scholl; Stangvik School; Swindon Advertiser; Teampro; The Prince's Trust; Thermorest; Thermos; Todalen School; Typhoo; Vinje Klaer; Wiltshire Rod & Gun Shop; Western Daily Press; Zippo.

Index